Building the Bombs:

A History of the Nuclear Weapons Complex

Building the Bombs:

A History of the Nuclear Weapons Complex

Charles R. Loeber

Edited by Lorna Gail Clark and Phil Brittenham

Illustrated by Michael Townsend

Designed by Jan Gaunce

Third Edition

Sandia National Laboratories

Albuquerque, New Mexico

Livermore, California

Sandia National Laboratories is a multi-program laboratory managed and operated by Sandia Corporation, a wholly owned subsidiary of Lockheed Martin Corporation, for the U.S. Department of Energy's National Nuclear Security Administration under contract DE-AC04-94AL85000.

SAND # 2012-7878P

Sandia National Laboratories
Albuquerque, New Mexico 87185
Livermore, California 94551

Printed 2002. 2003; 2nd edition, 2005; 3rd edition, 2012

CONTENTS

List of Figures ix

Preface xi

Acknowledgements xiv

Abbreviations and Acronyms xv

1. Einstein Opens the Door

Relativity 1

Atomic Structure 2

Bombarding the Nucleus 4

Binding Energy and Mass Defect 6

Anti-Semitism in Europe 8

Nuclear Fission 10

U.S. Government Involvement 11

Fissile Material Problem 14

Effort Accelerates 16

2. The Manhattan Project

Manhattan Project Begins 21

NWC in 1942 22

Prototype, Test, and Research Reactors 25

Fissile Material Production 27

NWC from 1943 to July 1945 29

Victory in Europe 31

Interim Committee 32

First Nuclear Weapons 32

Results of the Manhattan Project .34

NWC in September 1945 40

3. German Atomic Bomb Program

German Head Start 45

Alsos Project 46

Farm Hall 47

Heavy Water 52

Norwegian Commandos 55

4. Espionage During The Manhattan Project
Background 63
Klaus Fuchs 64
Ted Hall 67
David Greenglass 70
Venona Project 71
The Reckoning 72
Reasons for the Security Breakdown 75

5. Creating the Cold War
Atomic Energy Act of 1946 79
Cold War Begins, 1946 to 1950 80
U.S. Nuclear Warhead Stockpile: 1945-1961 83
NWC in 1947 84
NWC in 1948 85
NWC in 1949 86
NWC from 1950 to 1951 87
Tactical Nuclear Weapons 90

6. Two Scorpions in a Bottle
Development of Fusion 95
Fusion Processes in Weapons 96
NWC from 1952 to 1953 98
McCarthyism 101
Oppenheimer's Security Clearance 102
Atoms for Peace 106

7. Tests and Test Sites
First Thermonuclear Tests 113
Worldwide Nuclear Tests 116
Nuclear Test Sites 118
Nonnuclear Test Sites 120

8. Performance Improvements
Wooden Bombs 127
Sealed Pits 128
Neutron Generators 129
Limited-Life Components 131

NWC from 1954 to 1957 132
NWC in 1958 134
Radiation Hardening and Miniaturization 135

9. **To The Brink**
Cold War Intensifies, 1953 to 1962 139
Bay of Pigs 141
Berlin Wall 142
Strategic Nuclear Weapons 144
Cuban Missile Crisis 146
NWC from 1962 to 1967 147

10. **Safety and Security Improvements**
Permissive Action Link 151
Nuclear Weapon Accidents 153
Weapon Safety Improvements 155
NWC from 1975 to 1979 156
U.S. Government Organizations .156
Environment, Safety and Health Concerns 160
NWC from 1982 to 1989 161

11. **Ending the Cold War**
Negotiate from Strength 165
Cold War Ends, 1987 to 1991 167
Stockpile Reductions 168
Nonnuclear Reconfiguration Program 170
NWC in 1994 173
NWC Site Missions 174

12. **Maintaining Deterrence**
The Challenge 177
Stockpile Stewardship and Management 177
Storage and Disposition of Weapons-Usable
Fissile Material 178
Tritium Supply and Recycling 179
Stockpile Life Extension Program 180
National Nuclear Security Administration 182
NNSA Reorganization 184
Summary 186

Epilogue 189

Appendices

Appendix A: 1953 AEC/DoD Agreements 203

Appendix B: National Environmental Policy Act 209

Appendix C: Nonnuclear Reconfiguration Program 215

Appendix D: Nuclear Weapon Treaties 227

Glossary 233

Bibliography 239

Photograph Credits 249

Index 251

About the Author 265

LIST OF FIGURES

1.1	Albert Einstein in 1922	1
1.2	Niels Bohr in 1922	3
1.3	Atomic Structure	4
1.4	Enrico Fermi	6
1.5	Binding Energy and Mass Defect	7
1.6	Nuclear Fission	10
1.7	Albert Einstein and Leo Szilard	12
1.8	Franklin D. Roosevelt	13
1.9	Glenn Seaborg	14
1.10	U.S.S. Shaw Explodes During the Japanese Air Raid	16
1.11	J. Robert Oppenheimer in 1945	17
2.1	General Leslie R. Groves	21
2.2	NWC in 1942	25
2.3	Calutron	27
2.4	Pu-239 Production	29
2.5	NWC from 1943 to July 1945	31
2.6	Harry S Truman	32
2.7	First Nuclear Weapons	33
2.8	Oppenheimer and Groves at Trinity	35
2.9	Colonel Paul W. Tibbets	37
2.10	Little Boy	37
2.11	Fat Man	38
2.12	NWC in September 1945	40
3.1	Werner Heisenberg in 1927	46
3.2	Heisenberg and Bohr in 1934	50
3.3	Walther Bothe	51
3.4	Harold Urey	53
3.5	Heavy Water Plant at Vemork	56
3.6	Ferry "Hydro" at the Railhead on Lake Tinn	58
4.1	Quebec Conference	65
4.2	Klaus Fuchs	66
4.3	Ted Hall	68
4.4	David and Ruth Greenglass	70
4.5	Harry Gold	70
4.6	NSA Seal	71
4.7	Julius and Ethel Rosenberg	72
5.1	AEC Logo	80
5.2	U.S. Nuclear Warhead Stockpile: 1945 to 1961	83
5.3	NWC in 1947	84
5.4	NWC in 1948	86
5.5	NWC in 1949	87
5.6	NWC from 1950 to 1951	88

5.7 Shot Grable .90
5.8 Lance .91
6.1 Edward Teller .95
6.2 Boost Reservoirs .97
6.3 NWC from 1952 to 1953 .100
6.4 Dwight D. Eisenhower .106
7.1 Mike .114
7.2 Bravo .115
7.3 B2A Stealth Bomber at Tonopah .122
7.4 Davis Gun at Edgewood .124
8.1 Thermal Batteries .127
8.2 Manual Insertion .128
8.3 Motor-Driven Insertion .128
8.4 Sealed Pit .129
8.5 Neutron Generator Operation .130
8.6 Neutron Generators .130
8.7 Tritium Decay Curve .131
8.8 NWC from 1954 to 1957 .133
8.9 NWC in 1958 .134
9.1 John F. Kennedy .141
9.2 Castro and Khrushchev .141
9.3 Berlin Wall .144
9.4 B-52 Bomber .145
9.5 Soviet Missile Installations in Cuba .147
9.6 NWC from 1962 to 1967 .148
10.1 Permissive Action Link .151
10.2 Bomb Hoisted Aboard the U.S.S. Petrel .153
10.3 Enhanced Nuclear Detonation Safety .155
10.4 NWC from 1975 to 1979 .156
10.5 AEC, ERDA, and DOE Logos .158
10.6 DOE Organization for Weapon Program Management .160
10.7 NWC from 1982 to 1989 .162
11.1 Ronald Reagan .165
11.2 Trident II Missile Breaks the Water after a Submarine Launch .166
11.3 Berlin Wall Being Destroyed .167
11.4 Presidents Bush and Gorbachev .169
11.5 Nonnuclear Reconfiguration .172
11.6 NWC in 1994 .173
12.1 NNSA Logo .184
12.2 NNSA Reorganization .185

PREFACE
to the Second Edition

The Nuclear Weapons Complex (NWC) is a nationwide group of government-owned and contractor-operated laboratories and production plants that are administered by the National Nuclear Security Administration (NNSA) under the U.S. Department of Energy (DOE). The NWC is responsible for the design, development, production, modification, repair, assembly, disassembly, and testing of all U.S. nuclear weapons. The DOE's Albuquerque Operations Office (AL) was responsible for managing the weapon programs within the NWC.

The seed for this book was planted in the mid-1980s while I was working for AL. This office was growing at that time and had developed a one-week orientation program for new employees. This program included a presentation on the history and missions of the NWC sites. During this period, I was in charge of AL's production management organization and presented this portion of the orientation.

Long after this program ended, requests for my history presentation continued to arrive from various sites in the NWC and elsewhere. As time went on, and in response to questions from my audiences, I compiled more and more information about this history. It is a fascinating story, and my research evolved into a hobby. In 1994, I retired from the federal government and the following year went to work at Sandia National Laboratories. Requests for this presentation continued to arrive, and Sandia supported me in fulfilling them.

This book parallels my presentation and is intended to serve as a fairly brief orientation to the NWC. Consequently, it does not go into great detail on any individual topic. It includes discussions of the original missions assigned to each site and the major changes that were made thereafter. For the sake of brevity, it does not cover the multitude of smaller missions assigned to each site or the materials and components procured from private industry.

There are many excellent books and reports on individual sites and projects within the NWC. Anyone desiring more in-depth information on a given topic can find additional sources in the references at the end of each chapter and in the bibliography.

As with my presentation, the book is designed to serve not only scientists and engineers but also the average person who does not have advanced technical training. Toward that end, a glossary of technical terms is provided for easy reference. To improve readability, many of the technical details and anecdotes (some are quite humorous) have been put into shaded blocks below the related text. Also, more detailed information on four topics has been placed into appendices. The shaded blocks and appendices may be skipped with no loss in understanding the main story.

As a further aid to the reader, different shapes and colors have been used to signify three types of changes to the NWC: (1) a yellow rectangle indicates a new site, (2) a blue rectangle with an "x" through it indicates a site that has been closed, and (3) a green rectangle with rounded corners indicates a major change in mission for a site.

Over the years, I experimented with the organization of this material. In general, it is presented in chronological order. However, some topics, such as nuclear testing, extended over a long period and experience has shown they are best presented in one section. The book is arranged accordingly.

The NWC evolved as needed to meet our national security requirements, which were driven by World War II and the Cold War. This evolution was also shaped by the need to incorporate new technologies into the nuclear weapon stockpile and to maintain this stockpile after the Cold War was over.

The story begins with the publication of Einstein's Special Theory of Relativity and his famous equation, $E = mc^2$. There were several great scientific discoveries over the next few decades that set the stage for development of the first atomic bomb. The book outlines those discoveries. It then explains the original reason for establishing the NWC, the subsequent reasons for change within it, including the key events in the Cold War, and the sites that were affected by these changes.

This book also explains the basic principles on which nuclear weapons operate, along with the major technology changes that were incorporated to improve the performance, safety, and security of U.S. nuclear weapons. In addition, it contains information on several interesting topics related to the NWC such as Nazi Germany's atomic bomb program, espionage during the Manhattan Project, nuclear weapon accidents, and worldwide nuclear tests.

When the Cold War ended, the mission of the NWC changed from the design and production of new weapons for a very large stockpile to the maintenance of existing weapons in a much smaller stockpile. In many ways, as explained herein, this post-Cold War mission is considerably more difficult.

I usually concluded my presentations with a question and answer period. The questions often went beyond the bounds of the facts related to the NWC and solicited my opinion on a variety of issues. I have included twelve of the most interesting and challenging questions and my answers in an Epilogue. To the extent possible, I have tried to keep the facts separate from my opinions. Chapters 1 through 12 and the appendices contain the facts. My opinions are expressed in the Epilogue.

My presentations on the history of the NWC were always well received. Hopefully, my readers will find this history to be just as interesting and entertaining in book form. I also hope that this book serves as a valued reference in the future.

The second edition of this book includes two major changes that affect the NWC since the original publication in August 2002; specifically, the NNSA's reorganization of December 2002 and the Senate's ratification of the Moscow Treaty in March 2003. It also includes a new section on binding energy and mass defect in Chapter One along with some minor editorial changes.

The third edition includes several updates since the second edition was published in 2005, most notably, the name NWC has been changed to Nuclear Security Enterprise.

ACKNOWLEDGEMENTS

This book could not have been completed without the support and encouragement of many of my friends and colleagues at SNL. I especially want to thank Rebecca Ullrich for her advice on a variety of topics as well as her suggestions on organization and format; Myra O'Canna for her help in obtaining information and pictures from the SNL archives and elsewhere; Michael Townsend for his work in preparing the NWC-related figures and for designing the front and back covers; Douglas Mangum for his input on Permissive Action Link; Perry D'Antonio for his input on Enhanced Nuclear Detonation Safety; Albert Bendure for his input on the Albuquerque Microelectronics Operation; Allen Strouphauer for his input on the Stockpile Life Extension Program; Larry Walker and Richard Lucero for their inputs on nuclear-related treaties; Bruce Green and Ron Williams for their advice on classification issues; Glenda Sweatt, Adele Johnson, and Diana Kozelka for their help in researching various topics in the SNL Technical Library; and John Hogan, Andrew Rogulich, Brien Bopp, Clyde Layne, Carl Mora, and Tom Schultheis (retired) for their inputs and comments on my draft manuscript.

Special thanks goes to Lorna Clark and Philip Brittenham for their editorial suggestions, and to Jan Gaunce for converting my manuscript into a very attractive final product.

Thanks also goes to several people outside of SNL including James Rose in DOE Headquarters for his advice on the National Environmental Policy Act and its implementing processes; Robert Friedrichs at the Nevada Test Site for his inputs on nuclear tests; Geoff Netzley at the Savannah River Site for an update on tritium supply; and to Joan March at LANL, Maurice Smith at the Kansas City Plant, and Harry Mumma (retired) from DOE/AL for their inputs and comments on my draft manuscript.

Finally, I give thanks to my wife, Jerilynn, for her encouragement over these many years and for her patience in listening to my often-repeated stories.

ABBREVIATIONS & ACRONYMS

ABM	Anti-Ballistic Missile Treaty
ACF	American Car and Foundry
ADM	atomic demolition munition
AEC	Atomic Energy Commission
AF&F	arming, fuzing, and firing
AL	Albuquerque Operations Office
AMO	Albuquerque Microelectronics Operation
AMU	atomic mass unit
APT	accelerator production of tritium
CDM	Concurrent Design and Manufacturing
CDR	conceptual design report
CEQ	Council on Environmental Quality
CIA	Central Intelligence Agency
CLWR	commercial light water reactor
CTBT	Comprehensive Test Ban Treaty
DoD	Department of Defense
DOE	Department of Energy
EA	environmental assessment
EIS	environmental impact statement
ENDS	enhanced nuclear detonation safety
ERDA	Energy Research and Development Administration
ES&H	Environment, Safety and Health
FBI	Federal Bureau of Investigation
FCDA	Federal Civil Defense Administration
FMCT	Fissile Material Cut-off Treaty
FONSI	finding of no significant impact
GAC	General Advisory Committee
HERF	high energy rate forging
HEU	highly-enriched uranium

HUAC	House Un-American Activities Committee
ICBM	intercontinental ballistic missile
INEL	Idaho National Engineering Laboratory
INF	intermediate-range nuclear forces
IRBM	intermediate-range ballistic missile
KC	Kansas City Plant
KCSO	Kansas CIty Site Office
kt	kiloton
LAC	lightning arrestor connector
LANL	Los Alamos National Laboratory
LASO	Los Alamos Site Office
LEU	low-enriched uranium
LLC	limited life component
LLNL	Lawrence Livermore National Laboratory
LSI	large-scale integrated circuit
LSO	Livermore SIte Office
LTBT	Limited Test Ban Treaty
MDE	Manufacturing Development Engineering
MDL	Microelectronics Development Laboratory
MED	Manhattan Engineer District
MeV	million electron volts
MIRV	multiple independently-targeted reentry vehicle
MLC	Military Liaison Committee
MOX	mixed oxide
MRBM	medium-range ballistic missile
Mt	megaton
NATO	North Atlantic Treaty Organization
NCP	Nonnuclear Consolidation Plan
NEPA	National Environmental Policy Act
NIF	National Ignition Facility

NNSA	National Nuclear Security Administration
NNSS	Nevada National Security Site
NOA	notice of availability
NOI	notice of intent
NPT	Non-Proliferation Treaty
NRC	Nuclear Regulatory Commission
NSA	National Security Agency
NSE	Nuclear Security Enterprise
NSO	Nevada Site Office
NTS	Nevada Test Site
NV	Nevada Operations Office
NWC	Nuclear Weapons Complex
OAK	Oakland Operations Office
OASO	Office of Amarillo Site Operations
OCDM	Office of Civil Defense Mobilization
OKCSO	Office of Kansas City Site Operations
OKSO	Office of Kirtland Site Operations
OLASO	Office of Los Alamos Site Operations
OR	Oak Ridge Operations Office
OSRD	Office of Scientific Research and Development
PAL	permissive action link
P&PD	Production and Planning Directive
PEIS	programmatic environmental impact statement
PNET	Peaceful Nuclear Explosions Treaty
PX	Pantex Plant
PSO	Pantex Site Office
ROD	record of decision
RTG	radioisotopic thermoelectric generator
SALT	Strategic Arms Limitation Talks
SLBM	submarine-launched ballistic missile

SLEP	Stockpile Life Extension Program
SNL	Sandia National Laboratories
SORT	Strategic Offensive Reductions Treaty
SR	Savannah River Operations Office
SRBM	short-range ballistic missile
SRS	Savannah River Site
SRSO	Savannah River Site Office
SSO	Sandia Site Office
START	Strategic Arms Reduction Treaty
TEF	Tritium Extraction Facility
TTBT	Threshold Test Ban Treaty
TVA	Tennessee Valley Authority
UCRL	University of California Radiation Laboratory
YSO	Y-12 Site Office

CHAPTER ONE

Einstein Opens the Door

Relativity

Figure 1.1. Albert Einstein in 1922

In 1905, Albert Einstein published a paper entitled "On the Electrodynamics of Moving Bodies," which came to be known as his Special Theory of Relativity.[1] (Einstein's General Theory of Relativity was published in 1915.) This theory was revolutionary in that it provided a new understanding of the relationship between space and time, showing that time is a variable and a function of the relative velocity of one object to another. This concept is outside the range of normal human experience and is very difficult to comprehend. It has been said that only twelve people in the world understood relativity at that time and that eight of them lived in Berlin.[2]

Einstein's theory also shows the equivalence of mass and energy. Until this time, scientists believed that matter could be neither created nor destroyed. This statement is still true for almost all reactions on earth. For example, in a fire, all of the atoms in the burned material still exist. They have only undergone a chemical change (e.g., carbon combines with oxygen and becomes carbon dioxide) or a change of state (e.g., water absorbs heat and becomes steam). Einstein's famous equation, $E = mc^2$, states that mass (m) can be destroyed by conversion into energy (E). Because the speed of light (c) is a very large number (300,000,000 meters/second), c squared is an enormous number. In other words, the conversion of a very small mass yields an enormous quantity of energy.

Einstein was first nominated for the Nobel Prize for relativity in 1910. Einstein's nomination was passed over eight times even though he was acknowledged to be one of the greatest scientists of all time. Unfortunately, even the prestigious scientists on the Nobel Prize Committee had trouble understanding relativity and did not want to make an award before experimental issues had been clarified. Also, some anti-Semitic scientists opposed giving the prize to Einstein because he was Jewish.

When Einstein finally received the 1921 Nobel Prize, it was "for his services to theoretical physics and especially for his discovery of the photoelectric effect," not for relativity.[3]

Einstein retained his sense of humor during this period in spite of the growing anti-Semitism in Germany. For example, on April 6, 1922, in an address to the French Philosophical Society at the Sorbonne, he said, "If my theory of relativity is proven successful, Germany will claim me as a German and France will declare that I am a citizen of the world. Should my theory prove untrue, France will say that I am a German, and Germany will declare that I am a Jew."[4]

Atomic Structure

Over the next three decades, there were several major scientific discoveries that defined the basic structure of the atom. Three of the most important discoveries were as follows:

- 1911 – Ernest Rutherford, a British physicist, laid the foundation for the modern theory of atomic structure by showing that atoms have a nucleus, which contains positively charged protons surrounded by negatively charged electrons.[5]

- 1913 – Niels Bohr, a Danish physicist, modified Rutherford's model to incorporate the ideas of quantum physics. He showed that electrons exist in discrete energy levels. An atom's chemical properties are a function of the number and arrangement of its electrons.[6]

Figure 1.2. Niels Bohr in 1922

- 1932 – James Chadwick, a British physicist, discovered the neutron as another particle in the nucleus. The neutron has no electrical charge and, therefore, can be used effectively as a subatomic "bullet" to probe the interior of atoms.[7]

Some of the other key terms used to describe atomic structure are as follows:

Atomic number equals the number of protons in a nucleus. For example, hydrogen has one proton and is atomic number one, helium has two protons and is atomic number two, lithium has three protons and is atomic number three, etc.

Mass number equals the number of protons and neutrons in a nucleus.

Standard notation shows the atomic number as a subscript and the mass number as a superscript.

Isotopes are atoms with the same number of protons but different numbers of neutrons. Hydrogen, for example, has three isotopes – protium, deuterium, and tritium.

The resulting model of the atom is illustrated in Figure 1.3.

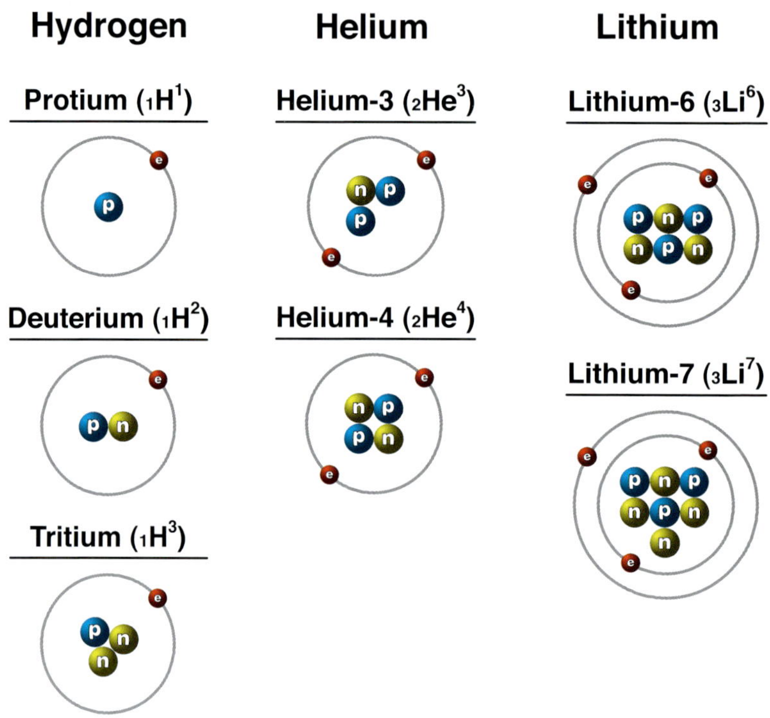

Figure 1.3. Atomic Structure

> *The hydrogen (H) in a molecule of ordinary water (H_2O) is mostly protium with only a very small amount of deuterium and trace quantities of tritium. Heavy water is deuterium oxide (D_2O).*

Bombarding the Nucleus

Other key scientific developments during this period were:

- 1919 – Ernest Rutherford achieved the first artificial transmutation of an element by bombarding atoms of nitrogen with alpha particles (i.e., helium nuclei). Some of the nitrogen atoms were transmuted into oxygen by having a proton from the helium become part of the nitrogen nucleus.[8]

- 1932 – Two British physicists, John Cockcroft and Ernest Walton, were the first to split the atom. They used very high voltage to accelerate protons into lithium nuclei. High voltage was required because nuclei are positively charged, and like charges repel. When a lithium nucleus captured a proton, it broke into two alpha particles. This was the first case of a nuclear disintegration brought about by purely artificial means.[9]

- 1934 – Leo Szilard, a Hungarian physicist, filed a patent application for the concept of using neutron-induced chain reactions to liberate energy. This application also described the key concept of critical mass and stated that "If the thickness is larger than the critical value…I can produce an explosion."[10] Although the mechanism for producing such reactions had not yet been discovered, Szilard was awarded a patent and thus legally could claim to be the inventor of the atomic bomb.

Szilard was awarded British Patent No. 630,726, entitled "Improvements in or Relating to the Transformation of Chemical Elements." As stated by Szilard, "This invention has for its object the production of radioactive bodies, the storage of energy through the production of such bodies and the liberation of nuclear energy for power production and other purposes through nuclear transmutation." [11] *Szilard did not patent this idea for personal gain. His motivation was to protect the idea in order to prevent its harmful use. In February 1936, he gave this idea to the British Admiralty so that it could be classified and protected under British secrecy laws.*[12]

Szilard subsequently tried to use his patent as a means by which to gain control of the decision-making process for the atomic bomb. He felt that the authority for such decisions should be in the hands of the best scientists in the field rather than government officials like General Groves. The U.S. government rejected his claim because he had not disclosed the existence of his patent before joining the Manhattan Project. [13] *Szilard's patent was not published until September 28, 1949.*

Figure 1.4. Enrico Fermi

- 1934 – Enrico Fermi, an Italian physicist, began bombarding many elements with neutrons. He discovered the principle of *moderation* whereby neutrons are slowed down by collisions with light atoms. He proved that slow neutrons were very effective in producing radioactive atoms. The slow neutrons were "captured" by a nucleus, which was then transmuted into a different isotope or atom. (Fast neutrons generally pass through a nucleus without being captured.) Although he did not know it at the time, this discovery became the key to nuclear energy. Fermi was awarded the Nobel Prize for this work in 1938.[14]

> *Light atoms are more effective at slowing neutrons than heavy atoms. Protium, which has atomic mass 1, would be the best moderator, but it absorbs too many neutrons. Deuterium with atomic mass 2 and carbon with atomic mass 12 hardly ever absorb neutrons and are very good moderators.*[15]

Binding Energy and Mass Defect

Francis W. Aston invented the mass spectrograph in 1919. It allows elements and isotopes to be separated by mass and to have these masses measured very accurately. He won the Nobel Prize in 1922 for this invention.

Aston found that atomic nuclei have masses that are very close to whole number multiples of protium ($_1H^1$). However, he also found that these mass numbers were always slightly below his prediction. It was like putting twelve one-pound balls together and finding the combined weight to be less than twelve pounds.

Aston knew that a very powerful force held nuclei together. One manifestation of this force is the "binding energy" of individual *nucleons* (protons and neutrons are also called nucleons). To acquire this energy, nuclei sacrifice some of their mass. This lost mass is known as the "mass defect." Aston plotted this data on a chart similar to the one shown in Figure 1.5 below.

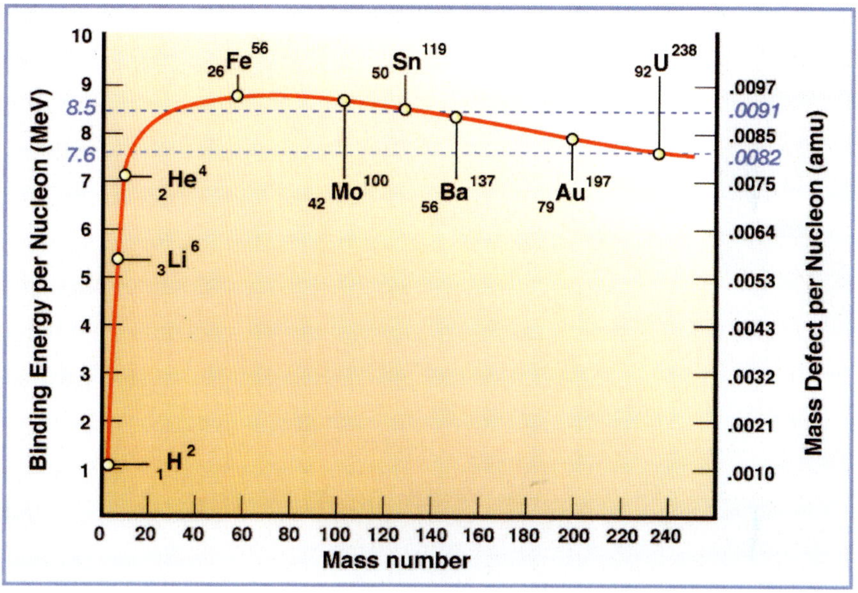

Figure 1.5. Binding Energy and Mass Defect

Elements/isotopes in the broad middle range of the periodic table, such as iron (Fe), molybdenum (Mo), tin (Sn), and barium (Ba) have *high binding energy* per nucleon and thus have a high mass defect. In other words, *their nucleons are relatively light.*

Conversely, elements/isotopes at each end of the periodic table, such as uranium (U) and deuterium ($_1H^2$), have *less binding energy* per nucleon. They have a smaller mass defect and their *nucleons are relatively heavy.*

In 1936, Aston explained that elements/isotopes at the ends of this curve have the potential to reduce their mass by transmuting into something closer to the center. [16] This process would release energy as per Einstein's equation, $E = mc^2$.

The mass of a nucleus is commonly expressed in terms of atomic mass units (amu). An amu is defined as one-twelth of the mass of the carbon 12 isotope ($_6C^{12}$). In the conversion of mass to energy, one amu is equivalent to 931 million electron volts (Mev).[17]

As shown in Figure 1.5, U-238 has a mass defect of .0082 amu/nucleon. This corresponds to a binding energy of 7.6 Mev/nucleon. If a U-238 nucleous split into two equal parts, each with a mass of 119 (such as Sn-119), the nucleons in these parts would have a mass defect of .0091 amu/nucleon. This corresponds to a binding energy of 8.5 Mev/nucleon.

Using the right side of Figure 1.5, there would be a loss of mass and release of energy as follows:
The change in mass is .0009 amu/nucleon (i.e., .0091 - .0082).
238 nucleons x .0009 amu/nucleon = .2 amu (about one-fifth of a proton mass) would be lost.
.2 amu x 931 Mev/amu = 200 Mev would be released.

Alternatively, the energy release can be calculated directly from the left side of Figure 1.5 as follows:
238 nucleons x (8.5 - 7.6 Mev/nucleon) = 200 Mev

As a point of reference, a typical chemical reaction, such as the combustion of one atom of carbon, produces about 4.1 electron volts (ev) of energy. By contrast, the nuclear reaction described above produces *fifty million* times as much energy.

Anti-Semitism in Europe

Anti-Semitism was not new to Europe in the 20th century. Its virulence waxed and waned over time in various countries as a function of their economic and social conditions and the temperament of their leaders. Anti-Semitism intensified in Europe following World War I, particularly during the economic depression that followed. Conditions were especially bad in Germany.

On January 30, 1933, Adolph Hitler, the leader of the Nazi party, was appointed Chancellor of Germany and began to implement anti-Semitic legislation. On April 7, 1933, the Law for the Restoration of the Professional Career Civil Service was passed. This law required civil servants of non-Aryan descent to retire. Because universities were state institutions, members of their faculties were civil servants. As a result of this law, one-fourth of the physicists in Germany were removed from their university positions. Eleven of these physicists had earned or would later earn Nobel Prizes.[18]

On September 15, 1935, the Nuremberg Laws were passed, making anti-Semitism the official policy of the German government. These laws deprived Jews of German citizenship. They also prohibited Jews from marrying non-Jews, from writing or publishing, from teaching in any educational institution, from working in a bank or hospital, from exhibiting paintings or giving concerts, and from entering any of the government's labor or professional bodies.[19]

By this time, many Jews realized that they would have to leave Germany in order to survive. The situation was becoming unbearable for Jews in other European countries as well. As a result, about one hundred physicists emigrated to the U.S. between 1933 and 1941.[20] Some of the most notable of these scientists were the following:

Hans Bethe – Germany *
Niels Bohr – Denmark *
Felix Bloch – Switzerland *
Albert Einstein – Germany *
Enrico Fermi – Italy * #
Otto Frisch – Austria
George Gamow – Russia
George Kistiakowski – Russia
John von Neumann – Hungary
Rudolf Peierls – Germany
Isidor I. Rabi – Austria *
Bruno Rossi – Italy
Emilio Segre – Italy *
Leo Szilard – Hungary
Edward Teller – Hungary
Stanislaw Ulam – Poland
Victor Weisskopf – Austria
Eugene Wigner – Hungary *

* *Nobel Prize winner.*

\# *Enrico Fermi's wife, Laura, was Jewish.*

Nuclear Fission

In November 1938, two German chemists, Otto Hahn and Fritz Strassman, bombarded uranium, atomic number 92, with neutrons. They were shocked to find that this resulted in the production of barium, atomic number 56. It appeared that the uranium atom had split, a theoretical impossibility at that time.

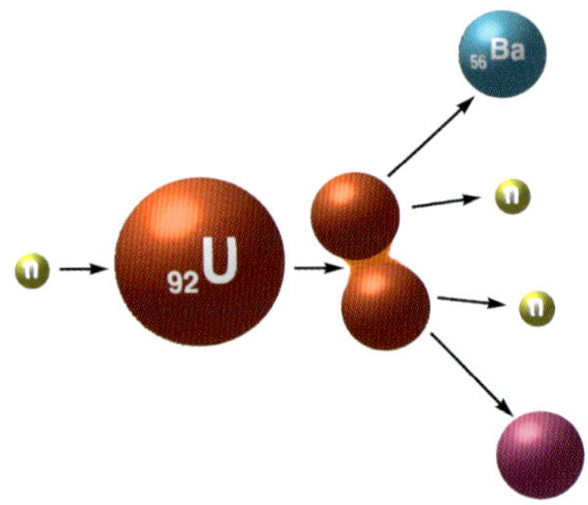

Figure 1.6. Nuclear Fission

They shared their results with two physicists, Lise Meitner and her nephew Otto Frisch, who gave a correct interpretation of the experiment and named the process "nuclear fission."[21] They were familiar with the work of Francis Aston and the concepts of binding energy and mass defect. Frisch borrowed the term "fission" from cell division in biology.[22]

Lise Meitner was born in Vienna in 1878 and had Jewish ancestry. She moved to Berlin in 1907 because it was the center of the world of physics. Meitner and Otto Hahn worked as friends and colleagues until 1938, when Germany annexed Austria. She then lost the protection provided by her Austrian citizenship against German anti-Semitism and was forced to flee to Sweden. Meitner had been collaborating with Hahn on the uranium bombardment experiment, and he continued to correspond with her.[23]

The Hahn-Strassman discovery was submitted to the German scientific magazine *Naturwissenschaften* in Berlin on December 22, 1938. Their paper was published on January 6, 1939.[24] The Frisch-Meitner interpretation of the Hahn-Strassman discovery was submitted to the English scientific magazine *Nature* on January 16, 1939. It was published on February 11, 1939.[25]

The Fifth Washington Conference on Theoretical Physics took place in Washington, D.C., in late January 1939. Many of the world's greatest physicists, including Niels Bohr, Enrico Fermi, Edward Teller, Hans Bethe, and Isidor Rabi, attended. Before Bohr sailed from Europe, Otto Frisch handed him a note with the conclusions that he and Lise Meitner had reached. On January 26, 1939, Bohr shared the news of nuclear fission at the conference.[26]

Bohr's announcement electrified the scientific community. The world's top physicists recognized the possibility that the fissioning of a heavy atom like uranium could produce fission fragments that, due to their lower atomic weights, would shed excess neutrons. The multiplying-neutron chain reaction envisioned and patented by Leo Szilard in 1934 had been realized. This reaction could release enormous quantities of energy as predicted in Albert Einstein's Special Theory of Relativity, that is, $E = mc^2$.

Theoretically, the energy release from one kilogram (about 2.2 pounds) of uranium 235 (U-235) would equal the energy from the detonation of 17,000 tons (17 kt) of TNT.[27]

U.S. Government Involvement

On August 2, 1939, Einstein signed a letter, written by Leo Szilard, to President Franklin D. Roosevelt alerting him to the possibility of making an atomic bomb and noting that Germany might be working to develop such a weapon.

On September 1, 1939, Germany invaded Poland and World War II began. The free flow of information among the world's scientists was shut down.

Roosevelt responded to Einstein's letter by establishing the Advisory Committee on Uranium under the leadership of Lyman J. Briggs, Director of the National Bureau of Standards. Although the Uranium Committee had a relatively small budget, the research efforts that they supported resulted in significant scientific progress.

Figure 1.7. Albert Einstein and Leo Szilard

This committee held its first meeting on October 21, 1939. Twelve days later (on November 1, 1939), the committee issued a report recommending the purchase of four tons of high purity graphite and fifty tons of uranium oxide (U_3O_8). This recommendation resulted in the first outlay of government funds for the atomic bomb effort in the amount of $6,000. The purpose was to support Enrico Fermi and Leo Szilard's uranium "pile" experiments, the goal of which was to produce a self-sustaining nuclear chain reaction.[28]

> *In July 1939, Enrico Fermi and Leo Szilard concluded that graphite could be used as a moderator in a chain-reacting "pile." However, the graphite had to be very pure. Impurities such as boron or cadmium would absorb neutrons and inhibit a chain reaction.*[29]

Shortly thereafter, Vannevar Bush, president of the Carnegie Foundation, became convinced of the need for the government to marshal the forces of science for a war that he believed would inevitably involve the United States.

On June 12, 1940, President Roosevelt established the National Defense Research Committee (NDRC) under the direction of Bush. The Uranium Committee operated under the Bush committee.

The NDRC gave nuclear fission an articulate lobby within the executive branch. The NDRC was subsequently chaired by James B. Conant, the President of Harvard University.[30]

A year later, on June 28, 1941, Roosevelt issued an executive order that established the Office of Scientific Research and Development and named Vannevar Bush to lead it. This office strengthened the presence of science in government even further. Bush now answered directly to the President and could invoke the prestige of the White House in his dealings with other federal agencies. The Uranium Committee became the Office of Scientific Research and Development Section on Uranium.[31]

Figure 1.8. Franklin D. Roosevelt

Fissile Material Problem

In September 1939, Niels Bohr and John Wheeler, an American theoretical physicist, published a paper in *Physical Review* entitled "The Mechanism of Nuclear Fission." One of their conclusions was that atoms with a high mass number that contain an even number of protons and an odd number of neutrons will fission rather easily (i.e., with slow neutrons). U-235 is an even-odd combination with 92 protons and 143 neutrons. By contrast, heavy nuclei with an even-even combination, such as U-238, would require fast neutrons to fission.[32]

Scientists subsequently concluded that an even-odd material like U-235, which produces two or three neutrons when it fissions and can thus sustain a chain reaction, was needed in order to make a bomb. This presented a great technical challenge because U-235 is extremely difficult to produce. U-235 and U-238 have identical chemical properties and, consequently, can be separated only by physical processes, that is, processes that take advantage of the slight difference in mass between the two isotopes. Further, natural uranium ore consists almost entirely of U-238 — only 0.7% is U-235.

Figure 1.9. Glenn Seaborg

As an alternative, the scientists theorized that Pu-239 could serve as an effective fissile material. Pu-239 is an even-odd combination with 94 protons and 145 neutrons. However, this material is almost non-existent in nature, and no man-made processes had been developed to produce it.

In January/February 1941, Glenn Seaborg used Ernest Lawrence's cyclotron at

Berkeley to produce Pu-239 by bombarding U-238 with neutrons. He then developed a chemical technique for separating it from the other elements.[33] By May 1941, Seaborg had shown that Pu-239 was 1.7 times more likely to fission than U-235.

Seaborg's discoveries made the Fermi-Szilard "pile"experiment more important than ever as they suggested the possibility of producing large amounts of fissionable Pu-239 by using plentiful U-238 and then separating it chemically. This process would be simpler and less expensive than isotope separation.[34]

Concurrent with the American efforts, the British were also doing research on uranium and fission. In the spring of 1940, they established the Military Application of Uranium Disintegration (MAUD) Committee to study the possibility of developing a nuclear weapon. In July 1941, Vannevar Bush received a copy of a MAUD Committee report estimating that a critical mass of only ten kilograms would be large enough to produce a nuclear explosion. Previous estimates had been much higher, which made the task of producing enough material seem impossible. This report helped turn the American bomb effort into a major project.[35]

On October 9, 1941, Bush met with Roosevelt and summarized the British findings. Roosevelt instructed him to move as quickly as possible but not to go beyond research and development. Bush also received Roosevelt's permission to explore construction needs with the Army.[36]

On December 6, 1941, the Uranium Committee met in Washington, D.C., and reorganized the work as follows:

- Harold Urey, at Columbia University, would work on a gaseous diffusion method for separating U-235 from U-238.
- Ernest Lawrence, at the University of California, would pursue an electromagnetic method for separating U-235 from U-238.
- Eger Murphee, Director of Research for Standard Oil of New Jersey, would supervise a centrifuge method for separating U-235 from U-238.

- Arthur Compton, at the University of Chicago, would manage the research required to design, build, and operate a plant for the conversion of uranium into plutonium. He would also be responsible for theoretical studies and design of the bomb.[37]

This work laid the foundation for the collection of laboratories and plants that would later become known as the Nuclear Weapons Complex (NWC).

Effort Accelerates

On December 7, 1941, without warning, the Japanese attacked the U.S. fleet at Pearl Harbor in Hawaii. Eighteen ships, including eight battleships, were sunk or heavily damaged. Also, 2,403 Americans were killed and 1,178 were wounded.[38]

Figure 1.10. U.S.S. Shaw Explodes during the Japanese Air Raid

The U.S. declared war on Japan on December 8. Germany and Italy were allied with Japan, and they declared war on the U.S. on December 11. The U.S. responded in kind on the same day. The need for the U.S. to build an atomic bomb before Nazi Germany was now all the more urgent.

During the first half of 1942, several methods to build an atomic bomb were explored. They all involved the need to obtain U-235 or Pu-239. By May 1942, Bush felt that production planning could wait no longer, and he decided to pursue all four of the fissile material production processes under consideration, specifically, electromagnetic separation, gaseous diffusion, gas centrifuge to produce enriched uranium, and a uranium "pile" (i.e., a reactor) to produce plutonium.

The decision to proceed with production planning led directly to the involvement of the Army. The need for security was a key reason for placing the program within one of the armed forces, and the construction experience of the Army Corps of Engineers made it the logical choice to build the production facilities.[39]

Figure 1.11. J. Robert Oppenheimer in 1945

In June 1942, Arthur Compton appointed J. Robert Oppenheimer, a brilliant physicist, to take over the responsibility for fast-neutron studies. These studies were a prerequisite to the design of an atomic bomb.[40]

During the summer of 1942, Oppenheimer assembled a small group of theoretical physicists at Berkeley. He called this group the "luminaries" because they were supposed to "throw light" on the design of an atomic bomb. This group included Hans Bethe, Edward Teller, Felix Bloch, Emil Konopinski, Robert Serber, and John Van Vleck. By the end of the summer, the luminaries had concluded that the development of an atomic bomb would require a massive scientific and technical effort.[41]

Little did they know how massive this effort would become.

Oppenheimer graduated summa cum laude from Harvard in three years. He spoke seven languages including Sanskrit, which he learned in order to read the Hindu scripture, the Bhagavad Gita, *in its original form. A contemporary once said, "There's a huge difference between a genius and a bright person. The reason Oppenheimer knows so much is that it's easy when you learn ten times as fast as other physicists and remember everything."*

Oppenheimer got his Ph.D. from the University of Göttingen in Germany. A colleague asked James Franck, one of the examiners at Oppenheimer's orals, how it had gone. Franck answered, "I got out of there just in time. He was beginning to ask me questions."[42]

References for Chapter 1

1. Denis Brian, *Einstein, A Life* (New York: John Wiley & Sons, Inc., 1996), 64.

2. Ibid., 86.

3. Ibid., 75, 144; and Abraham Pais, *Subtle is the Lord — The Science and Life of Albert Einstein* (Oxford: Oxford University Press, 1982), 506-510.

4. Alice Calaprice, *The Quotable Einstein* (Princeton: Princeton University Press, 1996), 7-8.

5. Samuel Glasstone, *Sourcebook on Atomic Energy* (Princeton: D. Van Nostrand Company, Inc., 1958), 93-94.

6. Ibid., 104-106, 202.

7. Ibid., 58-59.

8. Ibid., 242-243; and Rhodes, *The Making of the Atomic Bomb*, 137.

9. Ibid., 242-243.

10. Bernard T. Feld and Gertrude Weiss Szilard, eds., *The Collected Works of Leo Szilard: Scientific Papers* (Cambridge: The MIT Press, 1972), 642.

11. Ibid., 639.

12. Richard Rhodes, *The Making of the Atomic Bomb* (New York: Simon & Schuster, 1986), 224-225.

13. Ibid., 504-505.

14. Glasstone, *Sourcebook on Atomic Energy*, 288, 326, 345; and Per F. Dahl, *Heavy Water and the Wartime Race for Nuclear Energy* (Bristol and Philadelphia: Institute of Physics Publishing, 1999), 63, 72.

15. Arthur Holly Compton, *Atomic Quest*, (New York: Oxford University Press, 1956), 87-88.

16. Rhodes, *The Making of the Atomic Bomb*, 138-141, 260.

17. Gladstone, *Sourcebook on Atomic Energy*, 87, 390-391.

18. Dahl, *Heavy Water and the Wartime Race for Nuclear Energy*, 185.

19. Crane Brinton, John B. Christopher, and Robert Lee Wolff, *Modern Civilization* (Englewood Cliffs, NJ: Prentice Hall, Inc., 1961), 686.

20. Rhodes, *The Making of the Atomic Bomb*, 196.

21. Ibid., 247-261; and Glasstone, *Sourcebook on Atomic Energy*, 387-389.

22. F. G. Gosling, *The Manhattan Project: Making the Atomic Bomb,* DOE/MA-0001 (Washington, D.C.: U.S. Department of Energy, 1999), 2.

23. Ruth Lewin Sime, *Lise Meitner: A Life in Physics* (Berkeley: University of California Press, 1996), 1, 184-205.

24. Rhodes, *The Making of the Atomic Bomb*, 262.

25. Ibid., 264; and Jeremy Bernstein, *Hitler's Uranium Club: The Secret Recordings at Farm Hall* (Woodbury, NY: AIP Press, 1996), 11.

26. Rhodes, *The Making of the Atomic Bomb*, 264-271.

27. Los Alamos Public Relations Office, Los Alamos: 1943-1945; *Beginning of an Era* (1979; reprint Los Alamos: Los Alamos Historical Society, 1986), 19.

28. Gosling, *The Manhattan Project*, 6.

29. Rhodes, *The Making of the Atomic Bomb*, 300-302.

30. Gosling, *The Manhattan Project*, 6-7; and Rhodes, *The Making of the Atomic Bomb*, 337-338.

31. Gosling, *The Manhattan Project*, 9.

32. Glasstone, *Sourcebook on Atomic Energy*, 403-405; and Rhodes, *The Making of the Atomic Bomb*, 311.

33. Rhodes, *The Making of the Atomic Bomb*, 353-355.

34. Gosling, *The Manhattan Project*, 7-8.

35. Ibid., 9.

36. Ibid., 9.

37. Compton, *Atomic Quest,* 82-86; Rhodes, *The Making of the Atomic Bomb*, 388; and Leslie R. Groves, *Now It Can Be Told* (New York: Harper, 1962), 9, 60.

38. Gordon W. Prange, *At Dawn We Slept: The Untold Story of Pearl Harbor* (New York: McGraw-Hill Book Company, 1981), 539.

39. Gosling, *The Manhattan Project,* 11.

40. Rhodes, *The Making of the Atomic Bomb*, 410.

41. Ibid., 415-416, 420.

42. David Halberstam, *The Fifties* (New York: Villard Books, 1993), 32-33.

CHAPTER TWO

The Manhattan Project

Manhattan Project Begins

In June 1942, Vannever Bush gave a report to President Roosevelt that said it was possible to make an atomic bomb in time to influence the outcome of the war. Roosevelt gave his approval to proceed. Colonel James C. Marshall, of the U.S. Army Corps of Engineers, was directed to form a new engineer district. Marshall established his main office in Manhattan in New York City. At this time, Colonel Leslie R. Groves was the Deputy Chief of Construction for the Corps. Marshall and Groves did not want to arouse curiosity about the project and chose the name Manhattan Engineer District (MED).

Bush felt that Marshall was moving too slowly, and on September 17, 1942, the Army appointed Colonel Groves to head the effort. Groves, who was promoted to Brigadier General on September 23, was a very dynamic leader and can be credited with launching the project.[1]

Figure 2.1. General Leslie R. Groves

By this time, the Corps had developed criteria for selecting the sites needed to produce enriched uranium and plutonium and identified some potential sites. Their criteria included reasonable access to electric power, water, communications, and transportation, and the ability to provide security. Of these criteria, the availability of electric power was the most important.[2]

Between September and December 1942, General Groves selected the first three sites in the nationwide group of laboratories and production plants that came to be known as the Nuclear Weapons Complex (NWC).

NWC in 1942

On September 23, 1942, General Groves took an overnight train to Knoxville, Tennessee. In just a few hours of driving around the area, he chose Oak Ridge as the site to produce enriched uranium (i.e., uranium with a high concentration of U-235).[3]

Three major uranium enrichment plants were built at Oak Ridge, which were code-named Y-12, K-25, and S-50. The Y-12 plant used an electromagnetic separation process, the K-25 plant used gaseous diffusion, and the S-50 plant used thermal diffusion.

In 1944, the project leaders were having major problems in making the electromagnetic separation process operational. They were having even greater problems with the gaseous diffusion process because of the barrier material, which is a very specialized type of filter. The gas centrifuge project had been canceled because of technical problems. Consequently, they began to look at other previously discarded alternatives, one of which was liquid thermal diffusion. In the fall of 1944, Groves added the S-50 thermal diffusion plant to provide partially enriched uranium as feed material to the Y-12 plant.[4]

Thermal diffusion is based on the principle that lighter atoms tend to concentrate in regions of higher temperature. The thermal diffusion system consisted of a long, vertical externally cooled column with a hot concentric cylinder inside. The U-235 isotope would concentrate by the hot column and then move upward. Thermal diffusion was relatively slow and inefficient.[5]

Y-12 produced all of the enriched uranium needed for the first atomic bomb. The K-25 plant was not completed and operational until August 1945. However, before its completion, K-25 supplied some low-enriched material to the Y-12 plant.[6]

On October 15, 1942, General Groves appointed J. Robert Oppenheimer as the Director of a new bomb-design laboratory. Oppenheimer turned out to be an excellent choice. Shortly after his appointment, Oppenheimer recommended Los Alamos as the site for the laboratory. He owned a summer home near Santa Fe and had discovered the area some years earlier while on a pack trip. In November 1942, General Groves visited Los Alamos and approved it.[7]

The original specifications for this secret laboratory were as follows:

- It had to have adequate housing for 30 scientists.
- The land had to be owned by the government or be easy to acquire in secrecy.
- It had to be uninhabited and large enough to permit safe separation of sites for experiments.
- It had to allow easy access control for security and safety reasons.
- It had to have enough cleared land to locate the main buildings very quickly.

Los Alamos met all these specifications.[8]

On December 7, 1942, Secretary of War Henry L. Stimson sent a communiqué informing officials of the Los Alamos Ranch School that the government would be expropriating the property for a special project. Within the next two weeks, they purchased the land and school for $440,000. A contract for constructing laboratory buildings and temporary living quarters was let in December. On January 1, 1943, the University of California was selected to operate the new laboratory, and a formal nonprofit contract was established with the MED.[9]

Construction was initiated at these sites immediately after General Groves selected them. On March 15, 1943, Oppenheimer and some of his scientific staff moved to Los Alamos.[10] Under the Manhattan Project, Los Alamos was the main nuclear weapon design and production facility.

This site was originally called the Los Alamos Laboratory. In 1947, its name was changed to the Los Alamos Scientific Laboratory.[11] In 1979, it was renamed the Los Alamos National Laboratory.

Oppenheimer induced many of the world's finest scientists to join him in this effort, including many who fled from anti-Semitism in Europe. General Groves began a speech to all the Army officers at Los Alamos by saying, "At great expense we have gathered on this mesa the largest collection of crackpots ever seen."[12]

On December 2, 1942, Enrico Fermi achieved the first self-sustaining nuclear chain reaction in a "pile" experiment under the stands of Stagg Field at the University of Chicago.[13] Fermi's pile was a massive latticework of 400 tons of graphite (a form of carbon), six tons of uranium metal, and fifty tons of uranium oxide. This demonstration proved that it would be possible to produce Pu-239 in a nuclear reactor.

Arthur Compton conveyed news of this success in a telephone call to James Conant in the Office of Scientific Research and Development at Harvard.

Compton said, "The Italian navigator has just landed in the New World." Conant asked, "Were the natives friendly?" Compton replied, "Everyone landed safe and happy."[14]

At the end of December 1942, General Groves selected Hanford, Washington, as the site for Pu-239 production. He gave formal approval for this site on January 11, 1943, after completion of a real estate appraisal.[15]

Figure 2.2. NWC in 1942

Prototype, Test, and Research Reactors

Five prototype, test, and research reactors were built and operated under the Manhattan Project. These reactors provided important information and materials for the project.

CP-1: The first of these reactors was built by Enrico Fermi and his associates at the University of Chicago (as described previously). It was called Chicago Pile Number One (CP-1) and became operational in December 1942.

CP-2: By March 1943, CP-1 had been dismantled and rebuilt with modifications as CP-2 at the Palos Forest Preserve outside Chicago. It was a larger version of CP-1 and included shielding to protect workers from radiation. CP-2 operated until 1956.

CP-3: In May 1944, a heavy-water-moderated reactor called CP-3 became operational at Argonne, Illinois. It served as a pilot backup in case the graphite reactors at Hanford failed. Heavy water (deuterium oxide – D_2O) is a good moderator because it has a very low cross section for neutron absorption (additional details are provided in Chapter 3). CP-3 was also used for research on reactor physics and operated until 1956.[16]

During World War II, the U.S. obtained heavy water from a variety of sources including a pilot plant built by the Standard Oil Company in Louisiana. The first large heavy water plant in North America was built by the Consolidated Mining and Smelting Company in Trail, Canada. Three other plants were built by DuPont at Morgantown, West Virginia, Childersberg, Alabama, and Newport, Indiana. By 1944, there was more than enough heavy water for the 6.5 tons required by CP-3.[17]

X-10: In November 1943, a graphite-moderated reactor called X-10 became operational at Oak Ridge, Tennessee. X-10 served as a pilot plant for the large plutonium production reactors that were built at Hanford. It was also used to produce small quantities of plutonium and for research on shielding and the biological effects of radiation. In addition, X-10 was used to produce polonium 210 for weapon initiators.

After the war, X-10 was used for reactor research and isotope production for medical, industrial, and agricultural applications. In 1948, the X-10 site became Oak Ridge National Laboratory. The reactor was decommissioned in 1963. It is now a national historic landmark and is open to visitors.

305 Test Pile: In March 1944, another graphite moderated reactor called the 305 Test Pile became operational at Hanford, Washington. It was used to test materials such as graphite, aluminum, and uranium for the large production reactors at that site.

After the war, this reactor was used to test materials for the other reactors that were built at Hanford. The 305 Test Pile operated until 1972.[18]

Fissile Material Production

Oak Ridge produced highly enriched uranium by separating the U-235 isotope from the U-238 and other isotopes in natural uranium.

Most of the U-235 used in the Manhattan Project was produced by electromagnetic separation in a "calutron" (California University cyclotron). In this process, natural uranium was combined with chlorine to form uranium tetrachloride, which was ionized and injected into one end of a D-shaped vacuum chamber. The ions passed through slotted electrodes to accelerate them into the chamber. A very strong magnetic field (perpendicular to the chamber) forced the ions to go around a curve, and because of inertia, the heavier U-238 isotope traveled on a larger radius than the lighter U-235. The separated isotopes were captured on collection plates.[19]

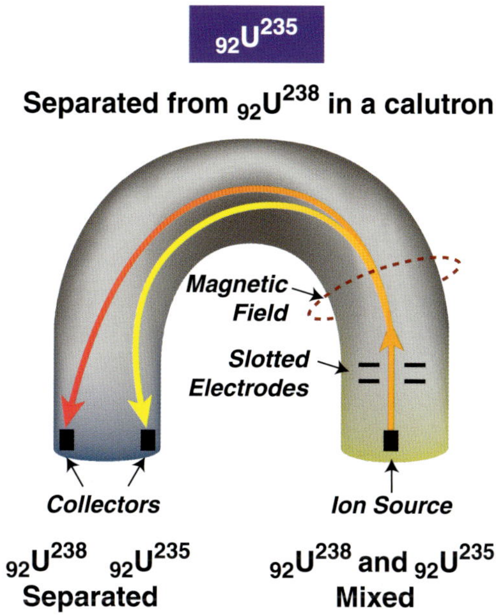

Figure 2.3. Calutron

There were two stages of calutrons. The Alpha stage produced a low-enrichment of U-235 (15%). This fed into the Beta calutrons that enriched the U-235 concentration up to weapons grade material. The Alpha stages were arranged into oval-shaped "racetracks" containing 96 calutrons. The Beta stages were arranged into square-shaped units containing 72 calutrons. At its peak, the Y-12 plant had 1,152 calutrons in operation — nine

Alpha stages with 864 calutrons and four Beta stages with 288 calutrons.[20]

The calutrons required an enormous quantity of electrical conductor material. There was a shortage of copper because of other defense requirements, so General Groves decided to borrow silver from the Treasury Department. Colonel Kenneth D. Nichols, of the Manhattan Project, told Daniel Bell, the Treasury Undersecretary, that they would need between five and ten thousand tons of silver. Bell gave an icy reply — "Colonel, in the Treasury we do not speak of tons of silver; our unit is the Troy ounce." They actually took 13,500 tons, which were returned in 1977.[21]

Thermal diffusion aided this process by supplying partially enriched uranium as feed material for electromagnetic separation. Gaseous diffusion is a more efficient process, but the production facilities were not fully operational until the end of the project. However, K-25 also supplied some partially enriched uranium to Y-12.[22]

Gaseous diffusion is based on the principle that a smaller atom (U-235) will pass through a barrier with tiny holes slightly faster than a larger atom (U-238). Each stage in the diffusion process raised the proportion of U-235 by a factor of only 1.0014. The entire process required about 4,000 stages coupled together in a very complex manner to reach the desired enrichment. The process used uranium hexafluoride because it is a gas at a relatively low temperature. Uranium hexafluoride is highly corrosive, and a great deal of time and effort went into developing a barrier material, made of nickel, that could withstand this environment.[23]

The Y-12 plant made the first delivery of enriched uranium to Los Alamos in March of 1944. This was just over a year after construction had started on the plant — an amazing accomplishment. By September 1944, Y-12 had delivered a full kilogram of highly-enriched uranium (63% U-235) to Los Alamos. By July 1945, 50 kilograms had been delivered and the enrichment had increased to 89%.[24]

Hanford produced Pu-239 by bombarding U-238 with neutrons in a nuclear reactor. The U-238 captured a neutron and transmuted into U-239. The U-239 transmuted via beta decay into neptunium 239. The neptunium then transmuted via beta decay into Pu-239.[25]

The U.S. eventually built nine plutonium production reactors at Hanford between 1944 and 1963. All nine were graphite-moderated, light-water–cooled reactors.[26]

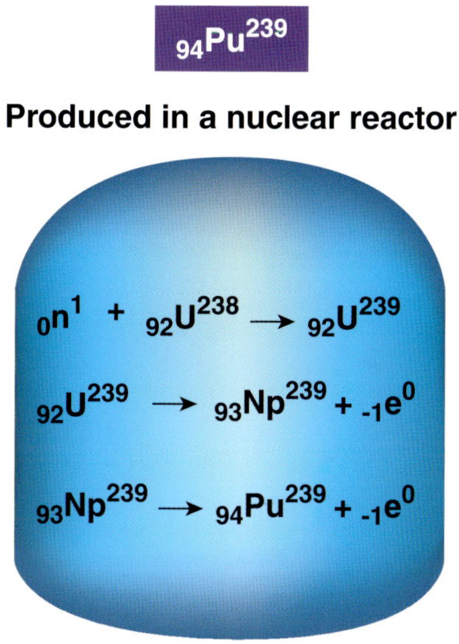

Figure 2.4. Pu-239 Production

NWC from 1943 to July 1945

In 1943, the designers realized that they were going to need a source of neutrons to initiate the fission chain reaction.[27] The first initiators, nicknamed "urchin," were made of polonium and beryllium.

> *Polonium was discovered by Marie and Pierre Curie in 1898. They named it after Marie's native country, Poland.*

Polonium 210 (Po-210) naturally decays into lead and an alpha particle ($_2He^4$). When an alpha particle hits beryllium (in the isotopic form of Be-9), it emits a neutron. The nuclear equation is as follows:

$$_4Be^9 + {}_2He^4 \rightarrow {}_6C^{12} + {}_0n^1$$

A barrier kept the polonium and beryllium apart until the moment that a critical mass was formed. These materials were then brought together and released neutrons.[28]

Po-210 is produced by bombarding bismuth 209 with neutrons. Initial production came from the small X-10 reactor at Oak Ridge.[29] *Po-210 was subsequently bred in the reactors at Hanford.*[30]

In 1943, the MED established a small polonium purification facility in Dayton, Ohio (see figure 2.5).[31]

This facility performed a chemical separation of the Po-210 from the fuel element that produced it. Los Alamos used this material in the production of polonium/beryllium initiators.

Charles A. Thomas, Research Director for Monsanto Chemical Company, borrowed the indoor tennis court on his mother-in-law's estate and converted it into a laboratory for polonium purification.[32]

Because Po-210 has a half-life of only 138 days, it must be replaced very frequently.[33] Also, these "urchin" initiators had to be inserted into the center of the fissionable material, which was very inconvenient.[34] It took several more years before an externally mounted neutron generator with a long life was developed.

By the summer of 1945, Los Alamos was bursting at the seams. There was a shortage of laboratory buildings, family housing, and water. Consequently, in July 1945, the Z Division of Los Alamos was established to perform production engineering and final weapons assembly work.[35] Los Alamos transferred the Z Division with 147 engineers and technicians to Sandia Base (formerly Oxnard Field) in Albuquerque.[36]

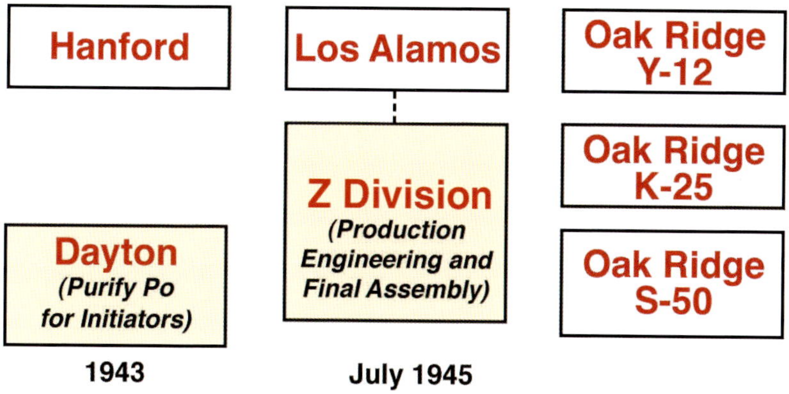

Figure 2.5. NWC from 1943 to July 1945

Oxnard Field was transferred from the Army Air Corps to the Manhattan Engineering District in 1945 and then became known as Sandia Base. Sandia Base was merged into Kirtland Air Force Base in 1971.

Victory in Europe

The German military was on the offensive for the first three years of World War II. The war began to turn against them in November 1942 when the Soviet army made a successful defense of Stalingrad and the Allies invaded North Africa. In July 1943, the Allies landed in Sicily and six weeks later moved to the mainland of Italy. Italy was effectively out of the war thereafter. On June 6, 1944, the Allies landed on the beaches of Normandy, France, and began fighting their way toward Germany. In February 1945, the leaders of the three great Allied powers, Roosevelt, Churchill, and Stalin, met at Yalta in the Crimea to confirm the final plans for the conquest of Germany. They agreed that the Soviets should have the honor of taking Berlin.

The Yalta agreements were subsequently criticized for allowing the Soviet Union to move too far westward. The Allies relied on Stalin's promises to permit free elections in Poland, Hungary, Czechoslovakia, and the Balkans. The Yalta agreements helped to set the stage for the Cold War.

Germany surrendered unconditionally on May 8, 1945. The threat of a German atomic bomb was over.[37] The U.S. could now turn its full attention to the war with Japan.

Interim Committee

On April 12, 1945, President Roosevelt died suddenly in Warm Springs, Georgia, and Vice-President Harry S Truman took his place.

On May 2, 1945, Henry Stimpson, the Secretary of War, proposed the formation of a group to develop recommendations on the proper use of atomic weapons. Truman approved this proposal and called this group the Interim Committee to avoid appearing to usurp congressional prerogatives.[38]

Figure 2.6. Harry S Truman

On June 1, 1945, the Interim Committee recommended that the atomic bomb be used against Japan as soon as possible, that it be used on a dual target (i.e., a military installation or war plant surrounded by workers' homes), and that it be used without warning. Truman could see no alternative and agreed reluctantly.[39]

First Nuclear Weapons

The Manhattan Project developed two types of nuclear weapons, which were named Little Boy and Fat Man as suggested by their relative shapes.

Little Boy was a relatively simple enriched uranium weapon. It consisted of a gun barrel with a subcritical mass of enriched uranium at each end. One mass had an explosive and a detonator behind it and served as a projectile. The other mass had an initiator in front of it and served as a target. When an electrical signal was sent to the detonator, it ignited the explosive, which quickly drove the one mass into the other to form a supercritical mass. At that point, the initiator gave off a burst of neutrons, which started (initiated) the fission chain reaction.

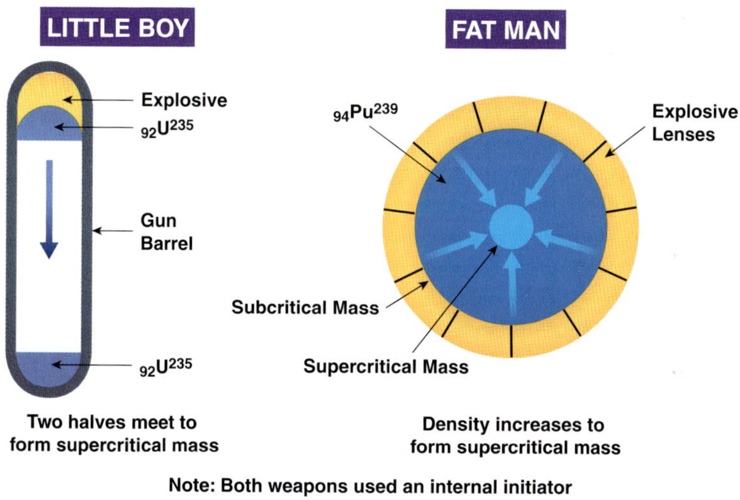

Figure 2.7. First Nuclear Weapons

Fat Man was a very complicated plutonium weapon. It consisted of a large sphere of plutonium with an initiator at the center. This sphere is commonly called a pit. A series of explosives with detonators surrounded the plutonium. When an electrical signal was sent to the detonators, they ignited the explosives, which compressed the plutonium to a much smaller diameter. The plutonium's density increased and formed a supercritical mass. The initiator gave off a burst of neutrons, which started the fission chain reaction.

> *The probability that a neutron will be captured by another atom and not escape from the mass is a function of a material's surface area and its density. A sphere is the optimum shape for a pit because it has the smallest ratio of surface area to volume. As the plutonium density increases, its atoms get closer together, which raises the probability of neutron capture. Also, as the surface area gets smaller, the probability of a neutron escaping is reduced.*

A gun assembly will not work for plutonium because it is too slow and results in a premature initiation of the chain reaction. The implosion design results in a much faster method of assembly. The primary cause of the premature initiation problem is Pu-240. Some of the plutonium produced in a reactor is in the form of Pu-240 rather than the desired Pu-239. Pu-240 has a high rate of spontaneous fission, which will cause the projectile and target of a gun assembly device to melt down and "fizzle" before they are joined.[40]

In 1942, the proposed bomb had a variety of names such as "the gadget," "the device," and "the thing." Later, when the probable dimensions of the weapon began to evolve, the scientists looked to President Roosevelt and Prime Minister Churchill for the source of their private language. The uranium bomb, since it was designed on the gun-barrel principle, was named the "Thin Man" after Roosevelt. The plutonium bomb would have to be the shape of a sphere and was called the "Fat Man" in line with the proportions of Churchill. The scientists reasoned that anyone overhearing conversations about the Thin Man and the Fat Man would conclude that it involved another Roosevelt-Churchill conference. In 1943, Emilio Segre determined that the subcritical uranium masses would not have to be brought together as quickly as previously thought, so the gun barrel could be shorter and lighter. When the barrel of the "Thin Man" was shortened, the name was changed to "Little Boy."[41]

Results of the Manhattan Project

In spite of incredible scientific challenges and immense technical difficulties, the Manhattan Project met its objective. On July 16, 1945, the first atomic device was tested at the Trinity Site near Alamogordo, New Mexico.

Oppenheimer gave the name Trinity to the test and test site. Oppenheimer was inspired by the poems of John Donne, in particular, the fourteenth of his Holy Sonnets, which explores the theme of a destruction that might also redeem. This sonnet opens with the line "Batter my heart, three person'd God."[42]

This device used a Fat Man-type implosion design with plutonium as the fissionable material. It had a yield of 21 kilotons (kt).[43]

> *On viewing the blast, Oppenheimer remembered a line from the Bhagavad-Gita, an epic poem of the Hindu faith: "Now I am become death, the destroyer of worlds."*[44]

The blast left a crater 2,400 feet across and about 10 feet deep. The intense heat had fused the sand in this crater into a glass-like solid, the color of green jade. It was given the name Trinitite.

The logistics for bringing the atomic bomb into the war were well planned. For the previous year, the 509th Composite Bomb Group, under the command of Colonel Paul Tibbets, had been preparing for the mission at a secluded site in Wendover, Utah.

On August 1, 1944, the coral island of Tinian was taken from the Japanese. This island, located 1,500 miles southeast of Japan, became the major airbase for the ensuing raids on Japan. On June 10, the 509th began moving to Tinian. It was chosen because of its long runways, which the heavily loaded bombers would require for take-off.

Figure 2.8. Oppenheimer and Groves at Trinity

Four hours after the Trinity test, the cruiser *Indianapolis* left San Francisco, carrying the "Little Boy" gun and enriched uranium projectile to Tinian.[45] It arrived there on July 26, 1945. After delivering its precious cargo, the *Indianapolis* went back to sea. The enriched uranium target rings were flown from Kirtland Field in Albuquerque to Tinian on three C-54s. They left on July 26 and arrived on July 28.[46]

> *On July 29th, the* Indianapolis *was torpedoed by a Japanese submarine, and it sank in just twelve minutes. The main radio room was destroyed, but they managed to send out a few weak distress signals, which were received at three U. S. Navy locations. Unfortunately, because of a series of errors, no immediate rescue actions were taken. Of the 1,196 men on board, about 900 got off. Only twelve small life rafts were located, so almost all the men were floating in their lifejackets. They were not found until August 2. During this four-day period, they were attacked repeatedly by sharks, and only 317 men survived.*[47]

On July 16, two B-29s left Hamilton Air Force base in California bound for Tinian with plutonium for the "Fat Man."[48] On the same day, Truman, Churchill, and Stalin held a conference in Potsdam, Germany, a suburb of Berlin, to discuss strategy for ending the war with Japan. This conference resulted in the Potsdam Declaration, which called for the Japanese to surrender unconditionally or face "prompt and utter destruction."

On July 26, Truman released the Potsdam Declaration to the press to give Japan "an opportunity to end this war." The Japanese rejected this offer. Based on experience in taking Iwo Jima and Okinawa, an invasion of the Japanese mainland would be very bloody. Estimates of American casualties ranged from a quarter million to one million. As a result, American policy makers concluded that the atomic bomb must be used.[49]

On August 6, 1945, Colonel Paul W. Tibbets took off from Tinian in a B-29 named the *Enola Gay* and dropped "Little Boy" on the Japanese city of Hiroshima.

Colonel Tibbets named his plane *Enola Gay* in honor of his mother.

Little Boy was 26 inches in diameter, 126 inches long, and weighed 8,900 pounds. It had a yield of 15 kt.[51] The scientists at Los Alamos were so confident this design would work that they never tested it beforehand.

Figure 2.9. Colonel Paul W. Tibbets

Approximately 70,000 people were killed and 130,000 wounded. Nevertheless, the Japanese leaders still refused to surrender.

By the end of 1945, the death toll had grown to 140,000 from radiation sickness and other injuries and reached 200,000 after five years.[50]

Figure 2.10. Little Boy

On August 9, Major Charles W. Sweeney took off from Tinian in a B-29 named *Bock's Car* and dropped Fat Man on the Japanese city of Nagasaki. This weapon was 60 inches in diameter, 128 inches long, and weighed 10,300 pounds. It had a yield of 21 kt.[52] *Bock's Car* was named for Frederick Bock, the usual commander of this plane, but piloted on this occasion by Major Sweeney.

Figure 2.11. Fat Man

Approximately 40,000 people were killed and 60,000 wounded. By the end of 1945, the death toll had grown to 70,000 and reached 140,000 after five years.[53]

Shigeyoshi Morimoto, a Japanese kite maker, lived in Nagasaki but had been working in Hiroshima for several months. He was in a paint store in Hiroshima and relatively close to the hypocenter when Little Boy went off. The walls of this store provided a good shield and he survived. Morimoto then struggled to get back to Nagasaki. He arrived at his home just in time to see a great flash of light from the Fat Man. He quickly pushed his wife and son into the cellar, and they survived. Morimoto is the only person known to have survived being in close proximity to both bombs.[54]

On the morning that Nagasaki was bombed, a crucial meeting of Japan's Supreme Council for the Direction of the War had been taking place in Tokyo. The meeting was deadlocked, with three powerful military commanders arguing fervently against surrender. General Anami, the War Minister, called for one last great battle on Japanese soil — as demanded by the national honor, as demanded by the honor of the living and the dead. "Would it not be wondrous for this whole nation to be destroyed like a beautiful flower?" he asked.

But when news of Nagasaki was brought in, the meeting was adjourned to convene that night with the Emperor Hirohito. It was Hirohito who decided that they must "bear the unbearable" and surrender. The Japanese government would accept the Potsdam Declaration with the understanding that the Emperor would remain sovereign.

The U.S. reply stated that the Emperor would remain but "subject to the Supreme Commander of the Allied Powers." If this was not unconditional surrender, it was very close to it. Meanwhile, Truman ordered no further use of atomic bombs without his express permission. (One more Fat Man bomb was available at this time.) The Japanese response reached Truman on August 14 at 6:10 p.m. Japan had accepted the Potsdam Declaration and surrendered. The largest war in history was over.[55]

World War II lasted ten minutes longer than necessary. The Japanese response would have arrived sooner, but a sixteen-year-old messenger, who picked it up at the RCA offices to deliver it to the Swiss legation had been stopped by the police for making a U-turn on Connecticut Avenue.[56]

Formal surrender papers were signed aboard the *U.S.S. Missouri* on September 2, 1945.[57]

General Groves offered this perspective on the bombings.

> *The most important result achieved by the Hiroshima bombing was not the physical damage, although over 50*

percent of the buildings were totally destroyed, nor was it the fifteen to twenty thousand Japanese soldiers who were killed or severely wounded, nor was it the thousands of other people killed and injured. The important result, and the one we sought, was that it brought home to the Japanese leaders the utter hopelessness of their position. When this fact was re-emphasized by the Nagasaki bombing, they were convinced that they must surrender at once. [58]

NWC in September 1945

In September 1945, the S-50 plant was shut down. This was the first plant closure in the NWC.

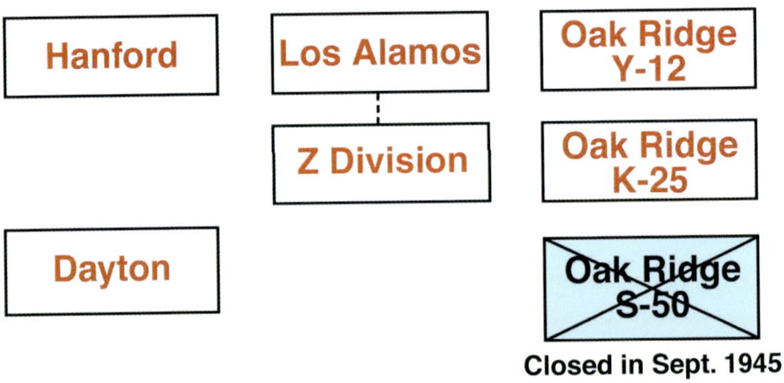

Figure 2.12. NWC in September 1945

As explained previously (under "Fissile Material Production"), the Alpha calutrons at the Y-12 plant provided low-enriched uranium to the Beta calutrons. Gaseous diffusion is a more efficient process for enriching uranium. By September 1945, the K-25 gaseous diffusion plant was producing enough low-enriched uranium to feed the Beta calutrons, and the Alpha calutrons were shut down.

By December 1946, the gaseous diffusion plant was producing highly-enriched uranium, and the Beta calutrons were shut down. Thereafter, all enriched uranium was produced by the gaseous diffusion process.[59]

References for Chapter 2

1. Leslie R. Groves, *Now It Can Be Told* (New York: Harper, 1962), 10-17; and F. G. Gosling, *The Manhattan Project: Making the Bomb,* DOE/MA-0001 (Washington, D.C.: U.S. Department of Energy, 1999), 13.

2. Vincent C. Jones, *Manhattan: The Army and the Atomic Bomb* (Washington, D.C.: United States Army, Center of Military History, 1985), 377.

3. William F. Burgess, Jo Anne McCormick, and Eileen Pingitore, *History of the Production Complex: The Methods of Site Selection,* Prepared by History Associates Inc. for the U.S. Department of Energy, DOE/NV/10594-H1 (Washington, D.C.: U.S. Department of Energy, 1987), 3-5.

4. Gosling, *The Manhattan Project,* 15, 26.

5. Samuel Glasstone, *Sourcebook on Atomic Energy* (Princeton: D. Van Nostrand Company, Inc., 1958), 230-231; and Groves, *Now It Can Be Told,* 119-121.

6. U.S. Department of Energy, Office of Environmental Management, *Linking Legacies,* DOE/EM-0319 (Washington, D.C.: 1997), 136-139.

7. Richard Rhodes, *The Making of the Atomic Bomb* (New York: Simon & Schuster, 1986), 449-451.

8. Los Alamos Public Relations Office, *Los Alamos: 1943-1945, Beginning of an Era* (1979; reprint Los Alamos: Los Alamos Historical Society, 1986), 9-11.

9. Ibid., 10.

10. Groves, *Now It Can Be Told,* 153.

11. Los Alamos Public Relations Office, *Los Alamos: 1943-1945,* 23.

12. Laura Fermi, *Atoms in the Family* (Chicago: University of Chicago Press, 1954), 226.

13. Gosling, *The Manhattan Project,* 16.

14. Arthur Holly Compton, *Atomic Quest* (New York: Oxford University Press, 1956), 144; Fermi, *Atoms in the Family,* 198; and Gosling, *The Manhattan Project,* 16.

15. Burgess, McCormick, and Pingatore, *History of the Production Complex,* 10; and Groves, *Now It Can Be Told,* 74.

16. Office of Environmental Management, *Linking Legacies,* 23, 161, 162; and Per F. Dahl, *Heavy Water and the Wartime Race for Nuclear Energy* (Bristol and Philadelphia: Institute of Physics Publishing, 1999), 184.

17. Office of Environmental Management, *Linking Legacies*, 21, 147; and Dahl, *Heavy Water and the Wartime Race for Nuclear Energy*, 176-184.

18. Office of Environmental Management, *Linking Legacies*, 162-163.

19. Office of Environmental Management, *Linking Legacies*, 138-139; and Rhodes, *The Making of the Atomic Bomb*, 487-489.

20. William J. Wilcox, Jr., *Some Highlights of Y-12's Early Years*, Videotape #1791 (Oak Ridge: Lockheed Martin Video and Motion Picture Services, March 3, 1999).

21. Groves, *Now It Can Be Told*, 107; and Rhodes, *The Making of the Atomic Bomb*, 490.

22. Glasstone, *Sourcebook on Atomic Energy*, 230-231; and Robert S. Norris, *Racing for the Bomb: General Leslie R. Groves. The Manhattan Project's Indispensable Man* (South Royalton, Vt; Steerforth Press, 2002), 367.

23. Ibid., 222-227; and Rhodes, *The Making of the Atomic Bomb*, 493-496.

24. Los Alamos Public Relations Office, *Los Alamos: 1943-1945*, 28; and Groves, *Now It Can Be Told*, 110.

25. Glasstone, *Sourcebook on Atomic Energy*, 484-489.

26. Office of Environmental Management, *Linking Legacies*, 165-167.

27. Rhodes, *The Making of the Atomic Bomb*, 670.

28. Richard Rhodes, *Dark Sun* (New York: Simon & Schuster, 1995), 187-188.

29. Rhodes, *The Making of the Atomic Bomb*, 579.

30. Office of Environmental Management, *Linking Legacies*, 22, 150.

31. Burgess, McCormick, and Pingatore, *History of the Production Complex*, 70.

32. Rhodes, *The Making of the Atomic Bomb*, 579.

33. Rhodes, *Dark Sun*, 277.

34. Ibid., 144.

35. Necah Stewart Furman, *Sandia National Laboratories: The Postwar Decade* (Albuquerque: University of New Mexico Press, 1990), 126-127.

36. Leland Johnson, *Sandia National Laboratories: A History of Exceptional Service in the National Interest*, SAND97-1029 (Albuquerque: Sandia National Laboratories, 1997), 15, 21.

37. Crane Brinton, John B. Christopher, and Robert Lee Wolff, *Modern Civilization* (Englewood Cliffs, NJ: Prentice Hall, Inc., 1961), 759-764, 769.

38. Rhodes, *The Making of the Atomic Bomb*, 628-629.

39. Ibid., 650-651.

40. Ibid., 548.

41. Fletcher Knebel and Charles W. Bailey II, *No High Ground* (New York: Harper & Brothers, 1960), 61; and Gosling, *The Manhattan Project*, 39-40.

42. Rhodes, *The Making of the Atomic Bomb*, 571-572; and Ferenc Morton Szasz, *The Day the Sun Rose Twice* (Albuquerque: University of New Mexico Press, 1984), 40-41.

43. U.S. Department of Energy, Nevada Operations Office, *United States Nuclear Tests: July 1945 through September 1992*, DOE/NV-20, Revision 15 (Las Vegas, NV: U.S. Department of Energy, 2000), 2-3; and Rhodes, *The Making of the Atomic Bomb*, 677.

44. Ibid., 676; and Ferenc Morton Szasz, *The Day the Sun Rose Twice* (Albuquerque: University of New Mexico Press, 1984), 89.

45. Ibid., 678.

46. Gosling, *The Manhattan Project*, 51; and Norris, *Racing for the Bomb: General Leslie R. Groves. The Manhattan Project's Indispensable Man*, 367.

47. Doug Stanton, *In Harm's Way: The Sinking of the USS Indianapolis and the Extraordinary Story of Its Survivors* (New York: Henry Holt and Company, 2001), 113, 132-137, 248-249; and Rhodes, *The Making of the Atomic Bomb*, 693-696.

48. Paul W. Tibbets, *Flight of the Enola Gay* (Columbus: Mid Coast Marketing, 1989), 195.

49. Rhodes, *The Making of the Atomic Bomb*, 656, 692, 693, 699; and John Ray Skates, *The Invasion of Japan: Alternative to the Bomb* (Columbia: University of South Carolina Press, 1994), 77, 234-244.

50. Rhodes, *The Making of the Atomic Bomb*, 733-734; and Gosling, *The Manhattan Project*, 51.

51. Nevada Operations Office, *United States Nuclear Tests*, vii; and Rhodes, *The Making of the Atomic Bomb*, 711.

52. Nevada Operations Office, *United States Nuclear Tests*, vii; and Rhodes, *The Making of the Atomic Bomb*, 740.

53. Rhodes, *The Making of the Atomic Bomb*, 741-742; and Gosling, *The Manhattan Project*, 53-54.

54. Keith Wheeler, *The Fall of Japan* (Chicago: Time-Life Books, 1983), 120-128.

55. David McCullough, *Truman* (New York: Simon & Schuster, 1992), 459-461.

56. McCullough, *Truman*, 461.

57. Gosling, *The Manhattan Project*, 54.

58. Groves, *Now It Can Be Told*, 319.

59. Office of Environmental Management, *Linking Legacies*, 142; and Norris, *Racing for the Bomb: General Leslie R. Groves. The Manhattan Project's Indispensable Man*, 448.

CHAPTER THREE

German Atomic Bomb Program

German Head Start

The U.S. launched its atomic bomb program primarily out of fear that the Germans might build one first. There were at least four good reasons for this fear.[1]

- The Germans discovered nuclear fission in 1938 and were presumed to have a lead in any race to a bomb.
- Germany had many outstanding scientists, including Werner Heisenberg, who was considered to be one of the world's greatest theoretical physicists. Heisenberg had won a Nobel prize in 1932 for his contributions to the invention of quantum mechanics and for the Heisenberg Uncertainty Principle.[2]

Heisenberg published his Uncertainty Principle in 1927. It helped to explain the fact that light and matter exhibit properties of both waves and particles. In brief, this principle states that it is impossible to simultaneously determine the position and velocity of a particle. Any attempt to measure one of these conditions immediately affects the other.[3]

- The Germans had a supply of uranium from the mines in Joachimsthal, Czechoslovakia, which they controlled.
- In May 1940, the Germans took control of the world's only heavy-water plant in Norway.

In 1938, the Germans established a program to study nuclear physics under the Heereswaffenamt — the Army Ordnance Research Department.

On September 26, 1939, Werner Heisenberg was conscripted by the Heereswaffenamt to join the War Office's Nuclear Physics

Figure 3.1. Werner Heisenberg in 1927

Research Group. This group was called the "Uranverein," or "Uranium Club."[4]

The Heereswaffenamt divided its work between two parallel groups — one with Heisenberg at the Kaiser Wilhelm Institute in Berlin and the other under Kurt Deibner at the Army's research laboratory at Gottow.[5]

Through 1940 and 1941, the German scientists focused on two lines of research — how to make a chain-reacting pile and how to separate U-235.[6]

In June 1942, Heisenberg became the de facto director of the German atomic bomb program. Although Heisenberg was a brilliant theoretician, he was not a good experimentalist and made some poor decisions that slowed their progress.[7]

Alsos Project

In late 1943, General Groves established an intelligence unit to provide information on the German atomic bomb program. The Manhattan Project had always carefully avoided drawing undue attention to its work or its people. Code names for their activities were deliberately innocuous. The first mission for this new unit was to enter Italy. Groves was horrified when he learned that the War Department's counterintelligence organization had given this mission the name "Alsos," which is Greek for "grove." His first inclination was to have the mission renamed, but then decided that would only draw more attention to it. This name was carried through all three of the missions, which took place successively in Italy, France, and Germany.[8]

Alsos 1 entered Italy in December 1943. This mission resulted in a good list of intelligence targets and dossiers on the top German scientists — where they worked, where they lived, and the location of their laboratories.[9]

Alsos 2 entered France on the heels of the Allies' invasion of Normandy on June 6, 1944. On August 25, the Allies liberated Paris, and the Alsos unit got into the Radium Institute. From there, a lead took them to the University of Strasbourg where they found papers that had been left behind by German physicist Carl Friedrich Von Weizsacker, who was one of Heisenberg's colleagues. These papers showed that the Germans were not even close to having an atomic bomb. Nevertheless, the Alsos unit wanted to be absolutely certain that no atomic activity was being conducted and continued their search. They also wanted to be sure that no prominent German scientist would evade capture or fall into the hands of the Soviet Union.[10]

Alsos 3 entered Germany on February 24, 1945. In April, they captured all of the German atomic scientists in or near the town of Hechingen in the Black Forest region of southwestern Germany. These scientists had been working on a small atomic pile in the nearby town of Haigerloch. This pile contained one and a half tons of heavy water and was used for neutron-multiplication studies. Heisenberg had calculated that a 50-percent increase in the size of this pile would produce a sustained chain reaction.[11]

As another success, Alsos 3 managed to have all of the heavy water and uranium ore in the German program shipped to the U.S. before the Soviet Union could get it.

Farm Hall

Ten German scientists were interned for six months (July 3, 1945 to January 3, 1946) at Farm Hall, an estate near Cambridge, England.[12] Farm Hall was wired to record their conversations. (The Farm Hall transcripts were not released to the public until February 1992.[13]) As a result of the documents found by the Alsos unit, interviews with the German scientists, and the Farm Hall transcripts, historians have concluded that there were three main reasons for the German failure to develop an atomic bomb:

1. Poor Leadership

Vannevar Bush gave his opinion for the German failure in a speech in 1949. He said the German scientists suffered from

> *... regimentation in a totalitarian system. Their war organization under that system was a botch. Palace politics, bemedaled nincompoops playing expert on subjects on which they were ignoramuses, overlapping power in the hands of parallel agencies — these were some of its characteristics. Finally, the whole structure was clogged with the suspicion, the intrigue and chicanery, and the poisonous fears that are to be expected in any system that functions at the whim of a dictator.* [14]

Samuel Goudsmit, the scientific director of the Alsos Project, held a similar opinion and said, "Goose-stepping Nazis had meddled in scientific matters they didn't understand." [15]

Both of these men had been actively involved in the war, and their words reflected the passion of that time. A more contemporary historian, Thomas Powers, reached much the same conclusion but used less derogatory language. He wrote that "those doing nuclear research in Germany never had a common chain of command, never worked in a common laboratory, never shared a common agenda or goal." Their program consisted of an "unruly mailing list of competing scientists whose only shared hope was to survive the war." [16]

Anti-Semitism, which became extreme under Hitler's leadership, was another factor contributing to the German failure. Some German scientists, such as Johannes Stark and Philipp Lenard, rejected relativity because it was developed by Einstein, a Jew. These men championed "Aryan physics" and opposed "Jewish physics." They influenced academic appointments during the 1920s and 1930s and thus damaged German science. For example, they blocked Heisenberg's appointment to replace Arnold Sommerfeld at the University of Munich in 1935. They attacked Heisenberg because he backed "Jewish physics," and for a time he was in personal danger. This foolishness began to change by the end of 1941 because the war placed a premium on physics that worked, whatever its origins.[17]

2. Lack of Desire

German efforts to build a bomb were damaged by the technical pessimism of leading German scientists who had no desire to build a bomb for Hitler. Heisenberg said that "the possibility of making atomic bombs created a horrible situation for all physicists, ... especially for us Germans ... because the idea of putting an atomic bomb in Hitler's hand was horrible." [18] Otto Hahn was another case in point. He reluctantly agreed to join the research effort. However, he said to his colleague Weizsacker, "but if my work should lead to a nuclear weapon I would kill myself." [19]

Historians have differed in their opinion about Heisenberg's efforts, and he remains somewhat of an enigma. Some historians, such as Goudsmit, felt that Heisenberg really tried to develop a bomb and failed. Goudsmit was Jewish and his parents died in a Nazi concentration camp, so he had a strong personal reason to be harsh in his views toward the Germans. Some later historians with less personal reason for hostility and with access to the Farm Hall transcripts feel that Heisenberg purposely killed the German atomic bomb effort. He did this by convincing German officials that the job was too big, would take too long, and was too uncertain of success.[20]

Albert Speer was the Minister of Armaments and War Production and had the authority to put the full weight of the German economy behind an atomic bomb program. In a meeting on June 4, 1942, Speer asked Heisenberg "how nuclear physics could be applied to the manufacture of atomic bombs." Heisenberg answered that, in theory, nothing stood in the way of building such a bomb, but it would take many years and enormous resources that Germany could not afford in wartime. Speer accepted Heisenberg's opinion and decided to continue work on a reactor project, but only on a modest scale. Germany never funded a massive program like the Manhattan Project.[21]

Heisenberg and Bohr had been close friends before the war. To Bohr's great distress, the German army occupied Denmark in April 1940.

In 1927, Niels Bohr developed the Complementarity Principle, which, in brief, states that particles and waves are mutually exclusive abstractions that complement each other. After much argument, Bohr and Heisenberg agreed that Uncertainty and Complementarity were different ways of saying the same thing. Uncertainty and Complementarity became the basis for the "Copenhagen School" of quantum mechanics.[22]

In September 1941, Heisenberg went to Copenhagen and met with Bohr. Both men had completely different interpretations of what transpired.

Figure 3.2. Heisenberg and Bohr in 1934

Heisenberg said he was trying to tell Bohr that Germany was not working on a bomb. He believed that the world's physicists could prevent such a weapon by agreeing not to work on it. Bohr felt that Heisenberg had been trying to pump him for information about the Allies' efforts on fission. Bohr was upset, and their friendship never regained its earlier warmth.[23]

An interpretation of the meeting between Bohr and Heisenberg has been captured in the play Copenhagen, *which won a Tony Award in 2000 as the best play in New York.*

The fact that the German government had given up on an atomic bomb was evident in the summer of 1943 when Speer approved an Army request to use uranium for armor-piercing shells. This was not depleted uranium as used in later years by the U.S. Rather, it was natural uranium that contained the precious U-235 isotope. Germany was clearly using the butt end of the rifle. The material that had caused so much concern to the U.S. and Britain was to be *thrown* at the enemy.[24]

3. Technical Errors

The Germans never got close to an atomic bomb because they were unable to produce the required fissile materials — enriched uranium (i.e., uranium with a high concentration of the U-235 isotope) or plutonium (Pu-239). They were unable to develop an effective process for separating U-235 from U-238. Consequently, they needed to produce plutonium.[25]

Pu-239 can be produced by bombarding U-238 with neutrons. The only way to get a significant supply of neutrons is in a nuclear reactor. A nuclear reactor requires "slow" neutrons in order to operate (as explained in Chapter One, slow neutrons are more likely to be captured by a nucleus). Neutrons can be slowed by the use of a moderator. Heavy water and very pure graphite are both good moderators.

Figure 3.3. Walther Bothe

In January 1941, Walther Bothe, a German physicist, erred in concluding that graphite would not work as a moderator. He failed to account for the fact that the graphite used in his experiments was contaminated with boron and cadmium, both ravenous neutron absorbers. As a result, the Germans decided they had to use heavy water as a moderator.[26]

In June 1939, while on a trip to the United States, Walther Bothe, who was almost fifty years old, met an attractive woman thirteen years his junior, Ingeborg Moerschner, and fell in love. He returned to work in Heidelberg, but continued this romance through correspondence. A year later, his letters said that he was feeling like a "drunken teenager" and that he had been "speaking of physics the entire day, while thinking only of you." As an intriguing speculation, Bothe may have been focusing on the feminine qualities of Ingeborg instead of on the nuclear qualities of his (impure) graphite.[27]

Heisenberg and his partner, Robert Doepel, built a heavy-water moderated reactor in their laboratory in Leipzig. On June 23, 1942, the heavy water leaked into the uranium and liberated hydrogen. The reactor exploded, and the laboratory was destroyed in the ensuing fire. All of Heisenberg's precious heavy water was lost. The destruction of Heisenberg's reactor was a turning point in the nuclear race. Up to this point, Germany had kept pace with the Allies in nuclear research.[28]

Dan Kurzman, the author of *Blood and Water: Sabotaging Hitler's Bomb*, made the following statement: "Fatefully, if not for a laboratory explosion and the mistake of a lovesick scientist, Germany might have beat the United States to a reactor and perhaps to a bomb." [29]

Heavy Water

In 1911, a large hydroelectric plant was built in Norway at the base of a 380-foot waterfall. Its generators produced 120,000 kilowatts of electrical power, making it the largest hydroelectric plant in the world at that time. Much of this power was used to separate nitrogen from the atmosphere in order to produce nitrate for fertilizer. This facility — known as the Norsk Hydro plant — was located in the Rjukan (pronounced Rookan) Valley, in the suburb of Vemork, about 75 miles west of Oslo.[30]

In 1932, Harold Urey, an American chemist, discovered the deuterium nucleus. Deuterium is one of three isotopes of hydrogen. The deuterium nucleus contains one proton and one neutron. Urey was awarded a Nobel Prize in 1934 for this discovery.

Figure 3.4. Harold Urey

Heavy water is deuterium oxide (D_2O). Ordinary water (H_2O) has a fairly high cross section (i.e., probability) for neutron absorption. By contrast, heavy water has a very low cross section for neutron absorption and thus serves as a good moderator. In ordinary water, only one part in 4,500 is "heavy." [31]

Urey found that H_2O was more likely to dissociate during electrolysis than D_2O. If 100,000 gallons of water were decomposed until only one gallon was left, this remaining liquid would contain about 99 percent pure heavy water. A large quantity of electrical power was required to produce heavy water by this process.

In 1934, the Norsk Hydro managers realized that they could produce heavy water as a by-product of their fertilizer manufacturing process, and they built a neighboring electrolysis plant.[32]

At the beginning of World War II, Norsk Hydro was the world's only commercial source of heavy water, most of which was sold to French and German scientists.[33]

In May of 1940, the Germans seized Norsk Hydro and forced its Norwegian operators to increase the production of heavy water. This plant had been producing about 10 kilograms of heavy water a month. By the fall of 1942, they were shipping ten times as much, or about 100 kilograms (220 pounds) a month to Germany.[34] Heisenberg and the other German scientists needed this heavy water to build a nuclear reactor.

The Norwegian underground reported this information to the British, who passed it on to General Groves. This information was compelling evidence that the Germans were trying to make a reactor, which would allow them to produce plutonium and, in turn, an atomic bomb.[35]

The Allies decided that the Norsk Hydro heavy water plant had to be destroyed. There were only two ways to demolish the heavy-water operation — bombing or sabotage. The Allies did not want to bomb out of fear of killing civilians who lived in the area and worked in the plant.[36]

The British devised a plan, which they called Operation Freshman, to sabotage the plant. On October 18, 1942, four Norwegian commandos parachuted into Norway to pave the way for a larger group of British commandos. They found a suitable place for the gliders to land and set up a radio direction finder.[37]

On November 20, 1942, two gliders carrying 41 British commandos were released in the vicinity of the Norsk Hydro plant. Unfortunately, the visibility was poor and both gliders crashed. Several of the commandos were killed and many were badly injured. The others surrendered without a fight in the belief that they would be treated as prisoners of war and that their comrades would receive medical attention.[38]

Unbeknownst to the British, on October 16, 1942, while enraged by other acts of sabotage in Norway, Hitler had issued an order to his commanders that opponents engaged in commando operations "are to be exterminated to the last man." General Nikolaus von Falkenhorst, the commander-in-chief of German forces in Norway was opposed to this order but felt that, as a soldier, he had to obey. The survivors were captured by the Germans, and although they were in British uniforms, all were shot. [39]

After the war, a British court convicted General von Falkenhorst of war crimes and sentenced him to death. However, he was pardoned in 1953.

Norwegian Commandos

The Allies decided to try another raid, which they labeled Operation Gunnerside, using Norwegian commandos, six of whom were trained at a secret camp in England.[40]

On February 16, 1943, the six Norwegian commandos were flown from Britain and dropped by parachute in the vicinity of the Norsk Hydro plant. On February 23, they met with the four Norwegian commandos who had previously been sent to Norway as a reception committee for Operation Freshman. On February 24, nine of the commandos left to attack Norsk Hydro. One stayed back to handle the radio and keep British intelligence informed of developments.[41]

The heavy-water plant was located at the edge of an almost perpendicular 600-foot cliff. The Germans had placed a strong guard force around the plant with mines, machine guns, and artillery protecting all approaches except the cliff because they did not believe anyone could scale it.[42]

Figure 3.5. Heavy Water Plant at Vemork

In spite of dark, cold conditions and 65-pound packs, the commandos managed to scale the cliff and sneak into the electrolysis building without alerting the guards. They then placed explosive charges on the eighteen heavy-water cells in the plant. Half a ton of the precious heavy water went down the drain, which was about five months' worth of production.[43]

General von Falkenhorst said that "the English bandits performed the finest coup I have seen in this war." (He assumed they were English.) Although ten thousand soldiers were sent out to find the commandos, all nine made a successful escape.[44]

After the raid, General von Falkenhorst signed an order that transferred the commander of the German security forces for the Norsk Hydro plant to the Russian front (an assignment dreaded by most German soldiers).

The heavy-water equipment was repaired by April 1943, and the plant reached full production again in August. The Germans also increased security at the plant, which ruled out another commando raid. The British and Americans reviewed the alternatives and decided to try precision bombing. To reduce civilian casualties, they planned for the bombs to be dropped between 11:30 and 11:45 A.M. when the workers would be at lunch, mainly in their well-protected basements.[45]

On November 15, 1943, 174 American aircraft, mostly B-17s along with some B-24s, dropped 828 bombs of the 1,000-pound and 500-pound variety on this plant. Only two of these bombs hit the electrolysis building, but the heavy-water equipment in the basement was untouched. However, damage to the rest of the plant was extensive. At that point, the Germans decided to dismantle the plant and rebuild it in Germany.[46]

The bombing cost the lives of 22 Norwegian civilians. Although tragic, this was a very small number compared to other large-scale bombing raids during the war.

Figure 3.6. Ferry "Hydro" at the Railhead on Lake Tinn

The Norwegian underground reported this decision to British intelligence. The British were less concerned with the plant itself than with the 14 tons of heavy water that had been saved.

The Germans loaded the heavy water into 49 drums and sent them by train to the town of Mael at the edge of Lake Tinn. This lake is about eighteen miles long, one mile wide, and 1,300 feet deep. They planned to transport the drums across the lake by a rail ferry named *Hydro* and then continue by rail to the port of Heroya, where they would be loaded aboard a ship and taken to Germany.[47]

One of the Norwegian commandos from the Vemork raid was in the area and learned of this plan. He enlisted two amateur helpers and succeeded in placing explosives aboard the ferry.

The saboteurs could not warn the ferry passengers of the danger without the risk of alerting the Germans. One of the saboteurs was horrified to learn that his mother planned to take the ferry on the 20th, and he could not convince her to do otherwise. He solved this dilemma by saturating her dinner on the 19th with a powerful laxative, and she was unable to travel the next morning.[48]

On February 20, 1944, the ferry and 45 of the 49 drums of the heavy water sank into the lake. Four of the drums were only partially filled and floated to the surface. Almost all of the precious heavy water had been lost.[49]

Of the 53 people on board the ferry, 18 lost their lives — 12 passengers, 2 crew members, and 4 Germans.

This event ended any chance for the Germans to achieve a self-sustaining nuclear chain reaction and an atomic bomb before the war ended.[50]

References for Chapter 3

1. Thomas Powers, *Heisenberg's War* (New York: Alfred A. Knopf, 1993), vii.

2. Ibid., 3.

3. Samual Glasstone, *Sourcebook on Atomic Energy* (Princeton: D. Van Nostrand Company, Inc., 1958), 76.

4. Ibid., 14-19.

5. Ibid., 82.

6. Ibid., 98.

7. Jeremy Bernstein, *Hitler's Uranium Club: The Secret Recordings at Farm Hall* (Woodbury, New York: AIP Press, 1996), 31-35, 39-41.

8. Leslie R. Groves, *Now It Can Be Told* (New York: Harper, 1962), 191.

9. Ibid., 193-198.

10. Richard Rhodes, *The Making of the Atomic Bomb* (New York: Simon & Schuster, 1986), 605-607.

11. Ibid., 609-610; and Groves, *Now It Can Be Told*, 238-243.

12. Bernstein, *Hitler's Uranium Club*, xxx.

13. Ibid., xv, 52.

14. Powers, *Heisenberg's War*, 481.

15. Ibid., viii.

16. Ibid., 79.

17. Ibid., 13, 316.

18. Ibid., 481-482.

19. Ibid., 15.

20. Ibid., 478.

21. Ibid., 146-149.

22. Rhodes, *The Making of the Atomic Bomb*, 131-132; and Powers, *Heisenberg's War*, 32-33.

23. Powers, *Heisenberg's War*, 114-127.

24. Ibid., 152.

25. Ibid., 99.

26. Ibid., 98-99; Bernstein, *Hitler's Uranium Club,* 25; and Per F. Dahl, *Heavy Water and the Wartime Race for Nuclear Energy* (Bristol and Philadelphia: Institute of Physics Publishing, 1999), 139-140.

27. Dan Kurzman, *Blood and Water: Sabotaging Hitler's Bomb* (New York: Henry Holt and Company, Inc., 1997), 40; and Dahl, *Heavy Water and the Wartime Race for Nuclear Energy,* 140-141.

28. Kurzman, *Blood and Water,* 38-39.

29. Ibid., 40.

30. Ibid., 5, 56; and Dahl, *Heavy Water and the Wartime Race for Nuclear Energy,* 36-40.

31. Kurzman, *Blood and Water,* 6; and Dahl, *Heavy Water and the Wartime Race for Nuclear Energy,* 41.

32. Kurzman, *Blood and Water,* 56.

33. Ibid., 7.

34. Ibid., 7, 42.

35. Ibid., 9.

36. Ibid., 111.

37. Ibid., 60-66.

38. Ibid., 78-109, 233.

39. Ibid., 67-68, 109, 236.

40. Ibid., 111, 118.

41. Ibid., 113, 126, 134.

42. Ibid., 135-136.

43. Ibid., 144-156; and Dahl, *Heavy Water and the Wartime Race for Nuclear Energy,* 206-207.

44. Kurzman, *Blood and Water,* 162, 166, 171; and Dahl, *Heavy Water and the Wartime Race for Nuclear Energy,* 208-209.

45. Kurzman, *Blood and Water,* 186, 193.

46. Ibid., 188, 209, 210, 233; and Rhodes, *The Making of the Atomic Bomb,* 513.

47. Kurzman, *Blood and Water*, 212; Rhodes, *The Making of the Atomic Bomb*, 514; Bernstein, *Hitler's Uranium Club*, 27; and Dahl, *Heavy Water and the Wartime Race for Nuclear Energy*, 224-226.

48. Kurzman, *Blood and Water*, 222, 234.

49. Dahl, *Heavy Water and the Wartime Race for Nuclear Energy*, 231-232.

50. Kurzman, *Blood and Water*, 224-232; and Rhodes, *The Making of the Atomic Bomb*, 513-517.

CHAPTER FOUR

Espionage During the Manhattan Project

Background

The Communist revolution of 1917 – 1918 in Russia was viewed as a blessing by the people who had suffered under the czars. Communism also appealed to many intellectuals who believed that it was a better, more equitable alternative to capitalism. The Great Depression of the 1930s tended to reinforce this view. At that time, the political oppression and economic weaknesses inherent to communism had not yet become evident or were overlooked by Western sympathizers. Also, the Soviets were allied with the U.S. and Great Britain in World War II. As a result, many people in Europe and the U.S. supported communism and the Soviet Union. A few were even willing to spy for the Soviets in the belief that they were helping to create a better world.

In the early 1940s, the Soviet Union was running an industrial espionage ring in the U.S. Agents stole technologies from laboratories and plants throughout the Northeast. Examples of these thefts included information on the production of film from Eastman Kodak and of nylon from DuPont. After the Soviets entered WWII, they intensified their espionage on defense technologies. For example, in 1942, they began to steal documents on the new secret technology of radar.

Several Americans served as couriers between the people who stole information and the Soviet agents. Three of these couriers were involved in the theft of atomic bomb information: Harry Gold, Lona Cohen, and Julius Rosenberg. Lona Cohen received assistance from her husband Morris, as did Julius Rosenberg from his wife Ethel. These individuals also helped to steal other information. For example, Morris Cohen recruited the spy who stole the radar secrets.[1]

Julius Rosenberg was also a source of information in his own right. While working as an engineer at Emerson Radio, he stole a working sample of a proximity fuze, one of the most innovative advances in American military technology during WWII.[2]

General Groves made great efforts to ensure the security of the Manhattan Project. Unfortunately, as was learned years after the project ended, his efforts were not entirely successful. Three spies at Los Alamos (Klaus Fuchs, Ted Hall, and David Greenglass) gave away atomic bomb information that was of immense value to the Soviet Union. The most damaging of these three spies was Klaus Fuchs.[3]

Klaus Fuchs

Klaus Emil Julius Fuchs was born in Germany in 1911. He joined the Communist party in the early 1930s and opposed Hitler. After the Reichstag fire in 1933, he went underground and left Germany for Paris. Later, when the Nazis put a price on his head, he escaped to England and worked at Bristol University. In 1937, he moved to the University of Edinburgh and went to work with Max Born, one of the pioneers of quantum mechanics, who was also a German émigré.

In 1940, Rudolph Peierls, another German émigré physicist, requisitioned Fuchs from Max Born. Peierls had been working on the British atomic energy program, which was code-named Tube Alloys. Because Fuchs was still an enemy alien who was known to have been an active Communist in his homeland, his clearance was delayed for several months. Fuchs started work on the atomic bomb in Birmingham, England, in May 1941.[4]

On June 21, 1941, Hitler launched Operation Barbarossa against the Soviet Union. Following this attack, Fuchs approached Jurgen Kuczynski, a German communist leader he knew in London, and asked how he could assist the Soviet war effort. For the next two years Fuchs passed everything he knew about Tube Alloys to Jurgen's

Figure 4.1. President Franklin Roosevelt and Great Britian's Prime Minister Winston Churchill at the Quebec Conference.

sister, Ursula Kuczynski, who was an agent of Soviet military intelligence.[5] Ironically, Fuchs was given British citizenship in May 1943 to facilitate and reward his work on the atomic bomb.[6]

In August 1943, at the Quebec Conference, Franklin Roosevelt and Winston Churchill established a Combined Policy Committee to facilitate U.S., British, and Canadian collaboration on the atomic bomb. The Quebec Agreement, which Roosevelt signed on August 17, established the official basis for collaboration between the United States and the United Kingdom on the atomic bomb. One of the first actions by the Combined Policy Committee was to transfer a group of fifteen British scientists to the U.S. This group included Fuchs.[7]

Fuchs arrived in the U.S. on December 3, 1943. He joined Rudolph Peierls and other British scientists in the U.S. effort to develop gaseous diffusion. This effort was led by Harold Urey and a team of physicists and chemists at Columbia University along with engineers from the Kellex Corporation.[8] Fuchs wrote thirteen papers on gaseous diffusion theory.

In March 1944, Fuchs began passing information on gaseous diffusion to Harry Gold, a courier for Soviet intelligence.[9] Gold, in turn, passed the information he received on to a Soviet agent. The material stolen in the first half of 1944 was not of critical importance to the Soviets. However, it did include valuable engineering details about the K-25 uranium diffusion plant at Oak Ridge, including the use of sintered nickel powder to make gaseous diffusion membranes.[10]

Hans Bethe, another German émigré physicist, was head of the Theoretical Division at Los Alamos. In January 1944, Bethe put Edward Teller, a Hungarian émigré physicist, in charge of a small group to work on implosion theory. As winter turned to spring, Teller began to neglect implosion calculations. Teller felt he had more important work to do, including early theoretical study of the possibility of using an atomic bomb to ignite a mass of deuterium for a weapon he called the "Super."

Figure 4.2. Klaus Fuchs

Bethe needed help on these calculations and requested that Rudolph Peierls transfer to Los Alamos. Peierls agreed to transfer and asked if he could bring along two assistants, one of whom was Fuchs.

Fuchs arrived at Los Alamos on August 14, 1944. While there, he produced a series of significant papers that dealt with the critical question of implosion. He also worked on initiators and wrote three papers on initiator theory.[11]

In the late 1944/early 1945 time frame, photographs were taken of everyone at Los Alamos for their identification badges. The picture of Klaus Fuchs in Figure 4.2 was taken for this purpose.

In February 1945, Fuchs passed a wealth of information on to Harry Gold who, in turn, gave it to Anatoly Yatskov, a Soviet agent in New York. This information included the principle of atomic bomb construction, the critical mass of plutonium, the implosion method of detonation, and the high rate of spontaneous fission in plutonium (which saved the Soviets a great deal of wasted effort by informing them that plutonium could not be used in a gun-type assembly but instead required the implosion method of assembly).[12]

On June 2, 1945, in Santa Fe, NM, Fuchs gave Harry Gold additional information on the plutonium bomb including a sketch of the bomb and its components along with important dimensions, a description and exact sketch of the initiator, the type of core, the importance of a tamper, and the intention to use the bomb against Japan. The information provided by Fuchs was extremely important to the Soviets and allowed them to save several years in the development of their own atomic bomb.[13]

Ted Hall

The second most damaging spy at Los Alamos was Theodore (Ted) Alvin Hall. Ted Hall finished his undergraduate work at Harvard when he was only eighteen. While at Harvard, he had taken Professor John Van Vleck's course on quantum mechanics. Van Vleck was one of the half dozen "luminaries" that Oppenheimer had assembled at Berkeley in the summer of 1942.

In 1943, Vannevar Bush, who was now Roosevelt's wartime chief of research and development, asked Van Vleck to recommend some physicists to work at Los Alamos. He recommended four candidates, one of whom was Ted Hall.[14]

Ted Hall joined the Manhattan Project in January 1944. He was the youngest physicist at Los Alamos. Hall was assigned to work

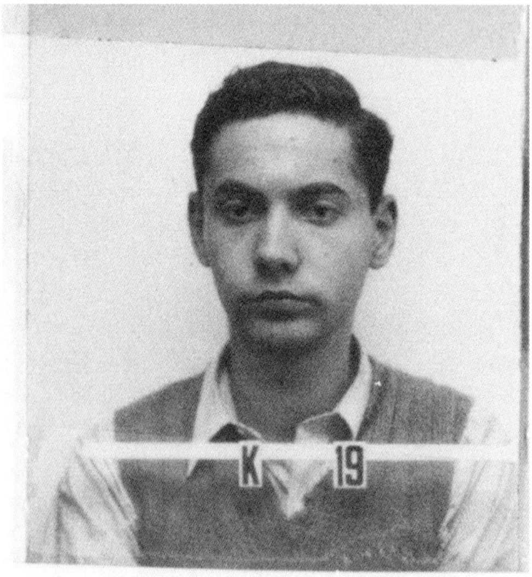

Theordore A. Hall

Figure 4.3 Ted Hall

in Bruno Rossi's laboratory. Rossi was another one of Oppenheimer's "luminaries." Although Hall was only a junior scientist, his work under Rossi exposed him to many of the most important secrets of the atomic bomb. The picture of Ted Hall was taken for his identification badge at Los Alamos.

Ted Hall's parents were Russian Jewish immigrants. They had suffered under the Romanov dynasty and were sympathetic to the revolution that resulted in a Communist state. They also strongly opposed the fascists in Germany, who were blaming their nation's troubles on the Jews. The U.S. depression of the 1930s pulled Hall's family even more firmly to the left. Young Ted picked up these sentiments.

At Harvard, a young man named Saville Sax was one of Ted Hall's roommates and a close friend. Sax's parents were also Russian Jewish immigrants who came to the U.S. to escape the pogroms of 1914. They had political views similar to those held by the Hall family. Sax became Hall's political collaborator and sometime espionage courier.[15]

Hall felt that an American monopoly of the atomic bomb would be dangerous and should be prevented. In October 1944, Hall and Sax made contact with a Soviet agent in New York. They told him that Hall was working at Los Alamos, that he was willing to steal atomic bomb information, and that Sax would serve as a courier.[16]

In December 1944, Hall met with Sax in Albuquerque and gave him information on the implosion concept. Sax passed this information on to a Soviet agent in New York. By the spring of 1945, the Soviets decided to replace Sax with Lona Cohen who was a more experienced courier. In August 1945, Hall met Lona Cohen at the University of New Mexico campus in Albuquerque and gave her several papers. She carried these papers back to New York hidden in a Kleenex tissue box and gave them to Yatskov.[17]

Lona Cohen's actions in carrying these papers out of New Mexico were a classic in espionage and became a part of the official history of the Russian Foreign Intelligence Service. Lona went to the train station in Lamy, NM, carrying a suitcase, a large bag, and a Kleenex box. Government agents were questioning and searching everyone getting on the train. She played the role of an innocent, disorganized scatterbrain. First, her train ticket disappeared. Then the zipper on her bag jammed and would not open. The train was waiting and time was running out. People tried to help her. The Kleenex box was hindering her search, so she handed it to an agent on the platform. She then found the ticket and started to board the train without the box. The agent chased Lona and handed the box to her.

The information that Ted Hall provided to the Soviets was similar to that provided by Klaus Fuchs with one exception; that is, it did not include anything on initiators. Hall had no knowledge of these devices. Although the information provided by Fuchs and Hall was somewhat redundant, that in itself was of great value to the Soviets. The Soviets were very concerned about receiving "disinformation" designed to lead them off track. As stated by Colonel Vladimir Barovsky of the KGB, "When you have two sources who aren't connected with each other and they bring information that intersects, then you can be certain they are reliable."[18]

David Greenglass

Figure 4.4. David and Ruth Greenglass

David Greenglass was the least damaging of the three spies. He was drafted in 1943 and sent to work as a machinist at Los Alamos. In August 1944, he was assigned to work in a facility that made models of the high-technology bomb parts being tested by various scientists.

David's sister was Ethel Rosenberg. Ethel's husband, Julius Rosenberg, convinced Ruth Greenglass to ask her husband, David, to provide them with some atomic bomb information. During a visit in November 1944, Ruth conveyed this request to David.

On June 3, 1945, in Albuquerque, NM, David Greenglass provided Harry Gold with a sketch of a high-explosive lens mold, which was used in an experiment to study implosion effects. David did not have a good understanding of any other important information. Gold had met with Fuchs the previous day.

Gold returned to New York, and, on June 4, he gave the information from Fuchs and Greenglass to Yatskov.[19]

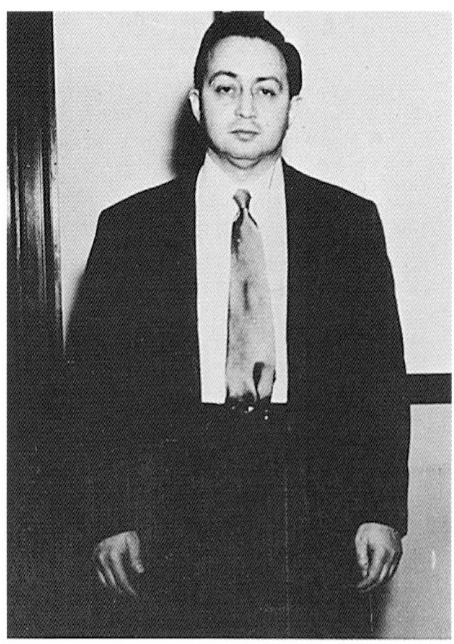

Figure 4.5. Harry Gold

Venona Project

The U.S. did not learn of these spies until years after the war. Uncovering them required a long, involved process that began in February 1943, when the U.S. launched the Venona Project under the Army Signal Intelligence Service. The purpose of this project was to decipher encrypted messages used in Soviet diplomatic cables.

In 1949, the Army Signal Intelligence Service, which included the Venona Project, was incorporated into the Armed Forces Security Agency. In 1952, President Truman issued a directive to form the National Security Agency within the Department of Defense. The Armed Forces Security Agency was included in the NSA. The NSA manages cryptological activities for the U.S.[23]

Figure 4.6. NSA Seal

The Soviets used an advanced cipher system that they thought was unbreakable. In December 1946, the Venona codebreakers managed to read a very suspicious cable that contained the names of several of the Manhattan Project scientists. Unfortunately, they had to work through a backlog of more than 10,000 messages, most of which contained routine trade information and had nothing to do with spies. Although some messages could never be deciphered, the codebreakers were able to read portions of more than 2,900 Soviet messages sent between 1940 and 1948.[20]

In September 1949, they deciphered a cable that showed the Soviets had stolen critical atomic bomb information. The FBI opened an investigation that linked this information to Klaus Fuchs. At the time, Fuchs was the Chief Scientist at England's top-secret Harwell Nuclear Center. The FBI informed British security services, which then began questioning Fuchs. Fuchs confessed on February 2, 1950.[21]

On May 22, 1950, the FBI located Fuch's courier, Harry Gold, who confessed. Gold also told the FBI that he served as a courier for a young soldier at Los Alamos.

On June 15, 1950, Gold identified David Greenglass from a photo provided by the FBI. Greenglass was arrested. He confessed and told the agents that he had been recruited by his wife, Ruth, who, in turn, had been drawn into espionage by her brother-in-law, Julius Rosenberg.[22]

It was subsequently learned that Julius and his wife Ethel had been involved in a variety of espionage activities.

The Venona Project remained in operation until 1980.

The Reckoning

Harry Gold pleaded guilty to espionage and received a 30-year prison sentence. He was paroled in 1966 after serving 16 years. He died during open-heart surgery in 1972.[24]

Klaus Fuchs went to trial in Britain on March 1, 1950. Because the Soviet Union had not been an enemy at the time of his espionage, he could not be accused of treason. Fuchs received the maximum penalty under British law, which was 14 years. Fuchs was released from prison in 1959 after serving nine years. Britain revoked his citizenship, and he flew to East Germany, where he became the Deputy Director and then Director of the Institute for Nuclear Research. He died in 1988 at age 77.[25]

David Greenglass agreed to testify against Julius Rosenberg if charges would not be brought against his wife, Ruth. He pled guilty to conspiracy to commit espionage and received a 15-year prison sentence.[26]

Julius and Ethel Rosenberg were convicted of conspiracy to commit espionage and sentenced to death on April 5, 1951. They died in the electric chair on June 19, 1953. Julius and Ethel Rosenberg were the only civilians ever to be executed under the General Espionage Act of 1917.[27]

Figure 4.7. Julius and Ethel Rosenberg

Morris and Lona Cohen escaped from the U.S. in 1950 before the FBI could catch them. In 1961, the Cohens were arrested in England. They had changed their names to Peter and Helen Kroger and were back into espionage. They were caught sneaking submarine technology out of the Portland Naval Research Base for delivery to the Soviets. They were convicted and sentenced to 20 years each.[28]

In 1969, the Cohens were released in a swap of prisoners with the Soviets. They were flown to Moscow and resumed working for the KGB. Lona Cohen died of cancer in Moscow in 1992. Morris died there in 1995. President Boris Yeltsin posthumously designated Morris and Lona Cohen as "Heroes of Russia," the only Americans known to have received this award.[29]

Ted Hall and Saville Sax were never brought to justice. In the spring of 1950, the Venona codebreakers told the FBI that these two had been involved in espionage. The FBI put them under surveillance but could find no corroborating evidence. Finally, in March 1951, the FBI questioned them, but they admitted to nothing. The FBI did not want to use the decrypted cables as evidence in court because that would have revealed the secret Venona Project. Without other evidence, they did not have a case against Hall and Sax and the case was moved to the back burner.[30]

Saville Sax never accomplished much. He did some teaching but suffered from bouts of depression and, for a while, was a heavy user of LSD. He died of a heart attack in 1980 at age 56.[31]

Ted Hall went on to achieve world-class status as a scientist in the field of biological microanalysis. In 1962, he transferred from the Sloan-Kettering Institute in New York to the Cavendish Laboratory at Cambridge University in England, where he used methods from nuclear physics to solve problems in cell biology. His most notable accomplishment was the development of an x-ray microanalysis technique to measure the concentration of trace elements in minute biological specimens. He took early retirement in 1984 at age 59.[32]

After the collapse of the Soviet Union in 1991, the KGB began to lift the curtain of secrecy surrounding its activities. The KGB wanted to demonstrate some of its past successes to justify its budget. The released information showed that an American spy who helped steal atomic secrets was still alive and at large.[33]

In July 1995, the NSA released the first group of decryptions from the Venona Project.[34] Among these was a November 1994 cable that linked Ted Hall and Saville Sax to Soviet intelligence. Various news organizations then began calling Ted Hall. In September 1995, two writers, Joseph Albright and Marcia Kunstel, who wrote the book *Bombshell*, met with Hall in Cambridge. They showed him how the evidence filtering out of the Russian archives dovetailed with the Venona decryptions. Hall began giving them his side of the story in January 1996. *Bombshell* was published in 1997. At that time, Hall had Parkinson's disease and inoperable kidney cancer.[35]

In March 1997, Hall provided a written statement to the authors of *Bombshell.* He still felt that the dangers of an American monopoly of atomic weapons justified his actions. An excerpt follows:

> *In 1944 I was nineteen years old — immature, inexperienced and far too sure of myself. I recognize that I could have easily been wrong in my judgement of what was necessary, and that I was indeed mistaken about some things, in particular, my view of the nature of the Soviet state. The world has moved on a lot since then, and certainly so have I. But in essence, from the perspective of my 71 years, I still think that brash youth had the right end of the stick. I am no longer that person; but I am by no means ashamed of him.* [36]

Hall was never prosecuted. He died of cancer in 1999 at age 74.

> *The Venona decryptions revealed the existence of two other spies in the Manhattan Project who were never identified. It appears that neither of them worked at Los Alamos. One spy had the Soviet code-name "Quantum" and turned over a detailed scientific description of a part of the process for enriching uranium through gaseous diffusion. The other spy initially had the code-name "Fogel," which was later changed to "Pers." Fogel/Pers provided the Soviets with a layout of one of the plants at Oak Ridge, Tennessee.*[37]

Reasons for the Security Breakdown

There were three major reasons for the security breakdown at Los Alamos, the first of which was the granting of security clearances without adequate background investigations. The population at Los Alamos grew much faster than anticipated, and the staff assigned to security investigations could not keep up with the demand. Also, the U.S. accepted the clearances on British scientists, which allowed Klaus Fuchs into the system.[38]

The second reason was the lack of compartmentalization of information. With compartmentalization, people have only the information needed to do their portion of a project. In order to accelerate the project, the scientists held weekly meetings in which all aspects of bomb design were discussed. As a result, even a junior scientist like Ted Hall or a machinist like David Greenglass could get a fairly complete picture of the overall effort.[39]

The third reason was the relaxation of travel restrictions at Los Alamos in September 1944. Although this improved morale, it allowed the spies to more easily pass stolen information to their outside contacts.[40]

In summary, the secrets were not stolen because of a sophisticated espionage effort by the Soviet Union. Rather, they were stolen because of the disloyal acts of three amateur spies who took advantage of a flawed security system.[41]

There is no doubt that the Soviet Union would eventually have developed an atomic bomb on its own. The issue is how much time and effort they saved by having the stolen secrets from Los Alamos. No one knows for sure (at least no one in the U.S.). However, it is generally believed that these thefts saved the Soviet Union somewhere between three and five years of development time.[42]

References for Chapter 4

1. Joseph Albright and Marcia Kunstel, *Bombshell* (New York: Times Books, 1997), 46-49.
2. John Earl Haynes and Harvey Klehr, *Venona: Decoding Soviet Espionage in America* (New Haven and London: Yale University Press, 1999), 303.
3. Richard Rhodes, *Dark Sun* (New York: Simon & Schuster, 1995), 121; and Leslie R. Groves, *Now It Can Be Told* (New York: Harper, 1962), 143.
4. Rhodes, *Dark Sun,* 54-57.
5. Albright and Kunstel, *Bombshell*, 78.
6. Rhodes, *Dark Sun*, 77.
7. Ibid., 129-130; *Groves, Now It Can Be Told*, 135-136; and Haynes and Klehr, *Venona: Decoding Soviet Espionage in America*, 304.
8. Rhodes, *Dark Sun*, 103.
9. Ibid., 109.
10. Albright and Kunstel, *Bombshell*, 78.
11. Rhodes, *Dark Sun*, 117-119.
12. Albright and Kunstel, *Bombshell*, 123-126.
13. Ibid., 138-139, 156-158.
14. Ibid., 6, 59-61.
15. Ibid., 7, 10-13.
16. Ibid., 90-95.
17. Ibid., 112-114, 134-135, 151-153.
18. Ibid., 129, 157.
19. Ibid., 107, 138-139; and Haynes and Klehr, *Venona: Decoding Soviet Espionage in America*, 308.
20. Robert Louis Benson and Michael Warner, eds., *Venona: Soviet Espionage and the American Response, 1939-1957* (Washington, D.C.: National Security Agency and Central Intelligence Agency, 1996), vii-viii.
21. Albright and Kunstel, *Bombshell*, 201-209; and Benson and Warner, *Venona: Soviet Espionage and the American Response, 1939-1957*, xxv-xxvi.
22. Albright and Kunstel, *Bombshell*, 218-220; and Benson and Warner, *Venona: Soviet Espionage and the American Response, 1939-1957*, xxvi.

23. Benson and Warner,*Venona: Soviet Espionage and the American Response, 1939-1957*, xlii-xliii.

24. Rhodes, *Dark Sun*, 581.

25. Ibid., 421-422, 581.

26. Ibid., 432.

27. Ibid., 480, 520-522; Albright and Kunstel, *Bombshell*, 240; and "1950-1954: Millenium Notebook," *Albuquerque Journal,* 16 July 1999, B8.

28. Albright and Kunstel, *Bombshell*, 261, 277, 285.

29. Ibid., 212, 233; Haynes and Klehr, *Venona: Decoding Soviet Espionage in America*, 316-317; and Benson and Warner, *Venona: Soviet Espionage and the American Response, 1939-1957*, xxvi.

30. Albright and Kunstel, *Bombshell*, 262-264.

31. Ibid., 254-256, 266.

32. Ibid., 267-274.

33. Benson and Warner, *Venona: Soviet Espionage and the American Response, 1939-1957*, v.

34. Albright and Kunstel, *Bombshell*, 278-280.

35. Ibid., 298.

36. Haynes and Klehr, *Venona: Decoding Soviet Espionage in America*, 310-314.

37. Richard Metzler, *Breakdown: How the Secret of the Atomic Bomb Was Stolen During World War II* (Sante Fe: Sunstone Press, 2000), 57.

38. Ibid., 66-67.

39. Ibid., 68-69, 75.

40. Ibid., 104-105.

41. Albright and Kunstel, *Bombshell*, xiii.

CHAPTER FIVE

Creating the Cold War

Atomic Energy Act of 1946

The Atomic Energy Act was signed by President Truman on August 1, 1946. This act transferred the responsibility for managing the design and production of nuclear weapons from the military-led Manhattan Engineer District to the civilian-led Atomic Energy Commission (AEC). The AEC was to be controlled by five appointed commissioners, the military would be linked through a Military Liaison Committee, and congressional oversight would be provided by a Joint Committee on Atomic Energy.

> *During the final deliberations of the Atomic Energy Act in July 1946, Representative Clare Booth Luce publicly fretted over the Commission appointments. She said, "Is not the danger that we shall be forced to put bureaucratic peewees into jobs that should be held only by supermen?" To his great credit, President Truman appointed AEC leaders of the highest caliber. Truman later looked back on these appointments and was justifiably proud that he had not clouded these appointments with politics. He had not even asked the political affiliations of his appointees.*[1]

The postwar optimism that atomic energy could be used for peaceful purposes was expressed in this act as follows:

> *It is hereby declared to be the policy of the people of the United States that, subject at all times to the paramount objective of assuring the common defense and security, the development and utilization of atomic energy shall, so far as practicable, be directed toward improving the public welfare, increasing the standard of living, strengthening free competition in private enterprise, and promoting world peace.* [2]

On January 1, 1947, the AEC took over the nation's atomic energy program from the Manhattan Engineer District.

AEC employees took great pride in their new organization as did contractor employees throughout the Nuclear Weapons Complex (NWC).

Figure 5.1. AEC Logo

Cold War Begins, 1946 to 1950

After the first atomic bombs were dropped to end World War II, many people felt that such terrible weapons should never be used again. The United Nations (UN) was viewed as the organization through which international disputes should be settled in the future.

Winston Churchill was a skeptic. On March 5, 1946, during a tour of the United States, Churchill made a speech in Fulton, Missouri, in which he issued a warning about Soviet aggression. He said that "from Stettin in the Baltic to Trieste in the Adriatic, an *iron curtain* has descended across the continent." The term "iron curtain" became synonymous with the split between East and West.[3] In spite of this warning, the United States continued to pursue peaceful relations with the Soviet Union.

On June 14, 1946, the U.S. presented the Baruch Plan to the UN. (Bernard Baruch was a long-term presidential advisor.) Baruch proposed the creation of an International Atomic Energy Authority, which would control all atomic energy activities potentially dangerous to world security. It would also have the power to control, inspect, and license all other atomic activities (e.g., reactors). When an adequate control system was established, the U.S. would stop producing atomic bombs, dispose of its existing bombs, and provide the Authority with full information for the production of atomic energy. On July 1, 1946, the Soviet Union rejected this plan. They claimed it was a trick to maintain the U.S. nuclear monopoly.[4] Meanwhile, the Soviet Union began to impose communist regimes on Eastern Europe.

On March 12, 1947, President Truman made a speech to Congress in which he requested authorization to send aid and advisors to Greece and Turkey to help these countries resist the spread of communism. This willingness to actively oppose communism became known as the Truman Doctrine.[5] The Soviets viewed this action as a declaration of Cold War.

On June 5, 1947, in a commencement address at Harvard University, Secretary of State George C. Marshall offered U.S. aid and cooperation in rebuilding Europe's shattered economy. He extended this offer to all of Europe including the Soviet Union. This offer grew into what came to be known as the Marshall Plan. Twenty-two days later, on June 27, 1947, the Soviet Union announced its rejection of the Marshall Plan. This rejection completed the economic and political division of Europe. At this point it became clear that the Cold War had really started.[6]

Bernard Baruch is credited by some historians with having coined the term "Cold War" during a 1947 speech to the South Carolina legislature. However, newspaper columnist Walter Lippmann gave the term wide currency with his influential book of essays titled The Cold War *in 1947.*

On February 25, 1948, the Soviet Union moved military forces into Prague and took over Czechoslovakia. Shortly thereafter, on June 24, 1948, the Soviet Union blockaded West Berlin, and the U.S. responded with the Berlin Airlift.[7] This was the first direct confrontation between the U.S. and the Soviet Union. In order to deal with this aggression, twelve western nations signed a document in April 1949 creating the North Atlantic Treaty Organization (NATO).[8]

On August 29, 1949, the Soviet Union tested its first atomic bomb, which has been nicknamed "Joe 1" after Joseph Stalin. On September 23, 1949, President Truman made an announcement to the news media that "within recent weeks, an atomic explosion has occurred in the USSR."[9]

As the Cold War got under way, the U.S. decided to set up a system for detecting an atomic bomb test in the Soviet Union. By April 1949, the U.S. Air Force had added "sniffer" devices to three squadrons of B-29s that they used for weather reconnaissance. The 375th Weather Reconnaissance Squadron was based in Alaska and regularly patrolled from Alaska to Japan, which was downwind of the Soviet Union. These devices trapped radioactivity on filters, which were sent back to a laboratory in Berkeley, California. The lab dissolved the filters and separated a selection of fission products such as radioactive isotopes of barium, cesium, molybdenum, zirconium, and lead. The lab then measured the rates of radioactive decay of these isotopes to determine when they had been created. If all the isotopes had the same birthday, then they must have been created in an atomic bomb.

On September 3, 1949, a WB-29 flying east of Kamchatka Peninsula detected a high level of radioactivity. The lab at Berkeley confirmed that this radioactivity was fission-derived and estimated that a Soviet explosion had occurred on August 29. The lab also determined that the bomb used a plutonium core and a natural uranium tamper. David Lilienthal, the AEC Chairman, gave this information to President Truman on September 20, 1949.[10]

During this period, communism was spreading in Asia as well as in Europe. On October 1, 1949, the Chinese Communists completed their victory over the Nationalists, and the People's

Republic of China was formed.[11] On June 25, 1950, North Korea invaded South Korea, and through the UN, the U.S. and its allies were drawn into the Korean War.[12]

U.S. Nuclear Warhead Stockpile: 1945 – 1961

As a result of the Cold War, the U.S. increased its stockpile of nuclear warheads. In June 1946, the U.S. had a stockpile of nine Fat Man–type nuclear weapons. The stockpile grew to 13 warheads in 1947, to 1,169 in 1953, and then to 22,229 in 1961. The production rate exceeded 7,000 weapons/year in 1959 and 1960.[13]

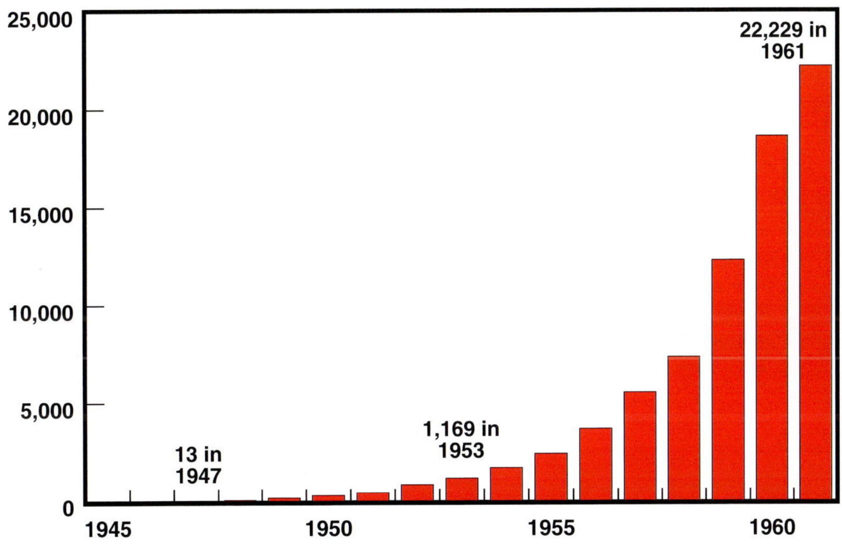

Figure 5.2. U.S. Nuclear Warhead Stockpile: 1945 to 1961

Also, between 1950 and 1963, the US added 39 new weapon systems to the stockpile — an average of three per year for thirteen years. Given the amount of time and effort required to develop each new system, this was a phenomenal accomplishment. (It is even more phenomenal that this was accomplished without computers.)

In 1947, the NWC began a period of great expansion in order to meet the new weapons development and production requirements.

NWC in 1947

Four sites were added to the NWC in 1947:

- A facility was established at the Naval Ordnance Test Station (NOTS), Salt Wells Pilot Plant, at Inyokern, California, to produce the high-explosive lenses required for implosion.[14]

- The Burlington Ordnance Plant in Iowa was converted to a nuclear weapons assembly plant. This plant also produced explosives. All the assembly functions performed by the Z Division at Sandia Base were transferred to this plant by 1949.[15]

- New facilities were established at the Rock Island Arsenal in Illinois to produce metal cases.

- The Mound Laboratory (the name was later changed to the Mound Plant) was established in Miamisburg, Ohio, to produce initiators. Mound took over the work from the Dayton facility, which was shut down at the end of 1948.[16]

  In subsequent years, Mound also produced a variety of other products including detonators, timers, transducers, firesets, and pyrotechnic devices.[17]

Figure 5.3. NWC in 1947

The number of employees in the NWC, both government and contractor, grew from approximately 55,000 in 1947 to over 142,000 in 1952. The Atomic Energy Act of 1946 required controls over access to restricted data and nuclear materials. Consequently, there was a great rush to implement a system for security clearances, and a Personnel Security Questionnaire (PSQ) was developed. A regulation then established three types of clearances based on an individual's need for access to restricted data. Single letters of the alphabet were taken from the PSQ to designate these clearances. "P" was for contractors having no access to restricted data or security exclusion areas. "S" was for frequent visitors to the NWC who would not have access to restricted data. "Q" was for employees with access to restricted data and security exclusion areas. Only the "Q" required a full Federal Bureau of Investigation background check. The "P" and "S" clearances were eliminated some years later, but the "Q" remained in effect.

Admiral Hyman G. Rickover invented the "L" designation when the Naval Nuclear Propulsion Laboratory was added to the AEC. Rickover did not want to comply with all of the requirements for the "Q" clearance, so the "L" was adopted as an alternative. It stands for limited access authorization. It originally applied only to naval nuclear information classified as confidential for research and development purposes. As used today, the "L" comes close to the original "S" clearance.[18]

NWC in 1948

There were four major changes to the NWC in 1948:

- In January, the AEC decided to establish a second site for initiator production at the Scioto Ordnance Works in Marion, Ohio.[19]

- In April, Z Division was declared a separate branch of Los Alamos Scientific Laboratory (LASL). Z Division's responsibilities had grown to an extent that a single division was no longer appropriate.[20]

- In November, the AEC selected the Pratt and Whitney airplane engine production plant in Kansas City as a site for the manufacture of electrical and mechanical components. In subsequent years, the Kansas City Plant also produced rubber and plastic components. This plant began operations in April 1949.[21]

- The Y-12 Plant began making uranium weapons parts, which, up to this point, had been made at Los Alamos.[22]

Figure 5.4. NWC in 1948

NWC in 1949

Three major changes occurred in 1949:

- The AEC negotiated with the U. S. Army to have detonators produced at Picatinny Arsenal in Dover, New Jersey.[23]

> *Many of the sites used by the AEC were not new, especially those owned by the Army. For example, Picatinny Arsenal is on land that once included the Mount Hope Iron Works, which produced cannon munitions for George Washington and the Continental Army.*

- In July, Hanford began building plutonium pits, which, up to this point, had been built at Los Alamos.[24]

Figure 5.5. NWC in 1949

- On May 13, President Truman sent a letter to the President of AT&T asking him to manage the LASL facility at Sandia Base. Truman appealed to his patriotism by stating "In my opinion, you have here an opportunity to render an exceptional service in the national interest."[25]

This statement became a founding principle for Sandia. On July 1, the President of AT&T officially accepted the contract to manage and operate the Sandia Laboratory.

Sandia Corporation began managing Sandia on November 1, 1949.[26] Sandia thus became a separate nuclear ordnance facility with the mission to design and produce nonnuclear components. Los Alamos designed the high explosive/nuclear system package while Sandia designed the rest of the nuclear bomb or warhead, including the arming, fuzing, and firing systems as well as other essential components.[27]

NWC from 1950 to 1951

Five sites were added to the NWC during 1950 and 1951:

- In 1950, the Savannah River site was established near Aiken, South Carolina, to be a second source for plutonium and to produce heavy water. This site also produced tritium for thermonuclear weapons. Tritium is produced by bombarding lithium with neutrons in a reactor.

The heavy water plant became operational in 1952. Heavy water was extracted from natural water, which contains small amounts of deuterium (0.015 percent). The heavy water was concentrated by a combination of three processes: (1) hydrogen sulfide–water chemical exchange, (2) water distillation, and (3) electrolysis. Each of these processes exploits the difference in the masses of the two isotopes.[28]

Five heavy water–moderated reactors were built and began producing plutonium at Savannah River between 1953 and 1955. They were more efficient and more flexible than the graphite-moderated reactors at Hanford.[29]

- In 1951, the Nevada Test Site (NTS) was established as the nation's on-continent nuclear weapons testing area. Prior to 1950, most tests were conducted in the Pacific. This was costly, time-consuming, and logistically difficult. NTS had been the Las Vegas Bombing and Gunnery Range and was chosen because it was a huge government-owned area with little water to contaminate and very few nearby residents. The first nuclear weapon tested at NTS, a one-kiloton bomb dropped from an airplane, was detonated on January 27, 1951.[30]

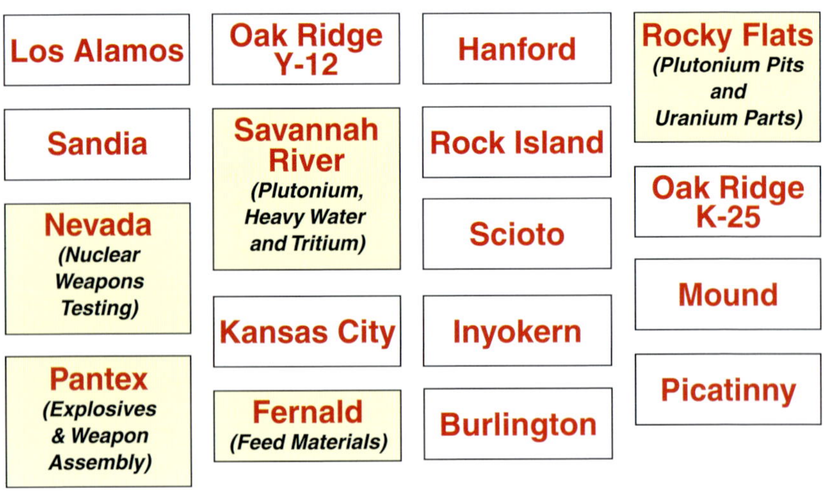

Figure 5.6. NWC from 1950 to 1951

- In 1951, the AEC acquired the Pantex Plant near Amarillo, Texas, to produce high explosives (HE) and assemble nuclear weapons. This site had been owned by the U.S Army originally and was sold to Texas Technological College in 1949.[31]

In 1951, the AEC planned to build another HE fabrication facility at Spoon River, Illinois. However, it was cancelled before construction began.

- In 1951, the AEC acquired the site for the Rocky Flats Plant near Denver, Colorado, to produce plutonium pits and uranium parts. The plant became operational in 1952. Subsequently, Rocky Flats also produced stainless steel and beryllium components.[32]

- In 1951, the AEC established the Feed Materials Production Center in Fernald, Ohio. This plant refined uranium ore into fuel for the reactors at Hanford and Savannah River.[33]

As production increased, the AEC became more concerned about the possibility of nuclear material being dispersed as a result of a high explosive detonation occurring during the assembly or disassembly of nuclear weaapons. As a result, in 1956, a test dubbed "Quick and Dirty" was conducted at Pantex to simulate the containment capability for an assembly cell concept. In essence, this concept consists of a cylindrical reinforced concrete structure with a cable-suspended roof covered with a thick layer of gravel. A detonation would cause the roof to lift and then collapse back into the structure. The gravel would filter out most of the nuclear material from the escaping gasses.

The name "Gravel Gertie" was adapted from a Dick Tracy comic character due to the large amount of gravel used in this design. Gravel Gerties were constructed at Pantex and became operational in 1958.[34]

Tactical Nuclear Weapons

The first nuclear weapons, Fat Man and Little Boy, were quite large and had relatively low yields. As time went on, designs were developed to make nuclear weapons smaller and more powerful. For example, in 1945, the Fat Man had a diameter of 60 inches, weighed approximately 10,000 pounds, and had a yield of 21 kt. By 1958, weapon designs had improved such that the B28 bomb had a diameter of only 20 inches, weighed approximately 2500 pounds, and had a yield in the megaton range. Miniaturization enabled the use of nuclear weapons in a wide variety of applications.

The United States decided to deploy nuclear weapons in Europe in the 1950s because of the West's weakness in conventional weapons. In 1950, NATO had 12 divisions to face an estimated 175 Soviet-led, Warsaw-Pact divisions. Tactical nuclear weapons were deployed with U.S. troops in Western Europe beginning in 1953. Tactical nuclear weapons have shorter ranges than strategic weapons, but their destructive power is very high.[35]

The first of these tactical weapons was a nuclear artillery shell for a 280-mm cannon. This was the W19, a gun-assembly–type

Figure 5.7. Shot Grable

weapon. The first live nuclear artillery test, Shot Grable, took place at the NTS on May 25, 1953. It had a yield of 15 kt.[36]

Nuclear artillery shells were subsequently deployed on 203-mm (8-inch) and 155-mm guns for the Army and on 16-inch guns for the Navy. In addition to artillery shells, the Army deployed a variety of tactical nuclear missile systems such as the Corporal, Honest John, Little John, Pershing, Sergeant, and Lance.

Figure 5.8. Lance

Lance was a highly mobile, guided surface-to-surface ballistic missile. It had a self-propelled tracked launcher with amphibious capability and could travel at 55 km/hour. It also had a two-wheeled launcher that could be towed behind a truck. It had a firing range up to approximately 100 km and offered multiple destructive yields in the kiloton class. Lance used the W70 warhead and was fielded in Europe in 1973.

The army also fielded the Davy Crockett with a projectile that weighed only 76 pounds and a variety of atomic demolition munitions (ADMs), which were small low-yield weapons designed to destroy targets such as bridges, tunnels, harbors, dams, airfields, and command posts.

Lance gained notoriety in 1977 as the "neutron bomb" after the Washington Post *reported that an enhanced-radiation version of the W70 warhead had been developed. This warhead could kill enemy personnel with great quantities of neutrons (even in hard targets like tanks), but it had reduced blast and heat effects. This was a major advantage in minimizing collateral damage to civilian areas. Congress approved funds for the production of this warhead in 1977. Other articles in the media called this warhead a capitalist tool because it could kill people but spare buildings. As a result of this adverse publicity, President Jimmy Carter deferred production of the enhanced-radiation warhead in 1978, and it was never fielded. Some people feel that this warhead would have gone into production if the* Washington Post *had labeled it the benign sounding "reduced-blast warhead" instead of the more frightening "neutron bomb."*[37]

On January 16, 1953, the AEC and the DoD approved the Missiles and Rockets Agreement, which defined their respective responsibilities for nuclear weapons. In brief, it said that:

- The AEC would be responsible for the warhead, including the nuclear components, detonators and the firing unit.
- The DoD would be responsible for all rocket or guided missile parts.
- Responsibilities for the "Adaption Kit," which included the arming and fuzing systems, power supply, and all hardware needed to install the warhead on a missile, were left in a gray area.

The Army gave the responsibility for the design and development of Adaption Kits on tactical nuclear weapons to Picatinny Arsenal. (Additional details on the Missiles and Rockets Agreement are provided in Appendix A.)

As these weapon systems kept getting smaller and more sophisticated, laboratory employees joked that they could design a "nuclear hand grenade." Their only problem was finding somebody dumb enough to throw it.

References for Chapter 5

1. Richard G. Hewlett, and Oscar E. Anderson, Jr., *The New World, 1939/1946* (University Park: The Pennsylvania State University Press, 1962), 620, 622.

2. Leland Johnson, *Sandia National Laboratories: A History of Exceptional Service in the National Interest,* SAND97-1029 (Albuquerque: Sandia National Laboratories, 1997), 1.

3. Jeffry Porro, ed., *The Nuclear Age Reader* (New York: McGraw-Hill, Inc., 1989), 32-33.

4. Ibid., 34-35; and Richard G. Hewlett, and Oscar E. Anderson, Jr., *The New World, 1939/1946* (University Park: The Pennsylvania State University Press, 1962), 576-579.

5. Porro, *The Nuclear Age Reader,* 41.

6. Ibid., 42-43.

7. Richard Rhodes, *Dark Sun* (New York: Simon & Schuster, 1995), 324.

8. Ibid., 354.

9. Ibid., 374.

10. Ibid., 369-373.

11. Ibid., 385.

12. John Spanier, *American Foreign Policy Since World War II,* 12th ed., rev. (Washington: CQ Press, A Division of Congressional Quarterly, Inc., 1992), 23.

13. U.S. Department of Energy, Classification Bulletin WNP-90 (Washington, DC: U.S. Department of Energy, July 29, 1994).

14. U.S. Department of Energy, Office of Environmental Management, *Linking Legacies,* DOE/EM-0319 (Washington, DC: U.S. Department of Energy, 1997), 26, 187.

15. Ibid., 26, 27, 187; and Ann Arnold Lemert, *First You Take a Pick and Shovel: The Story of the Mason Companies* (Lexington, KY; the John Bradford Press, 1979), 160-162.

16. William F. Burgess, Jo Anne McCormick, and Eileen Pingatore, *History of the Production Complex: The Methods of Site Selection,* Prepared by History Associates Inc. for the U.S. Department of Energy, DOE/NV10594-H1 (Washington, D.C.: U.S. Department of Energy, 1987), 71.

17. Necah Stewart Furman, *Sandia National Laboratories: The Postwar Decade,* (Albuquerque: University of New Mexico Press, 1990) 381-382.

18. Richard G. Hewlett and Francis Duncan, *Atomic Shield, 1947/1952* (University Park and London: The Pennsylvania State University Press, 1969), 23-25, 675; and *Sandia Lab News* (Albuquerque: Sandia National Laboratories, June 30, 2000), 12.

19. Office of Environmental Management, *Linking Legacies*, 26, 187, 188; and Burgess, McCormick, and Pingatore, *History of the Production Complex*, 73.

20. Furman, *The Postwar Decade*, 258.

21. Burgess, McCormick, and Pingatore, *History of the Production Complex*, 81; and Office of Environmental Management, *Linking Legacies*, 189.

22. Office of Environmental Management, *Linking Legacies*, 26, 185.

23. Ibid., 27, 187.

24. Ibid., 26, 183.

25. Furman, *The Postwar Decade*, 342, 345.

26. Johnson, *A History of Exceptional Service in the National Interest*, 31.

27. Ibid., 3.

28. Office of Environmental Management, *Linking Legacies*, 21, 147-149.

29. Ibid., 165-166.

30. Ibid., 204; and U.S. Department of Energy, Nevada Operations Office, *United States Nuclear Tests: July 1945 through September 1992*, DOE/NV-209, Revision 15 (Las Vegas, NV: U. S. Department of Energy, 2000), 2-3.

31. Burgess, McCormick, and Pingatore, *History of the Production Complex*, 65; and Lemert, *First You Take a Pick and Shovel: The Story of the Mason Companies*, 168-169.

32. Furman, *The Postwar Decade*, 379; and Office of Environmental Management, *Linking Legacies*, 26.

33. Office of Environmental Management, *Linking Legacies*, 155.

34. Lemert, *First You Take a Pick and Shovel: the Story of the Mason Companies*, 170.; and Carr, B. H., *Pantex History: 1942 to 1992* (Amarillo: Pantex Plant Report, 1992), 15.

35. Porro, *The Nuclear Age Reader*, 121-123.

36. Nevada Operations Office, *United States Nuclear Tests*, 4-5.

37. Walter Pincus, "Neutron Killer Warhead Buried in ERDA Budget," *Washington Post*, 6 June 1977, A1.

CHAPTER SIX

Two Scorpions in a Bottle

Development of Fusion

Fusion is the joining of two light nuclei to form one heavier nucleus with a release of energy. It is very difficult to make two nuclei join because of the electrostatic repulsive force between them (i.e., both nuclei are positively charged and like charges repel). For the fusion process to take place, the two nuclei must approach each other fast enough and close enough that the strong, attractive short-range nuclear forces overcome the electrostatic forces of repulsion.

The speed of a nucleus depends upon the temperature of the material of which it is a part. Also, the distance between nuclei is a function of the material's density. In nature, the combination of high temperature and high density that will enable fusion to take place exists in the interior of the sun. Consequently, fusion weapons are commonly called "thermonuclear weapons," and because the fusion process involves isotopes of hydrogen, they are also called "hydrogen bombs."

Figure 6.1. Edward Teller

Edward Teller had been interested in a fusion weapon since the days of the Manhattan Project. In 1946, he invented a relatively simple single-stage design for a thermonuclear weapon. He called it the "alarm clock" to awaken the world to the possibility of a new generation of nuclear explosives.[1]

The U.S. never tested this design. It would have had a fairly low yield and could more properly be called a fusion-boosted fission device rather than a true thermonuclear weapon.

As the Cold War intensified, Teller pushed hard for the U.S. to develop such a weapon. His efforts eventually bore fruit.

On January 13, 1950, President Truman announced to the world that he was directing the AEC to work on the hydrogen bomb.[2]

This announcement distressed the scientists at Los Alamos because no one knew how to build one. Their efforts up to the end of 1950 were not encouraging. Chemical explosives could not exert enough compression to cause fusion. In December 1950, Stanislaw Ulam thought of a way to increase compression by orders of magnitude. In effect, he proposed to use the fission reaction to compress a secondary.[3]

Ulam passed his idea on to Edward Teller in January 1951. Teller then proposed to use the X-rays coming off the fission primary — rather than the other products — to compress the fusion secondary. This process would allow a faster and longer-sustained compression of the fusion fuel. On March 9, 1951, Teller and Ulam wrote a joint report describing this concept (commonly called the Teller-Ulam concept). Thereafter, Teller pushed Ulam aside and refused to deal with him any longer. Teller found it intolerable to share credit for this concept. Another Los Alamos scientist, Herbert York, said "I think Teller has slighted Ulam, but I think also Teller does deserve fifty-one percent of the credit."[4]

Teller, Ulam, and other scientists at Los Alamos then established plans for some tests to verify this new concept. These plans were incorporated into the upcoming Greenhouse test series.

Fusion Processes in Weapons

There are two basic fusion processes used in nuclear weapons. One process is gas "boosting" in which deuterium (D) and tritium (T) are stored at high pressure in reservoirs outside the primary (pit). Shortly before detonation, a mixture of deuterium and tritium is injected into the pit. The implosion of the pit along with the onset of the fissioning process heats the mixture to a temperature at which the D-T nuclei undergo fusion. This reaction releases 17.6 million electron volts (MeV) of energy.

$${}_{1}D^{2} + {}_{1}T^{3} \rightarrow {}_{2}He^{4} + {}_{0}n^{1} + 17.6 \text{ MeV}$$

The principle of boosting fission weapons with deuterium and tritium was known as early as November 1945.

Boost reservoirs are made of very high-strength stainless steel and come in a variety of shapes and sizes.

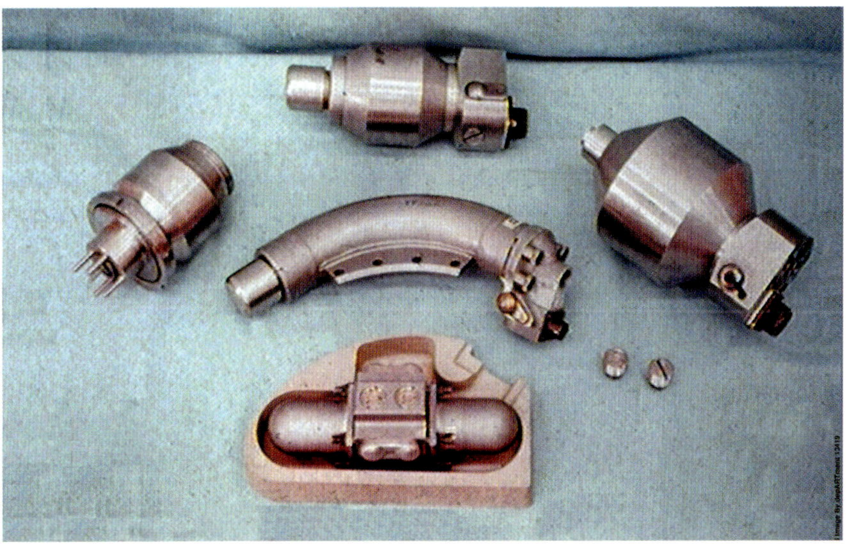

Figure 6.2. Boost Reservoirs

The other fusion process is through the use of a secondary assembly. The secondary is composed of lithium deuteride and other materials. The primary explosion activates the secondary. As the secondary implodes, the lithium, in the isotopic form of lithium-6, is converted to tritium by neutron interactions. The tritium then undergoes fusion with the deuterium.

$${}_{3}Li^{6} + {}_{0}n^{1} \rightarrow {}_{2}He^{4} + {}_{1}T^{3} + 4.78 \text{ MeV}$$

All modern nuclear weapons require deuterium, tritium, and lithium-6.

NWC from 1952 to 1953

Eight changes occurred in the 1952 to 1953 time frame:

- In 1952, a plant was established in Albuquerque, New Mexico, to produce metal cases and weapon-handling equipment.[5] It was commonly called the South Albuquerque Works and was operated by American Car and Foundry (ACF) Industries. The South Albuquerque Works was originally owned by the Eidal Manufacturing Company, which built trailers for the army. The AEC leased this plant in 1952 and then bought it in 1953.

- In 1952, the metal case production work at Rock Island Arsenal was transferred to Albuquerque. The AEC's operation at Rock Island Arsenal was then closed.

- In 1952, the University of California Radiation Laboratory (UCRL) joined the NWC as a design laboratory. Its mission was to compete with Los Alamos in physics package design, which supposedly would lead to faster and cheaper breakthroughs. This laboratory was established largely because of the efforts of Edward Teller. Teller felt that the leaders at Los Alamos, especially Oppenheimer, were not sufficiently enthusiastic about thermonuclear weapons, and he began a campaign to open a second nuclear weapon design laboratory. Gordon Dean, the Chairman of the Atomic Energy Commission, resisted this campaign for nine months but finally capitulated after Teller began lobbying the Air Force to take this mission. Ernest Lawrence supported Teller's proposal and arranged to house the new organization temporarily within his Radiation Laboratory at Berkeley. It soon moved to Livermore, California, the site of a former World War II air base. Livermore's first director was Herbert York, not Edward Teller. The new laboratory's first assignment was to perform thermonuclear diagnostic studies.[6] After the death of Ernest O. Lawrence (a Nobel Laureate) in 1958, the name was changed to the Lawrence Livermore Laboratory.

A significant rivalry developed between the two laboratories. When the media gave credit for the first successful test of a multi-megaton device (Mike in 1952) to Livermore — an error that the laboratory was prevented from correcting because of national security rules — Los Alamos scientists were deeply resentful. When Livermore staged its own first tests in 1953, Ruth and Ray, they both were "fizzles" — the weapon scientists' term for failures. In Livermore's first test, Ruth, the metal tower, which normally would have been vaporized by the nuclear blast, was only bent. The Los Alamos scientists then enjoyed teasing their Livermore counterparts by asking if they could borrow their tower after future tests.[7]

The two laboratories also tried to protect their ideas from each other. A Los Alamos scientist once joked that the levels of classification were "confidential," "secret," "top secret," and, the strictest of all, "hide from Livermore."[8]

- In 1952, the AEC established another source for heavy water at the Dana Plant in Newport, Indiana.[9]
- In 1952, construction began on the Portsmouth Gaseous Diffusion Plant in Piketon, Ohio, to produce enriched uranium. Construction was completed in 1956.[10]
- In 1953, construction began on the Paducah Gaseous Diffusion Plant in Paducah, Kentucky. Construction was completed in 1954.[11]
- In 1953, the AEC decided that the Scioto site was no longer needed as a second source for initiators, and it was closed.[12]
- In 1953, the Y-12 Plant at Oak Ridge began producing lithium-6 (Li-6) and "secondaries" for the newly developed thermonuclear weapons. Lithium deuteride was the key material. Natural lithium is about 7.5 percent Li-6 and 92.5 percent Li-7. The Y-12 Plant began to develop lithium isotope separation processes in 1950.[13]

> *Three processes were explored, COLEX, ELEX, and OREX. The COLEX process supplied most of the enriched lithium needed by the NWC. The COLEX process (the name is a contraction of "column exchange") is based on the fact that isotopes of lithium are partially separated when transferring between an aqueous solution of lithium hydroxide and a lithium-mercury amalgam.*[14]

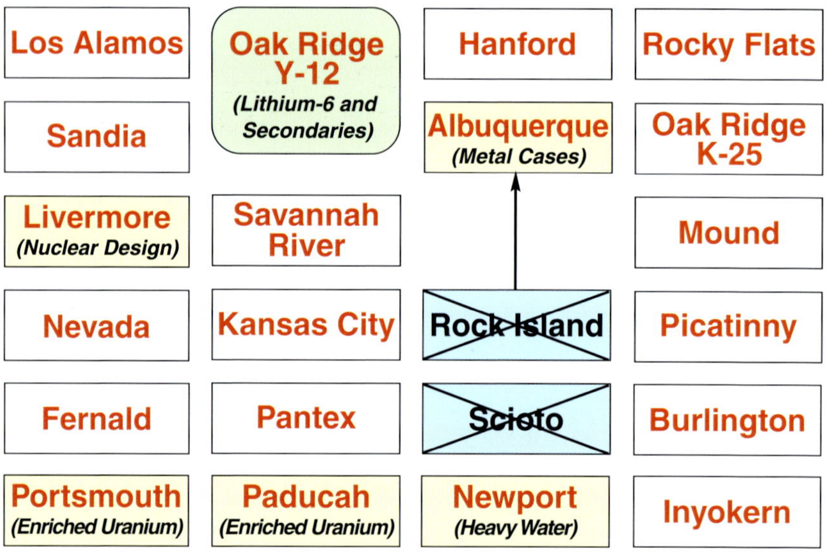

Figure 6.3. NWC from 1952 to 1953

As a result of these newly established capabilities, the U.S. was able to begin production of thermonuclear weapons. The first thermonuclear warhead, the B14, entered the stockpile on an emergency basis in 1954. It was replaced by the B15 in 1955.[15]

Two other developments occurred in this time frame:

- In May 1952, Sandia created a pre-production group to assist in translating its designs into products to be used in weapons. This group became the Manufacturing Development Engineering (MDE) Department. In 1969, Sandia decided to concentrate its resources on research and closed the MDE

Department. The production engineering function was then transferred to the plants.[16]

- In 1953, the AEC and DoD reached some agreements on the division of responsibilities between them. These agreements have had a significant impact on the NWC ever since. The details of these agreements are contained in Appendix A.

McCarthyism

The American people were shocked and frightened by the early Cold War events, especially the communist takeovers in Eastern Europe and China and the development of a Soviet atomic bomb. This fear was reflected throughout American society. The period between 1948 and 1954 was characterized by a national paranoia toward communism and is often labeled after its most prominent demagogue, Wisconsin Senator Joseph R. McCarthy. Any deviation from a strong anti-communist line was considered suspect. McCarthyism stood for an era in which fundamental American freedoms were suppressed in the name of national security.[17]

In August 1948, the House Un-American Activities Committee (HUAC) began to investigate alleged communist penetration of the government. Hearings were held against Alger Hiss, a former government official in various agencies including the State Department. Hiss was accused of espionage by a former associate, Whittaker Chambers. Hiss was subsequently indicted and brought to trial. In January 1950, after two trials, Hiss was convicted of perjury, not espionage, and sentenced to five years imprisonment. The Hiss case had the effect of licensing a hunt against communists.[18] Many politicians jumped on the bandwagon.

On February 3, 1950, the arraignment of Klaus Fuchs made headlines throughout the world. Six days later, Senator Joseph McCarthy began a witch hunt with a speech in which he claimed to have a list of 205 Communists who worked in the State Department. This claim turned out to be a big lie, but it gave McCarthy national attention. McCarthy made similar headlines in

April 1954 claiming communists in government had delayed U.S. research on the hydrogen bomb by eighteen months.[19]

During this period, 145 suspected communists were indicted and 108 were convicted. In retrospect, the U.S. had suppressed legitimate political activities on extremely thin grounds. In addition, individuals refusing to testify under the Fifth Amendment privilege against self-incrimination were then fired from their jobs and/or blackballed from employment.[20]

As time went on, the paranoia broadened such that government or government contractor employees could be fired for being "security risks." Previously, people were challenged for having had suspect associations in the past. This new security risk category included anyone who might disclose classified information in the future because of carelessness or blackmail. During the Eisenhower administration, approximately 6,000 civil servants quit and 1,500 were dismissed. Vice President Richard Nixon announced: "We're kicking the Communists and fellow travelers and security risks out of the Government...by the thousands."[21]

This period ended on December 2, 1954, when Senator McCarty was censured by the U.S. Senate.[22] Unfortunately, before it was over, the excesses of this period contributed to the decisions to execute the Rosenbergs and to bring charges against J. Robert Oppenheimer.

Oppenheimer's Security Clearance

The Atomic Energy Act of 1946 authorized the General Advisory Committee (GAC) of scientists appointed by the President to provide the AEC Commissioners with technical guidance. President Truman appointed James Conant, Enrico Fermi, I. I. Rabi, Cyril Smith, Glenn Seaborg, and Robert Oppenheimer to this committee. The first meeting of the GAC was held on January 3, 1947, at which time the other members elected Oppenheimer as chairman.[23]

On September 23, 1949, President Truman announced that an atomic explosion had occurred in the Soviet Union. Lewis Strauss, one of the AEC Commissioners, felt that it was not enough for the U.S. to have a larger nuclear weapon stockpile than the Soviet Union. Rather, he wanted the U.S. to make a quantum leap forward by developing the "super" (i.e., the hydrogen bomb). Toward that end, he concluded that the AEC should consult with the GAC as to how they could "proceed with expedition."[24]

In October 1949, the GAC issued a report that recommended against developing a hydrogen bomb. Unlike fission weapons, fusion weapons have essentially unlimited explosive potential. The GAC felt that fusion weapons would be too dangerous for the world and that atomic bombs were an adequate deterrent to aggression. This report infuriated Teller and many other people of influence. Some of them began to question Oppenheimer's loyalty.[25]

On January 13, 1950, the Joint Chiefs of Staff sent a memorandum to the GAC stating that they considered it "necessary to have within the arsenal of the United States a weapon of the greatest capability, in this case the super bomb." The Secretary of Defense sent this memorandum directly to President Truman. On January 31, 1950, Truman announced that he was directing "the Atomic Energy Commission to continue its work on all forms of atomic weapons, including the so-called hydrogen or super-bomb."[26]

In February 1952, Oppenheimer made a speech before the Council on Foreign Relations in which he said, "We may be likened to two scorpions in a bottle, each capable of killing the other, but only at the risk of his own life."

This speech was published in the June 1952 issue of *Foreign Affairs*.[27]

Secret FBI interviews with Teller dating from May 1952 provided several new allegations against Oppenheimer. Teller told the FBI that Oppenheimer had opposed the development of the hydrogen bomb since 1945, that the hydrogen bomb would have been a reality by 1951 or earlier if Oppenheimer had not opposed it, and that Oppenheimer wrote the majority opinion for the October 1949 GAC report and was the dominating influence on the committee.[28]

Oppenheimer's term as a member of the GAC ended on August 8, 1952, and he was not reappointed. Several influential people felt that the GAC should have members who supported the President's policy on the hydrogen bomb.[29]

President Eisenhower appointed Lewis Strauss as Chairman of the AEC in May 1953. Strauss distrusted Oppenheimer because he had failed to report fully on the wartime espionage approaches of Haakon Chevalier, who was an old friend, and because he continued to oppose development of the hydrogen bomb after President Truman had authorized it. On December 21, 1953, Strauss handed Oppenheimer a list of charges against him. Oppenheimer had the choice of resigning from his position as a consultant to the AEC or requesting a security hearing. Oppenheimer told Strauss that he wanted a hearing.[30]

The hearing began on April 12, 1954. Oppenheimer was challenged in two areas, the first of which was his failure to fully report on Haakon Chevalier. General Groves testified that he thought Oppenheimer wanted to protect his friend of long standing. During relentless cross-examination, Oppenheimer made some contradictory statements about this affair. Although this was embarrassing to Oppenheimer, it was not likely to result in the loss of his clearance.[31]

The second challenge involved his opposition to the development of the hydrogen bomb. Many of the nation's scientific elite were called to testify. Most were Oppenheimer's friends, including Gordon Dean, David Lilienthal, Vannevar Bush, Hans Bethe, and Isidor Rabi. Seven were his enemies and testified against him. The most damaging testimony came from Edward Teller.[32]

Teller did not believe that Oppenheimer was disloyal. Rather, he felt that Oppenheimer had been providing bad advice regarding the development of a hydrogen bomb. Teller felt that Oppenheimer had great influence within the scientific community and that his opposition to the hydrogen bomb was endangering the nation. Teller's concluding testimony included the following exchange:

> Question: *Do you feel that it would endanger the common defense and security to grant clearance to Dr. Oppenheimer?*
>
> Answer: *To the extent that your question is directed toward intent, I would say I do not see any reason to deny clearance. If it is a question of wisdom and judgment, as demonstrated by actions since 1945, then I would say one would be wiser not to grant clearance.* [33]

The hearing ended on May 6, 1954. On May 27, the Security Board recommended against reinstating Oppenheimer's security clearance. Oppenheimer appealed the Security Board's findings to the AEC Commissioners.

Lewis Strauss released the 992 page transcript for publication on June 15. Oppenheimer's conflicting statements thus became public, but so did Edward Teller's testimony. Many of Teller's scientific colleagues were appalled.[34]

On June 29, the AEC Commissioners, led by Strauss, found that "Dr. Oppenheimer is not entitled to the continued confidence of the Government and of this Commission because of the proof of fundamental defects in his character." Oppenheimer was devastated by the withdrawal of his clearance. He continued to direct the Institute for Advanced Study at Princeton for another decade but was suffering from extreme frustration.[35]

None of the thousands of messages decrypted during the Venona project contained anything to suggest that Oppenheimer was disloyal. In fact, if Oppenheimer had been a Soviet source, it is very likely that the quality and quantity of Manhattan Project secrets stolen by the Soviet Union would have been much greater.[36]

The author, Richard Rhodes provided the following story in his book, *Dark Sun*:

> *Edward Teller became a pariah within the larger scientific community. The summer after the Oppenheimer verdict, Teller attended a conference of nuclear scientists at Los Alamos. On the first day, Teller went to the dining room for*

lunch where he spied Robert Christy and I. I. Rabi. He eagerly went over to their table, hoping to join in the easy camaraderie of old colleagues. While a room full of prominent scientists looked on, both Christy and Rabi refused to shake Teller's extended hand. Then Rabi congratulated Teller on the extremely clever way in which he had phrased his testimony. As if slapped in the face, Teller retreated and went immediately to his room. He did not return to Los Alamos for nine years. [37]

On December 13, 1963, President Lyndon Johnson invited Oppenheimer to the White House and presented him with the Enrico Fermi Award, which was the AEC's highest honor. Sadly, the AEC continued to regard Oppenheimer as a security risk and deny him a clearance. Oppenheimer retired from the Institute for Advanced Study in 1966, when illness weakened him. He died of throat cancer on February 18, 1967.[38]

Atoms for Peace

In January 1953, Dwight D. Eisenhower became President of the United States. For the first two years of his administration he was plagued by the excesses of McCarthyism. It was a very difficult time for anyone in the U.S. to suggest anything that might inhibit nuclear weapons development or production. Nevertheless, Eisenhower had the courage to make nuclear disarmament a primary objective of his Administration.

Figure 6.4.
President Dwight D. Eisenhower

Eisenhower was a "five star" general and knew the face of war first hand. He had been the supreme commander of the Allied Expeditionary Force that invaded Normandy in 1944 and went on to defeat Germany in World War II. He had also been the supreme commander of Allied forces in Europe (i.e., NATO) from 1950 to 1952. No one could seriously question his loyalty to the U.S.

After Stalin's death in March 1953 and the end of the Korean War in July, Americans hoped for some change in the Soviet Union's foreign policy toward the United States.[39]

On December 8, 1953, in a speech at the United Nations, Eisenhower proposed an Atoms-for-Peace plan, which included a recommendation to establish an International Atomic Energy Agency. He pledged that the U.S. would devote "its entire heart and mind to find the way by which the miraculous inventiveness of man shall not be dedicated to his death, but consecrated to his life."

This speech received enthusiastic response from every continent. There was general agreement that Eisenhower had delivered one of the most significant speeches of the postwar era. But it was also recognized that Eisenhower's vision would become reality only if there were good faith on all sides.[40]

The plan had three goals: (1) to allocate fissionable materials to peaceful uses in medicine, agriculture, and research; (2) to promote the production of power using atomic fuel; and (3) to divert uranium stockpiles from the nuclear arms race. This plan included an atomic bank for nuclear materials. The U.S. contended that an atomic bank would siphon off nuclear material from national stockpiles and thus reduce the amount available for weapons. Nuclear power was to save the world from nuclear devastation.[41]

The U.S. presented its plan for the international agency to the Soviets on March 19, 1954. The Soviets rejected it. They claimed that the small amount of nuclear materials allocated to the international agency would not significantly reduce the stock available for weapons, and the widespread use of nuclear power would result in the proliferation of weapon-grade material. They felt that a ban on nuclear weapons was needed first.[42] Such a ban was politically impossible in the U.S. because of the Soviet Union's hostile actions in Berlin and elsewhere.

The Atoms-for-Peace plan also posed a security dilemma for the U.S., that is, the need to safeguard technical information on nuclear weapons against the desire to promote the use of nuclear technology for peaceful purposes.[43]

By June 1954, Eisenhower decided to proceed without the Soviets if necessary, and the U.S. began entering into bilateral agreements with other nations. On August 30, 1954, he signed a new Atomic Energy Act (which superseded the Atomic Energy Act of 1946) that provided more encouragement to the peaceful application of nuclear energy. For example, it allowed nuclear reactors to be privately owned under suitable licensing arrangements.[44]

In September 1954, Eisenhower made a radio and television address on his Atoms-for-Peace plan and announced that American initiatives had been "cynically blocked in the councils of the world." He went on to say that the U.S. would continue to work for an international agency while negotiating bilateral agreements with other countries. In 1955, the first agreement was established. It provided for American assistance in establishing research reactors abroad.

Similar efforts to promote peaceful uses of nuclear energy took place within the U.S. In 1957, the first commercial electrical power reactor in the U.S. went into operation at Shippingport, Pennsylvania. In 1959, the world's first nuclear-powered cargo ship, the Savannah, was launched at Camden, New Jersey. Mrs. Eisenhower attended the launching and christened the new ship.[45]

The U.S. had two ships named Savannah. The first was launched in 1819 and became the first ship to cross the Atlantic using steam power. The second Savannah was a technical success but a commercial failure. High costs discouraged any successors.

Eisenhower's Atom's-for-Peace plan met its first two goals but failed at the third, that is, as a means to curtail the nuclear arms race. As a result, nuclear weapons development and production accelerated throughout the 1950s. These requirements drove the expansion of the NWC.

Eisenhower's last major attempt to curb the nuclear arms race occurred on October 31, 1958, when he announced a unilateral nuclear testing moratorium. (Additional details are provided in Chapter Seven, in the Section on Worldwide Nuclear Tests.)

On January 17, 1961, President Eisenhower gave his farewell address to the nation. He said, "We face a hostile ideology — global in scope, atheistic in character, ruthless in purpose, and insidious in method."

He explained that keeping the peace would continue to require a strong military establishment and an armaments industry unprecedented in America's peacetime history. Eisenhower then warned the nation that

> *In the councils of government, we must guard against the acquisition of unwarranted influence, whether sought or unsought, by the military-industrial complex .....Only an alert knowledgeable citizenry can compel the proper meshing of the huge industrial and military machinery of defense with our peaceful methods and goals, so that security and liberty may prosper.* [46]

References for Chapter 6

1. Richard Rhodes, *Dark Sun* (New York: Simon & Schuster, 1995), 256.
2. Ibid., 407.
3. Ibid., 462.
4. Ibid., 466-471; and Peter Goodchild, *Edward Teller: The Real Dr. Strangelove* (Cambridge: Harvard University Press, 2004), 179-180.
5. Necah Stewart Furman, *Sandia National Laboratories: The Postwar Decade,* (Albuquerque: University of New Mexico Press, 1990), 379.
6. Rhodes, *Dark Sun,* 496; and Goodchild, *Edward Teller: The Real Dr. Strangelove,* 182-184.
7. Hugh Gusterson, *Nuclear Rites: A Weapons Laboratory at the End of the Cold War* (Berkeley: University of California Press, 1996), 24.
8. Ibid., 256.
9. U.S. Department of Energy, Office of Environmental Management, *Linking Legacies,* DOE/EM-0319 (Washington, DC: U.S. Department of Energy, 1997), 21, 147.
10. Ibid., 142.
11. Ibid., 142.
12. William F. Burgess, Jo Anne McCormick, and Eileen Pingatore, *History of the Production Complex: The Methods of Site Selection,* Prepared by History Associates Inc. for the U.S. Department of Energy, DOE/NV10594-H1 (Washington, D.C.: U.S. Department of Energy, 1987), 73.
13. Office of Environmental Management, *Linking Legacies,* 21, 143 and 185.
14. Ibid., 21 and 143-144.
15. Stephen I. Schwartz, ed., *Atomic Audit* (Washington, DC: Brookings Institution Press, 1998), 86.
16. Leland Johnson, *Sandia National Laboratories: A History of Exceptional Service in the National Interest,* SAND97-1029 (Albuquerque: Sandia National Laboratories, 1997), 50-52, 150.
17. Bernard A. Weisberger, *Cold War, Cold Peace: The United States and Russia Since 1945* (New York: American Heritage, 1984), 105.
18. Ibid., 108.

19. Rhodes, *Dark Sun*, 413, 543.

20. Weisberger, *Cold War, Cold Peace*, 111, 118.

21. Ibid., 121

22. Ibid., 104-105.

23. Rhodes, *Dark Sun*, 280.

24. Ibid., 374, 381.

25. Ibid., 400-403.

26. Ibid., 406-407.

27. Richard G. Hewlett and Jack M. Holl, *Atoms for Peace and War: 1953-1961* (Berkeley and Los Angeles: University of California Press, 1989), 53-54.

28. Rhodes, *Dark Sun*, 536.

29. Ibid., 496.

30. Ibid., 530, 536-538.

31. Ibid. 544-549.

32. Ibid., 530, 550.

33. Ibid., 553-555; and Goodchild, *Edward Teller: The Real Dr. Strangelove*, 244.

34. Rhodes, *Dark Sun*, 556-557.

35. Ibid., 557-558.

36. John Earl Haynes and Harvey Klehr, *Venona: Decoding Soviet Espionage in America* (New Haven and London: Yale University Press, 1999), 329-330.

37. David Halberstam, *The Fifties* (New York: Villard Books, 1993), 353.

38. Rhodes, *Dark Sun*, 577-578.

39. Hewlett, *Atoms for Peace and War*, 214, 565.

40. Ibid., 209.

41. Ibid., 72, 309, 360.

42. Ibid., 221, 308-309.

43. Ibid., preface.

44. Ibid., 226.

45. Ibid., 227, 236, 357-358, 506-507.

46. Ibid., 562-563.

CHAPTER SEVEN

Tests and Test Sites

First Thermonuclear Tests

On May 9, 1951, the U.S. tested the world's first thermonuclear device at Enewetak Atoll in the Marshall Islands, about three thousand miles west of Hawaii. This test was a part of the Greenhouse series and was code named George. It had a yield of 225 kt. George proved that the Teller-Ulam concept was valid.[1]

Edward Teller had a very limited role in subsequent activities at Los Alamos. Although Teller was a brilliant scientist, he was a notoriously poor administrator. As a result, on September 17, 1951, Norris Bradbury, the Los Alamos Director, appointed Marshall Holloway to head the thermonuclear program. A week later Teller resigned in a huff. Bradbury later said, "Just as the going gets tough — in spite of Edward's protestations about national need and so on — Edward quits, because I wouldn't give him control of the program." Bradbury claimed that half or two-thirds of his division leaders would have quit if Teller had been put in charge. He went on to say, "Edward couldn't follow one course of action for two consecutive days — jump here, jump there. I couldn't put him in charge of the program here. I had to tell him so. I wished he would stay. I tried to persuade him to stay, but I couldn't put him in charge, and I wouldn't put him in charge." [2] Over the next year, Los Alamos made very significant progress.

On October 31, 1952, the U.S. tested the world's first *staged* thermonuclear device at Enewetak. This device, code name *Mike,* had a yield of 10.4 megatons (Mt), which was about 700 times more powerful than the *Little Boy* which destroyed Hiroshima.

Mike used the *fission–fusion–fission* concept, in which the reaction begins with fission in a Pu primary that ignites a liquid-deuterium

Figure 7.1. Mike

secondary. Fusion in the secondary produces high-energy neutrons that cause U-238 around the secondary to fission.

Teller felt bitterness and jealousy toward his Los Alamos colleagues and did not travel to Enewetak. Instead, he stayed in Berkeley and monitored this test with a seismograph.[3]

The *Mike* device could not serve as a deliverable weapon because it required very large cryogenic equipment to cool the liquid deuterium. *Mike* was almost seven feet in diameter, 20 feet long, and weighed 82 tons.[4]

On August 12, 1953, the Soviet Union tested its first thermonuclear device. The U.S. gave it the code name *Joe 4*. It had a yield of 400 kt. It was thought to be a relatively simple single-stage device similar to Teller's "alarm clock." The Soviets had not yet incorporated the idea of X-ray compression, which made high-megaton yields possible in a device of reasonable size.[5]

On March 1, 1954, the U.S. tested its first *deliverable* thermonuclear weapon at Bikini Atoll in the Marshall Islands.

The test had the code name *Bravo*. It used solid lithium deuteride in the secondary and had a yield of 14.8 Mt.[6] *Bravo* was the largest yield thermonuclear device ever tested by the U.S. It was almost 1000 times more powerful than the *Little Boy* which destroyed Hiroshima.

Figure 7.2. Bravo shot

The Bravo test surprised the scientists because it was expected to yield about 5 Mt. *Bravo* used lithium enriched to 40 percent lithium-6. The scientists who measured lithium fusion cross sections had failed to notice an important fusion reaction in lithium-7, the other 60 percent of the lithium fuel component. With lithium-7, there is an n, 2n reaction (i.e., one neutron entering a lithium nucleus knocks two neutrons out). When this occurs, the atom becomes lithium-6, and thus enriches the fuel.[7] The nuclear equation for this reaction is as follows:

$$_{3}Li^{7} + {}_{0}n^{1} \rightarrow {}_{3}Li^{6} + {}_{0}n^{1} + {}_{0}n^{1}$$

Worldwide Nuclear Tests

The first nuclear test was conducted by the U.S. at the Trinity site near Alamogordo, NM. Since then, seven other countries have conducted nuclear tests. It is estimated that there have been 2,070 nuclear tests worldwide. These figures include "peaceful nuclear explosions" of which 42 were conducted by the U.S. and 116 by the Soviet Union.

The date of the first test by each country and the number of tests are as follows:[8]

Country	Date	Number of Tests
United States	July 16, 1945	1,030
Soviet Union	August 29, 1949	715
United Kingdom	October 3, 1952	57 (includes 24 joint US/UK tests)
France	December 3, 1960	210
China	October 16, 1964	44
India	May 18, 1974	6 (5 on May 11-13, 1998)
Pakistan	May 28, 1998	6 (all on May 28-30, 1998)
North Korea	October 9, 2006 May 25, 2009	2

On October 31, 1958, the United States entered into a unilateral testing moratorium, which was announced by President Eisenhower with the understanding that the Soviet Union would also refrain from conducting tests. This moratorium was upheld until the Cold War intensified and the Berlin Wall was erected in August of 1961.[9]

The U.S. conducted 215 tests in the atmosphere (including five under water tests). The U.S. also conducted 815 tests underground, 63 of which involved multiple simultaneous detonations. These multiple tests resulted in 95 additional detonations. In total, the U.S. had 1,125 detonations.

The Soviet Union conducted 219 tests in the atmosphere (including five under water tests). They also conducted 496 tests underground, many of which involved multiple simultaneous detonations. These multiple tests resulted in 254 additional detonations. In total, the Soviet Union had 969 detonations.

India used plutonium obtained from domestic nuclear power reactors for its devices. Inadvertently, the U.S. helped India with this technology under the "Atoms for Peace Program," which was started during the Eisenhower administration in 1953.

Pakistan used enriched uranium for its devices. It appears that Pakistan obtained uranium enrichment technology from a variety of sources, most notably China.[10]

The Soviet Union resumed testing on September 1, 1961, with a series of the largest tests ever conducted. In response, the United States also resumed testing. On October 30, 1961, the Soviet Union detonated the largest nuclear device ever tested, 58 Mt.[11]

On August 5, 1963, the United States and the Soviet Union signed the Limited Test Ban Treaty, which prohibited underwater, atmospheric, and outer space nuclear tests. This treaty did not ban underground tests.

Worldwide, there have been 541 nuclear tests in the atmosphere or underwater. Since June 1962, all U.S. nuclear tests have been underground. The last atmospheric test in the world occurred on October 16, 1980, in China.[12]

The last U.S. nuclear test was conducted on September 23, 1992.[13]

Nuclear Test Sites

The U.S. conducted tests at 15 sites. These tests can be placed into three categories:

- **Weapons Tests** to gather data on nuclear devices and to determine the effects of nuclear detonations on military systems were conducted at nine sites.[14]

Weapon Test Site	Number of Tests
Alamogordo, New Mexico	1 test
Bikini Atoll (South Pacific) (an atoll is a coral reef enclosing a lagoon)	23 tests
Enewetak Atoll (South Pacific)	43 tests
Johnston Atoll (mid-Pacific)	12 tests
Christmas Island (South Pacific)	24 tests
Amchitka, Alaska	2 tests
Central Nevada	1 test
Nellis Air Force Range, Nevada	5 tests
Nevada Test Site (NTS)	896 tests (including 24 joint US/UK tests)

Tests were also conducted at other locations (not land-based sites) in the Pacific (four tests) and in the South Atlantic (three tests).

The first nuclear test after World War II was conducted at Bikini Atoll on June 30, 1946. Five days later, on July 5, 1946, French fashion designer, Louis Reard, created a scandal by unveiling his latest creation, the bikini bathing suit. It consisted of four tiny triangles of fabric and a handful of string The Vatican denounced the suit as immoral, and it was prohibited in Spain and Italy. Reard chose the name bikini because it was "an explosive fashion."

- **Vela Uniform Project** used seismic equipment to improve the capability to detect, identify, and locate underground and underwater nuclear explosions. Seven tests were conducted at four sites.[15]

Test Site	Number of Tests
Hattiesburg, Mississippi	2 tests
Fallon, Nevada	1 test
Amchitka, Alaska	1 test
NTS	3 tests

Project VELA was created to help verify compliance with the Limited Test Ban Treaty of 1963 and, subsequently, the Threshold Test Ban Treaty of 1974. It consisted of three major programs: VELA Uniform, as explained above; VELA Hotel, which used satellites to detect nuclear explosions in space or on the earth's surface; and VELA Sierra, which used earth-based equipment to detect explosions in the atmosphere or in space. Vela is a Spanish word meaning watchfulness or vigil.[16]

- **Plowshare Program** to investigate the use of nuclear explosions for the extraction of natural gas and oil and for earth moving projects. There were 33 of these tests with 35 detonations conducted at five sites.[17]

Test Site	Number of Tests
Carlsbad, New Mexico	1 test
Farmington, New Mexico	1 test
Grand Valley, Colorado	1 test
Rifle, Colorado	1 test (included 3 simultaneous detonations)
NTS	29 tests

In total, there were 928 tests conducted at the NTS. The NTS is the only U.S. nuclear test site that is still open.

Nonnuclear Test Sites

A typical nuclear weapon has about 200 nuclear components and over 6,000 nonnuclear components. These nonnuclear components range from the tiny electronic parts in the arming, fuzing, and firing systems to the large metal structures in the outer case of a weapon. All these components must be tested in the environments they might experience in actual use. Consequently, the NWC has had seven nonnuclear test sites.

Five sites were used to test the ballistics and other characteristics of nuclear weapons:

- **Wendover** – In September 1944, the Army Air Force decided it was time to organize and train a unit to deliver atomic bombs and began to form the 509th Composite Group out of the 393rd Bombardment Squadron and other units. Colonel Paul W. Tibbets — the man who piloted the *Enola Gay* and dropped *Little Boy* on Hiroshima — was given command of this group. Tibbets was given his choice of three bases to serve as home for the 509th and chose Wendover Army Air Force Base in Utah. Tibbets liked this location because it was very remote, which he felt would offer fewer distractions from their mission and provide better security.

Bob Hope, the famous WWII entertainer, visited Wendover in the winter of 1945 and gave it the nickname "Leftover Field."[18]

  The 509th Composite Group was activated officially on December 17, 1944. Some of its training involved dropping 5,500-pound, orange-colored simulated atomic bombs, which were nicknamed pumpkins. In May/June 1945, Tibbets and his command moved to Tinian Island in the Marianas.[19]

  Also in May 1945, a new organization, the 216th Army Air Base Unit (Special), was activated and assigned to Wendover. This unit was responsible for further ground work associated with the flight test program of the atomic bomb project. Between the beginning of May and the end of July, the 216th

Unit assembled 71 test weapons.[20] From September to November 1945, the weapons assembly operations were transferred from Wendover to Oxnard Field in Albuquerque. This portion of Oxnard Field subsequently became a part of Sandia National Laboratories.[21]

- **Los Lunas** – Shortly after World War II, Sandia decided that the Kirtland airfield practice bombing range at Los Lunas, New Mexico, could serve as a test range for nonnuclear components. In December 1945, Sandia began the first ballistic tests of the Mark III bomb, the first postwar nuclear weapon. These tests provided information needed to improve the control of the bomb's trajectory and accuracy. Ballistic tests were conducted on the Mark IV bomb in late 1946. The Los Lunas Test Range was not fully satisfactory because it is 5,000 feet above sea level, which affects a bomb's ballistics.[22]

- **Salton Sea** – In 1946, the Army Manhattan Engineer District acquired use of the Salton Sea base in southern California from the Navy. This site became the new test range for Sandia, and the Los Lunas Test Range was phased out. Salton Sea is 235 feet below sea level and thus allowed questions to be answered about ballistics in dense atmospheres.

  Sandia completed its first test drop at Salton Sea on March 12, 1947. Most of the tests at this site were high-altitude, subsonic drops of various ballistic shapes, including both production units and experimental models of newer, more aerodynamic designs.

When the field test director joked that every bomb shape had been tried at Salton Sea except the kitchen sink, some prankster kicked a kitchen sink out of an open bomb-bay during the next test run. [23]

As the bombers progressed from propeller-driven to jet-powered aircraft, the staff at Salton Sea began having increasing problems in tracking these planes because of range limitations. Also, because of the population growth in southern

California, they began to have problems with commercial air lanes, highways, fishermen, boaters, and air pollution. Testing was terminated at Salton Sea in 1960.[24]

- **Yucca Flats** – In 1954, Sandia established the Yucca Flats area of the Nevada Test Site to test contact fuzes. Unfortunately, several problems soon became apparent, including conflicts with the nuclear test program and the mountains on three sides, which obstructed aircraft approaches for low-altitude bomb drops. Testing was terminated at Yucca Flats in 1956.[25]

- **Tonopah** – As a result of the problems at Salton Sea and Yucca Flats, Sandia began to search for a new site. In 1956, the AEC established the Tonopah Test Range in the northwest sector of the Air Force's Las Vegas Bombing Range. This site was so remote that commercial aircraft, highway traffic, and urban development were insignificant.

  The first drop test at this new site was conducted on February 8, 1957. Rocket testing began on July 27, 1957.

  During the 1960s, about 500 tests were conducted annually at Tonopah.[26]

Figure 7.3. B2A Stealth Bomber at Tonopah

Over the years, many other defense-related projects were tested at Tonopah. For example, in the 1970s and 1980s, many tests were conducted on the W33, W48, W79, and W82 artillery-fired atomic shells for the Army. Sandia also tested materials used in the nosecones of missiles for the Air Force. In 1988, Tonopah became famous when the Air Force announced that it had used this site for a decade as the development testing range for Stealth fighters.[27]

Two sites were used for other nuclear weapon-related tests:

- Kauai – In 1962, in response to Soviet violation of the nuclear test moratorium, a rocket launching facility was established on Kauai in the Hawaiian Islands. This site was initially called the Barking Sands Rocket Complex because nearby coral sand, when stepped on, made crunching noises similar to a yapping dog. In the 1970s, it was renamed the Kauai Test Facility. This site was subsequently used to support a NASA project for study of the upper atmosphere. It was also used to launch scientific experiments for the Los Alamos and Lawrence Livermore National Laboratories and for some universities.[28]

- Edgewood – In 1968, a test range was established at Edgewood, New Mexico, about twenty miles east of Albuquerque.

  Many of the tests at this site involved *terradynamics*, which concerns the ballistics of weapon shapes as they pass through soils.

  Some of these tests used an enormous recoilless rifle, called a Davis gun, which was designed at Sandia. This gun had a 35-foot-long barrel and could fire projectiles into the ground at up to 3,000 feet per second. A weapon that can drive deeply underground before detonating can destroy an enemy tunnel complex or subsurface bunker.

  Testing at Edgewood during the 1960s and 1970s related chiefly to soil implantation of seismic sensors capable of detecting the passage of enemy equipment and troops.

Figure 7.4. Davis Gun at Edgewood

As part of its nuclear testing verification program, Sandia had developed sensors for detecting nuclear underground blasts. These devices were so sensitive that they could record the footsteps of passing troops. During the 1960s, Sandia combined these sensors with ground penetration projectiles that could be dropped from aircraft to imbed in soils. The sensors relayed signals to a central command station for analysis. The military deployed thousands of these seismic penetrators in Vietnam. The Edgewood Test Range was phased out of the NWC in 1975.[29]

References for Chapter 7

1. Richard Rhodes, *Dark Sun* (New York: Simon & Schuster, 1995), 473-474.

2. Ibid., 478-479; and Peter Goodchild, *Edward Teller: The Real Dr. Strangelove*, (Cambridge: Harvard University Press, 2004), 190.

3. Rhodes, *Dark Sun*, 505-512.

4. Ibid., 494-495.

5. Ibid., 524-525.

6. Ibid., 525, 541.

7. Ibid., 541

8. U.S. Department of Energy, Nevada Operations Office, *United States Nuclear Tests: July 1945 through September 1992*, DOE/NV-209, Revision 15 (Las Vegas, NV: U. S. Department of Energy, 2000), xii-xv; and Sir Frederick Warner, ed., *Nuclear Test Explosions* (Chichester, England: John Wiley & Sons Ltd., 2000), 30-31.

9. Nevada Operations Office, *United States Nuclear Tests: July 1945 through September 1992*, vii.

10. Praful Bidwai and Achin Vanaik, *New Nukes: India, Pakistan and Global Nuclear Disarmament* (New York: Interlink Publishing Group, Inc., 2000), 94-103; and Raja Menon, *A Nuclear Strategy for India* (New Delhi: Sage Publications, Inc., 2000), 68-72, 85-88, 95-97, 101-103, 113-114.

11. Leland Johnson, *Sandia National Laboratories: A History of Exceptional Service in the National Interest*, SAND97-1029 (Albuquerque: Sandia National Laboratories, 1997), 113.

12. Warner, *Nuclear Test Explosions*, 31; and Nevada Operations Office, *United States Nuclear Tests: July 1945 through September 1992*, vii.

13. Nevada Operations Office, *United States Nuclear Tests: July 1945 through September 1992*, 88.

14. Ibid., xv, xvi.

15. Ibid., xvi, 30-31, 36-37, 44-45, 48-49, 58-59, 62-63.

16. Johnson, *A History of Exceptional Service in the National Interest*, 110-113, 130; and Stephen I. Schwartz, ed., *Atomic Audit: The Costs and Consequences of U.S. Nuclear Weapons Since 1940* (Washington, D. C.: Brookings Institution Press, 1998), 219.

17. Nevada Operations Office, *United States Nuclear Tests*, xvi, 16-17, 24-67.

18. Paul W. Tibbets, *Flight of the Enola Gay* (Columbus, Ohio: Mid Coast Marketing, 1989), 161-162.

19. Ibid., 163, 181-182.

20. James Les Rowe, *Project W-47* (Livermore: JA A Ro Publishing, 1978), xvi, 176.

21. Necah Stewart Furman, *Sandia National Laboratories: The Postwar Decade* (Albuquerque: University of New Mexico Press, 1990), 125.

22. Leland Johnson, *Tonopah Test Range: Outpost of Sandia National Laboratories,* SAND96-0375 (Albuquerque: Sandia National Laboratories, 1996), 11-12.

23. Ibid., 13-16.

24. Ibid., 24.

25. Ibid., 26-27.

26. Ibid., 27, 31-36, 39, 49.

27. Ibid., 62, 69-70, 79.

28. Ibid., 57-59.

29. Ibid., 60-61

CHAPTER EIGHT

Performance Improvements

Wooden Bombs

As the stockpile grew during the 1950s, the military wanted to reduce the maintenance requirements on nuclear weapons and improve their readiness and reliability. They also wanted these weapons to be smaller, lighter, and more versatile. The laboratories translated these desires into a "wooden bomb" concept, that is, a nuclear weapon that could lie in storage for twenty years or more without major maintenance, yet could be pulled from the stockpile and used at a moment's notice.[1]

Sandia took steps to implement this concept by replacing many of the reusable components in the arming, fuzing, and firing systems with one-shot components. For example, lead-acid batteries that required charging and had to be replaced every few years were replaced by thermal batteries, which did not require charging and could be stored for decades. These batteries come in various shapes and sizes.

Figure 8.1. Thermal Batteries

Otto Erb, a German scientist, had planned to incorporate thermal battery technology into the V-1 and V-2 rockets during World War II. He provided this information to British intelligence after the war, and it was passed on to the United States.[2]

Other examples include explosive switches in place of relays and explosive-to-electric transducers in place of conventional power supplies.

Sealed pits and neutron generators were two other major improvements in the wooden bomb concept.

Sealed Pits

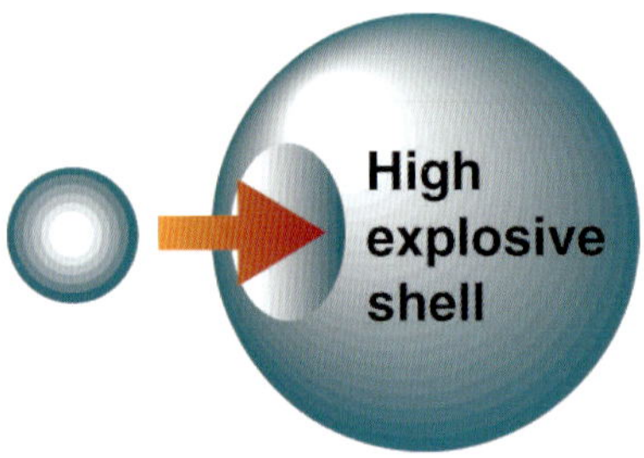

Figure 8.2. Manual Insertion

In the early days of nuclear weaponry, the capsule containing the fissile material and the initiator were kept separate from the rest of the weapon system and had to be inserted when the weapon was to be used. From 1945 to 1951, this insertion was done manually.

This technique was somewhat hazardous to personnel, created logistics problems, and allowed the fissile material to become contaminated.

In 1951, designs were introduced whereby the capsule was inserted by a motor driven screw. Although this technique was an improvement, it still had some of the above disadvantages.

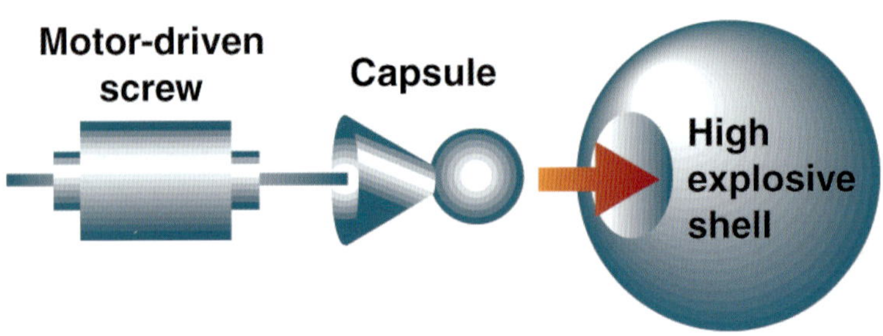

Figure 8.3. Motor-Driven Insertion

In 1957, Los Alamos introduced the first sealed pit weapon. With this new approach, the capsule was sealed hermetically and contained permanently within the pit at the center of the weapon.

Figure 8.4. Sealed Pit

This innovation allowed the pit to be used as an interchangeable building-block component in different weapons systems. The W25 warhead, an air-to-air rocket called Genie, was the first system to use a sealed pit.[3]

Neutron Generators

In 1950, Los Alamos proposed the concept of replacing the internally mounted Po/Be initiators with externally mounted neutron generators. In 1953, Sandia began the engineering development of this concept in conjunction with the General Electric X-Ray Department in Milwaukee, Wisconsin. The first neutron generators were produced at this plant in 1954. [4]

Neutron generators provide high-energy neutrons to initiate nuclear weapons and test devices. They consist of a miniaturized linear accelerator assembled with a pulsed electrical power supply for their operation. Their principle of operation is as follows: Deuterium atoms are entrapped in a source material located at one end of a high-vacuum tube. Tritium atoms are entrapped in a target material at the other end. This tube is connected to an electronic circuit.

The weapon system provides an input signal to a timer in the neutron generator. The timer is synchronized with the weapon system's fuzing circuitry to ensure that neutrons are released at the precise time for initiation. A high current is sent to the source and ionizes the deuterium into a plasma. A very high voltage is placed between the source and the target and accelerates the deuterium ions into the tritium. A very high voltage is required in order to overcome the electrostatic repulsive force between the deuterium and tritium nuclei. Fusion reactions occur between the deuterium and tritium nuclei and produce neutrons (see the D-T reaction explained on page 97). The operation of a neutron generator is illustrated in Figure 8.5.

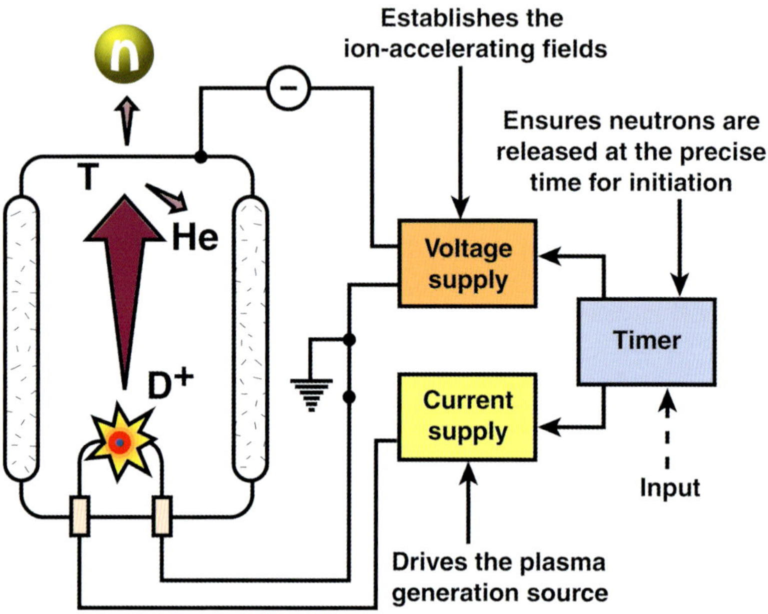

Figure 8.5. Neutron Generator Operation

There are two basic types of neutron generators, electronic and explosive. The major difference between them is in the method employed to produce the high voltage. An electronic generator stores electrical energy in a large capacitor. This energy is released by a switch. An explosive generator stores energy in a metal/ceramic component called a ferroelectric. This energy is released by shattering the ferroelectric with a small detonator. Explosive generators are about the size of a twelve-ounce beverage can. They are used where space and weight are at a premium, such as in missile warheads. Electronic generators have an advantage because they can be used after a function test. Explosive generators are destroyed in a function test.

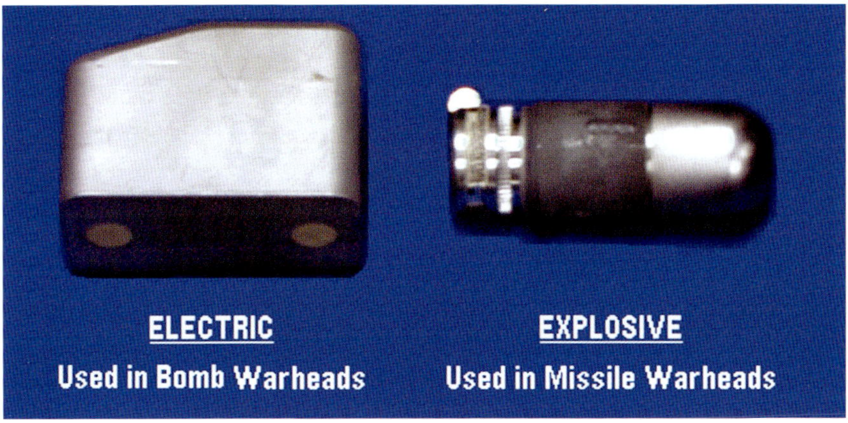

Figure 8.6. Neutron Generators

Limited-Life Components

Tritium decays radioactively with a half-life of 12.3 years. Because neutron generators contain tritium, they are limited-life components that must be replaced periodically. Replacement is required when the neutron output falls below the weapon system requirement, as illustrated in the following figure.

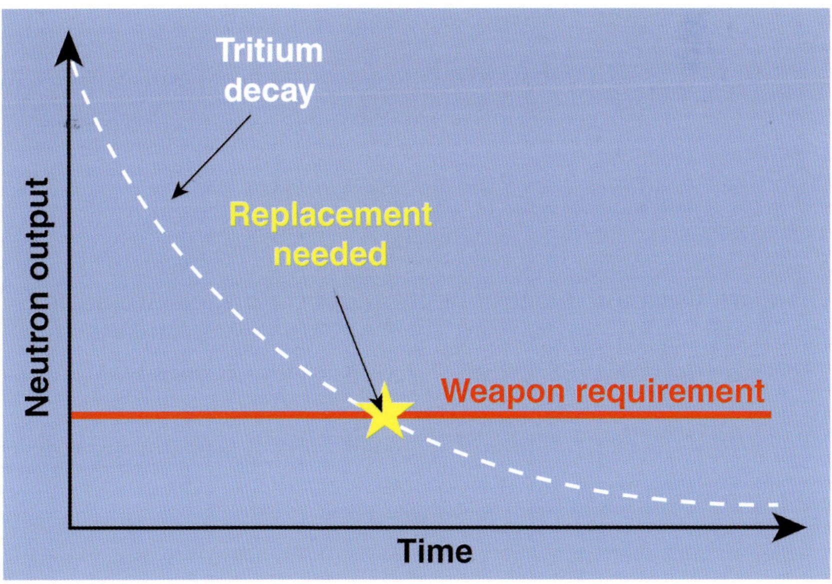

Figure 8.7. Tritium Decay Curve

Reservoirs used for gas boosting are also limited-life components because they contain tritium.

NWC from 1954 to 1957

Seven important changes occurred in the 1954 to 1957 time frame.

- In 1954, the AEC decided that the products from the Salt Wells plant at Inyokern, California, were no longer needed, and it was closed.[5]
- In 1955, the Savannah River Plant began to fill components with tritium.[6] Savannah River also made its first shipment of plutonium.
- In 1956, the Weldon Spring plant was established near St. Louis, Missouri. This plant provided feed materials for reactors, the same mission as Fernald.[7]
- In 1956, at the direction of the AEC, Sandia established a facility in Livermore, California. Its mission was to provide ordnance engineering support to the Lawrence Livermore Laboratory.[8]
- In 1957, the Pinellas Plant in St. Petersburg, Florida, was added to the NWC to produce neutron generators. These externally mounted devices were a major improvement over the internally mounted polonium/beryllium initiators that had been produced at Mound. The DoD had to return weapons to the NWC in order to have internally mounted initiators replaced. The DoD could replace externally mounted neutron generators in the field.[9]

Not all sites were chosen solely on the basis of their technical or economic merit. In 1955, John Smith, the Manager of General Electric's X-Ray Department asked Addison F. Persons, who lived in the harsh, cold climate of Syracuse, New York, to serve as the manager of a proposed new plant to manufacture neutron generators. In February 1952, Persons had taken a vacation to St. Petersburg, Florida, and found the climate to be very desirable. Persons told Smith that he would be interested if the plant could be located near St. Petersburg. The Pinellas site was chosen largely to satisfy Persons.[10]

Pinellas was built by General Electric in 1956 under a contract letter of intent with the AEC. In 1957, the AEC exercised its option in this contract and purchased the plant.[11]

The first externally mounted neutron generators went into the stockpile on the W34, a nuclear depth bomb, in June 1958, and on the B28 bomb in August 1958. In subsequent years, Pinellas was given the mission to produce other components including thermal batteries, radioisotopic thermoelectric generators (RTGs), lightning arrestor connectors, capacitors, and neutron detectors.

- In 1957, the mission to produce reservoirs for deuterium-tritium gas boosting of weapons was added to the South Albuquerque Works.[12]
- In 1957, the Dana Heavy Water Plant in Newport, Indiana, was closed.[13]

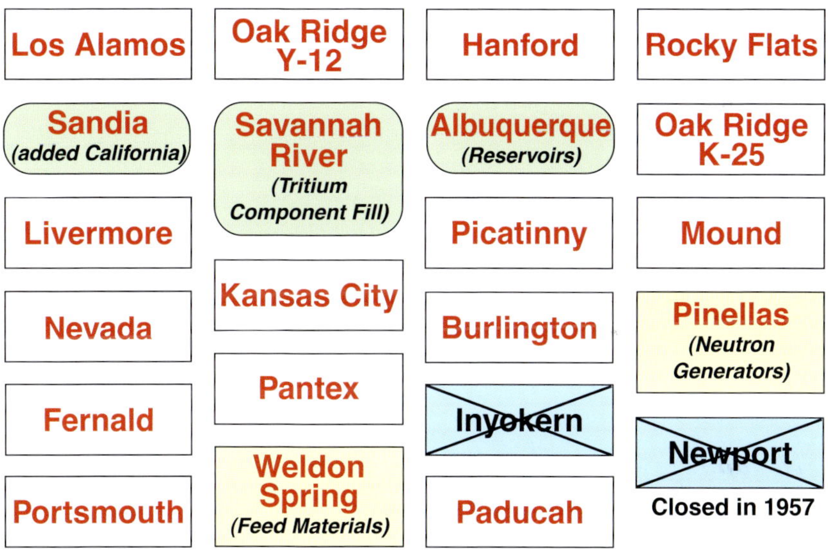

Figure 8.8. NWC from 1954 to 1957

> *In 1956, the NWC's electrical consumption peaked at 60.7 billion kilowatt-hours, which was approximately 12 percent of the country's total output. This high usage was largely for uranium enrichment activities at the three gaseous diffusion plants, which consumed more electricity than was produced by the Hoover, Grand Coulee, and Bonneville dams plus the entire Tennessee Valley Authority (TVA) system combined.*[14]

NWC in 1958

Four major changes occurred in 1958:

- The mission to produce beryllium components was added to the Rocky Flats Plant. This work had previously been done at Los Alamos.[15]

- The AEC's operations at Picatinny Arsenal were closed, and the detonator work was transferred to the Mound Plant.[16]

> *Picatinny Arsenal continued to be involved with nuclear weapons because of the 1953 Missiles and Rockets Agreement. As explained in Appendix A, Picatinny Arsenal had the mission to provide "adaption kits" for army tactical nuclear weapons. However, because this work was under the DoD, Picatinny was no longer considered a part of the NWC.*

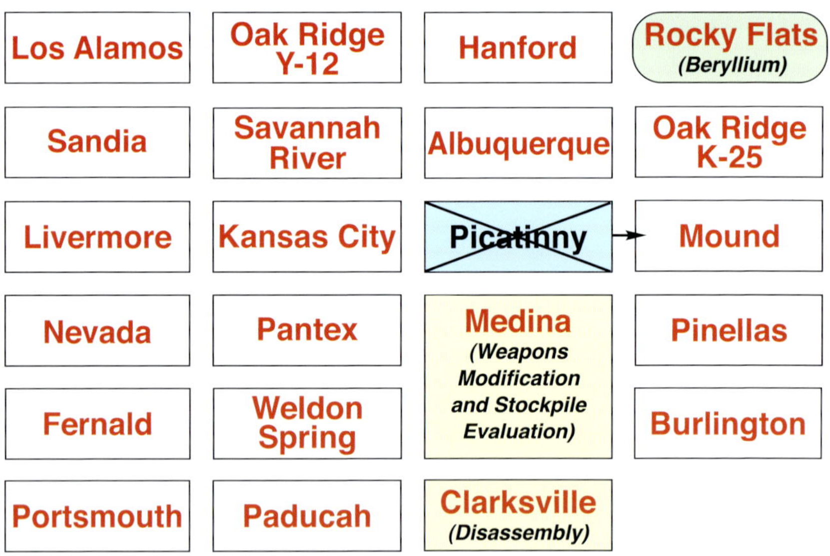

Figure 8.9. NWC in 1958

- The Clarksville Modification Center, located on the Fort Campbell Military Reservation in Clarksville, Tennessee, was established to disassemble retired weapons prior to their disposal.

- The Medina Modification Center, located on the Lackland Training Annex of Lackland Air Force Base in San Antonio, Texas, was established to do weapon modification and stockpile evaluation testing.[17]

From 1955 to 1958, Medina served as a nuclear weapons storage facility and was operated jointly by the AEC and DoD. Storage operations ceased when Medina became a modification center; and thereafter, it was operated solely by the AEC.

Radiation Hardening and Miniaturization

In 1961, in an effort to obtain increased reliability and miniaturization, the design staff at Sandia turned away from vacuum tubes and wiring to solid-state semiconductor electronics and printed wiring boards. This effort was very successful.

By 1970, Sandia completed the arming, fuzing, and firing (AF&F) package for the Navy's Mark 3 reentry body, which is built around the W68 warhead. The Mark 3 was used on the Poseidon C3 submarine-launched ballistic missile (SLBM). This AF&F design set new standards for miniaturization and provided improved protection against radiation.[18]

Improvements continued, and by the late 1970s SNL developed an even smaller and better AF&F for the Mark 4 reentry vehicle, which is build around the W76 warhead. The Mark 4 was used on the Trident I C4 SLBM.[19]

By the early 1980s, Sandia had a need for custom-made, radiation-hardened, large-scale integrated circuits (LSIs) for the AF&F used on the Navy's Mark 5 reentry body. This football-sized AF&F package has 3,276 components.

Miniaturization and sophistication reached their zenith with the Mark 5, which was built around the W88 warhead. Eight of these reentry bodies can fit on a single Trident II D5 SLBM.

At this point in time, private industry was not interested in supplying radiation-hardened LSIs because the market was too small, the technology was too complex, and the demand for other integrated circuits was very high. Consequently, to meet the Trident II development milestones, Sandia began producing these products in-house.[20]

The DOE's Kansas City plant had the mission to provide electronic components within the NWC. In September 1982, DOE/AL and Sandia asked Allied Signal, the management and operating contractor at the Kansas City plant, to run the radiation-hardened LSI production operation. They accepted this challenge and, in 1983, established the Albuquerque Microelectronics Operation (AMO). In 1985, the AMO assumed responsibility for production operations and began to support the Trident II program and other weapon program schedules.[21]

In 1986, the Sandia microelectronics development staff relocated to the newly constructed Microelectronics Development Laboratory (MDL), leaving the existing facility to be operated by the AMO for radiation-hardened production in support of DOE weapons programs. By 1989, Harris Semiconductor in Melbourne, Florida, had demonstrated the ability and interest to fabricate radiation-hardened LSIs. Subsequently, Harris supplied these devices for a variety of nuclear weapon applications.

The DOE then initiated studies to assess options for the long-term approach to supporting radiation-hardened microelectronics for weapon programs. The outcome of these studies was a decision to phase out the AMO, which ceased operations in December 1991, after completing all LSI production required for the Trident II program.[22]

The MDL continued to make radiation-hardened microelectronics for specialized purposes, such as satellites for the DoD and space probes for the National Aeronautic and Space Administration. By the late 1990s, there was again a nuclear weapon requirement for some microelectronic devices that were not available from commercial sources. In 1999, the MDL began delivering these devices to the DOE.

References for Chapter 8

1. Leland Johnson, *Sandia National Laboratories: A History of Exceptional Service in the National Interest*, SAND97-1029 (Albuquerque: Sandia National Laboratories, 1997), 57-58; and Necah Stewart Furman, *Sandia National Laboratories: The Postwar Decade* (Albuquerque: University of New Mexico Press, 1990), 660-661.

2. Furman, *The Postwar Decade*, 662-665.

3. Ibid., 661-662; and Johnson, *A History of Exceptional Service in the National Interest*, 61.

4. Johnson, *A History of Exceptional Service in the National Interest*, 58-59.

5. U.S. Department of Energy, Office of Environmental Management, *Linking Legacies*, DOE/EM-0319 (Washington, D.C.: U.S. Department of Energy, 1997), 26.

6. Ibid., 192.

7. Ibid., 154.

8. Johnson, *A History of Exceptional Service in the National Interest*, 70.

9. Ibid., 58; and Office of Environmental Management, *Linking Legacies*, 26, 192.

10. Addison F. Persons, first manager of the Pinellas Plant, "Some Personal Observations About the Evolution of the General Electric Operation on Bryan Dairy Road, Pinellas County, Florida," memoir, February 22, 1977, 3-7, copy in author's collection.

11. Ibid., 12, 17.

12. Richard D. Faulkner, former member of the management staff at the ACF-operated plant in Albuquerque, interview by author, July 10, 1997.

13. Office of Environmental Management, *Linking Legacies*, 147.

14. Stephen I. Schwartz, ed., *Atomic Audit: The Costs and Consequences of U. S. Nuclear Weapons Since 1940* (Washington, D.C.: Brookings Institution Press, 1998), 356.

15. Office of Environmental Management, *Linking Legacies*, 26.

16. Ibid., 187.

17. Ibid., 27, 198; and Ann Arnold Lemert, *First You Take a Pick and Shovel: the Story of the Mason Companies* (Lexington, KY, The John Bradford Press, 1979), 177-178.

18. Johnson, *A History of Exceptional Service in the National Interest*, 112, 155.

19. Ibid., 193, 195.

20. Ibid., 238-239.

21. H. T. Weaver, *Lessons Learned from Early Microelectronics Production at Sandia National Laboratories*, SAND98-0269 (Albuquerque: Sandia National Laboratories, 1998), 14.

22. Dale Clements, Albuquerque Microelectronics Operation (AMO) (Albuquerque: AMO, [1991]), 1-4, copy in author's collection; and Albert Bendure, former employee of the AMO, interview by author, November 14, 2000.

CHAPTER NINE

To The Brink

Cold War Intensifies: 1953 to 1962

Several events occurred between 1953 and 1962 that intensified the Cold War. The Truman Administration's policy for containment of Soviet power relied on both nuclear and conventional weapons. The Eisenhower Administration, which took office in January 1953, felt that Truman's policy was too expensive and decided to take a different approach. The need for a strong containment policy was heightened in June 1953, when an anti-Communist uprising in East Berlin and other East German cities was crushed by tanks of the Soviet Union.[1]

As a result, on January 12, 1954, U.S. Secretary of State John Foster Dulles made a speech in which he defined a new policy of "massive retaliation." Through this policy, the U.S. threatened to launch a massive nuclear strike against the Soviet Union in case of another attack against Western interests like that in Korea. The intent of "massive retaliation" was to provide greater security at lower cost.[2]

In October 1956, there was a national anti-Communist revolt in Hungary. This revolt was crushed by Soviet tanks.[3] The next month, on November 18, 1956, in a statement to Western diplomats at the Kremlin in Moscow, Soviet Premier Nikita Khrushchev told the West, "whether you like it or not, history is on our side. We will bury you."[4]

In October 1957, the Soviet Union launched "Sputnik," the world's first orbiting satellite. The fact that the Soviets were ahead in space technology was a great shock to the U.S. Khrushchev decided to offset the U.S. lead in strategic bombers by emphasizing the Soviet lead in missilery. The U.S. became very concerned about a "missile gap."[5]

In November 1958, the Soviet Union set the stage for the second Berlin crisis (which occurred in 1960-61) by announcing a plan to end the four-power occupation of East Berlin and hand control of East Berlin and the routes leading into West Berlin to the East Germans. The Soviet goal was to force an Allied withdrawal from West Berlin. This was the most serious confrontation between the U.S. and the Soviet Union since the Berlin blockade of 1948-1949. In September 1959, Khrushchev visited the U.S. and met with President Eisenhower. After this meeting, Khrushchev withdrew his threat to take unilateral action in Berlin in return for American willingness to negotiate on the problems in Berlin. They arranged for a summit meeting in Paris in May 1960.[6]

On May 2, 1960, an American U-2 reconnaissance aircraft was shot down 1300 miles inside the Soviet Union. The Soviets captured its pilot, Francis Gary Powers, who confessed to being on a spy mission. The U.S. initially denied knowledge of this flight but then tried to justify its actions, saying that Soviet secrecy made it necessary to gather information by this means to prevent a surprise attack. Khrushchev was outraged and cancelled the Paris summit conference.[7]

On July 9, 1960, Soviet Premier Khrushchev, in a speech to the All-Russian Teachers' Congress, warned the United States that, if it attacked Cuba, the Soviet Union would come to Cuba's assistance. Khrushchev pointed out that the Soviet Union had missiles that could hit targets in the United States. In response, President Eisenhower issued a statement that said the United States would do whatever was necessary to oppose communist intervention in Latin America, despite the Soviet threat.[8]

On January 6, 1961, at a meeting of the Communist parties in Moscow, Soviet Premier Khrushchev pledged support for "wars of national liberation." This statement alarmed President-elect Kennedy and was a source of tension in Soviet-American relations.[9]

On January 20, 1961, in his inauguration address, President Kennedy said, "let every nation know, whether it wishes us well or ill, that we shall pay any price, bear any burden, meet any hardship, support any friend, oppose any foe to assure the survival and the success of liberty." He also cautioned the Soviets against "aggression or subversion anywhere in the Americas" and went on to say, "we dare not tempt them with weakness. For only when arms are sufficient beyond doubt can we be certain that they will never be employed."[10]

Figure 9.1. President John F. Kennedy

These events and statements set the stage for three confrontations in 1961 and 1962 that brought the world to the brink of nuclear war.

Bay of Pigs

On January 1, 1959, in Cuba, a group of rebels led by Fidel Castro overthrew the dictatorship of Fulgencio Batista. During the revolutionary struggle, Castro had identified himself with democratic government and social and economic justice and had gained widespread popularity among the Cuban people.

Before long, Castro betrayed the revolution's original democratic promises and established a dictatorship with centralized control over all activities in the country. All parties were abolished except one, the Communist party, upon whose organizational strength Castro had become increasingly dependent. Castro also linked Cuba closely to the Communist bloc.

Figure 9.2. Castro and Khrushchev

Castro and Soviet Premier Khrushchev developed a close working relationship.

In April 1961, the new Kennedy administration supported an invasion of Cuba by 1,400 Cuban exiles in an attempt to overthrow Castro. The Central Intelligence Agency (CIA) had developed the plans for this operation and supervised its execution. The CIA assumed that, once the exiles had gained a beachhead in the Bay of Pigs, some units of Castro's army and the Cuban population would welcome the invaders as liberators. The operation was a dramatic and appalling failure.

American prestige sank to a new low. From the Soviet Union's standpoint, the failure of the U. S. to intervene with its own military forces was seen as a major weakness. This view served to invite further Soviet adventures.[11]

Berlin Wall

Between 1948 and 1960, over 2.5 million East Germans migrated to the West. This was 20 percent of East Germany's population. This exodus included many highly-trained professionals and deprived the German Democratic Republic (East Germany) of the people it needed to compete with the Federal Republic of Germany (West Germany). Over 200,000 people escaped during the first half of 1961.[12]

Khrushchev could no longer tolerate watching East Germans make Communism look bad as they streamed into the prosperous West. He wanted a new treaty that would remove NATO troops from Berlin and recognize East Germany as an independent nation (but under Soviet control). In June 1961, Khrushchev said he would sign a separate peace with East Germany if there were no agreement within six months (i.e., by December 1961) to change the status of Berlin. This plan was unacceptable to the U.S. and its allies.

On July 25, 1961, after returning from a confrontation with Khrushchev in Vienna, President Kennedy gave a nationally televised address concerning the escalating crisis over Berlin. In his speech, Kennedy urged his fellow citizens to take actions to save themselves: "in the event of an attack, the lives of those families which are not hit in a nuclear blast and fire can still be saved if they can be warned to take shelter and if that shelter is available....We owe that kind of insurance to our families and to our country....The time to start is now."[13] The fear of a nuclear war was very real.

In 1951, President Truman created the Federal Civil Defense Administration (FCDA), which produced a series of pamphlets, films, and television shows to educate the public about the effects of nuclear weapons and potential ways of surviving an attack. Popular magazine articles such as "When an Atomic Blast hits Your Home or Auto" contributed to the notion that, with careful planning, everything would be okay. Popular Mechanics published blueprints for a basic backyard bomb shelter. In 1958, President Eisenhower replaced the FCDA with the Office of Civil Defense Mobilization (OCDM). He then issued a national shelter policy, providing leadership and advice on shelters but stipulating that citizens were responsible for their own protection. By 1960, only 1500 shelters had been built. Kennedy's speech caused a great demand for home shelters, and by December 1961, about 200,000 families had taken Kennedy's advice. The public lost interest in shelters after the enactment of the Partial Test Ban Treaty in 1963.[14]

On August 13, 1961, the Communists began building the Berlin Wall to eliminate the escape hatch for East Germans. Although the wall violated the quadripartite status of Berlin, the West did not knock it down out of fear that such an action might trigger a military conflict with the Soviet Union.[15]

Because the West's conventional forces were very weak, a conflict would result in either surrender or escalation to nuclear war. Kennedy told his aides, "it's not a very nice solution, but a wall is a hell of a lot better than a war."[16]

On October 27, 1961, East Germany closed Checkpoint Charlie in the Berlin Wall. American and Soviet tanks sighted each other across this divide for 16 hours and then moved back. In November, Kennedy and Khrushchev agreed to talk about Berlin. Khrushchev then withdrew his demand for the West to pull out of Berlin and tensions began to ease.

Figure 9.3. Berlin Wall

The West's lack of action over the Berlin Wall intensified Khrushchev's conviction that the United States would not fight and that he could eventually drive the West out of Berlin. It also led Khrushchev to believe that the Soviets could continue to exploit American strategy so long as they kept their challenges below the level that would trigger a nuclear response.

President Kennedy saw the tension over Berlin as a reason to build up American military power. He was determined to show Khruschev that the United States was not bluffing when it declared its intentions to defend West Berlin. Kennedy moved in two directions. One aim was "flexible response." The United States needed more options than nuclear war or surrender. Increased flexibility was to be achieved by building larger conventional forces. The other aim was to reduce the vulnerability of the United States' nuclear forces.

Strategic Nuclear Weapons

Strategic nuclear weapons have the capability to attack the homeland of an enemy from long range. They are delivered by three principal means: land-based intercontinental ballistic missiles (ICBMs), submarine-launched ballistic missiles (SLBMs), and long-range bombers. These three capabilities are commonly known as the "triad." Each leg of the triad has advantages and disadvantages as a deterrent. For example, one advantage to bombers is that they can be recalled after takeoff.

ICBMs and SLBMs use multi–staged rockets with ranges of 5000 miles or more. The term "ballistic" is derived from the free-fall trajectory that these missiles follow while they are outside the earth's atmosphere. The warheads in ballistic missiles are contained in reentry vehicles (so-named because they "reenter" the atmosphere). Ballistic missiles can carry multiple reentry vehicles, which can be directed to different targets, and are thus called multiple independently–targeted reentry vehicles (MIRVs).

In 1960, the United States had most of its nuclear eggs in one basket — bombers. Because bombers are very vulnerable on the ground, they provide attractive targets for a surprise attack. By contrast, missiles in hardened (i.e., reinforced concrete underground) silos or on submarines are much more difficult to destroy.

Invulnerable second-strike forces (i.e., forces that can withstand a first-strike) were believed to be the basis for stable mutual deterrence.[17] Consequently, the United States began to change its mix of nuclear weapons to deemphasize bombers in favor of

Figure 9.4. B-52 Bomber

hardened land–based and mobile sea–based missiles. Deployment was accelerated on the Minuteman ICBM and the Polaris SLBM. By 1968, the United States had a much more survivable triad of nuclear forces with bombers, ICBMs and SLBMs.[18]

The NWC designed and built the nuclear warheads for these new missile systems.

Cuban Missile Crisis

Once the Soviets saw that the Communist regime was tolerated in Cuba, they began to establish a missile base there. In the fall of 1962, photographs from a U-2 reconnaissance aircraft showed that the Soviets were building launch sites for approximately seventy medium- and intermediate-range ballistic missiles.

That Khruschev had dared to move his missiles so near the United States and expected no counteraction beyond diplomatic protests was a dangerous sign. President Kennedy felt compelled to take a strong stand. If the United States failed to defend its interests close to home, Khruschev was likely to present even greater challenges in Berlin and elsewhere.

Kennedy placed a blockade around Cuba to prevent any additional missile shipments and demanded the removal of the missiles already in place. American firmness and determination left Moscow little choice. Kennedy told the nation about this crisis.

The United States had great superiority in conventional forces in the Caribbean and could also have mounted an invasion of Cuba if it had been necessary. Khruschev's only way of defending Cuba and the missile sites was by risking nuclear war, which he was unwilling to do.

At that time, the United States had a huge bomber force along with 200 ICBMs. The Soviets had fewer than 50 first–generation (i.e., technically unsophisticated) missiles, all of which were exposed above ground. The United States' strength set a clear upper limit on the pressure the Soviets could exert on the United States. As a result, Khruschev backed down and took the missiles out of Cuba. The U.S. had clearly won this confrontation. However, the Soviet leaders decided they would never be humiliated again and began a major effort to build up their nuclear power. By the end of the decade, the Soviet Union had reached a rough parity with the U.S.[19]

Figure 9.5. Soviet Missile Installations in Cuba

The Cuban missile crisis is generally considered to have been the most dangerous period in the entire Cold War.

NWC from 1962 to 1967

By the early 1960s, the U.S. had an enormous stockpile of nuclear weapons and production rates began to drop. Although the NWC was still very busy, the focus was on improving, rather than creating, the stockpile. The AEC conducted studies analyzing the effectiveness and economics of operating such a large complex. As a result of these studies, actions were initiated to consolidate operations and phase out certain facilities.

Six major site changes and two important mission changes occurred in 1962 – 1967.

- In 1962, the AEC decided to consolidate uranium component production at the Y-12 Plant, and those capabilities at Rocky Flats were transferred to Y-12.[20]

- In 1964, the AEC discontinued production of highly-enriched uranium (HEU) at the three gaseous diffusion plants because it had accumulated sufficient stocks. These plants continued to produce HEU for other AEC programs, including civilian nuclear power research and the U.S. Navy propulsion program. The K-25 Plant continued to be involved with weapons by producing low-enriched uranium for use as fuel in production reactors. The Portsmouth and Paducah Plants were thus closed out of the NWC.[21]

> *In 1992, Congress passed the Energy Policy Act and, under its provisions, uranium enrichment at the Portsmouth and Paducah Plants were leased by the DOE to the newly-created United States Enrichment Corporation.*[22]

- In 1965, the AEC decided to consolidate plutonium pit production at Rocky Flats, and those capabilities were transferred from Hanford.[23]

- In 1965 and 1966, respectively, the Clarksville and Medina Modification Centers were closed and their operations were transferred to the Pantex and Burlington Plants.[24] Also in 1966, the Weapons Evaluation Test Laboratory (WETL) was added to Pantex.

- In 1966, the Weldon Spring Plant, which produced feed materials for nuclear reactors, was closed after losing out in competition with Fernald.[25]

- In 1966, the South Albuquerque Works began to transfer its operations to other facilities; specifically, large metal case work went to the Y-12 Plant, smaller metal manufacturing went to the Kansas City Plant, and stainless steel reservoir manufacturing went to the Rocky Flats Plant. The South Albuquerque Works was closed in 1967.[26]

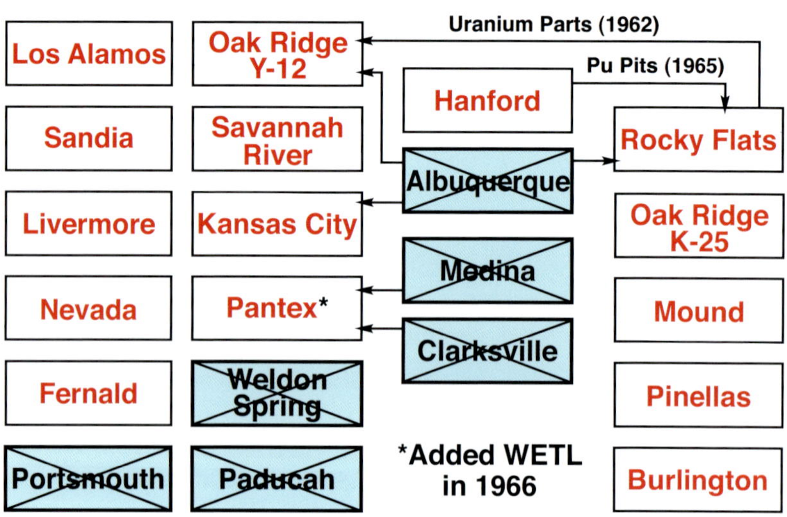

Figure 9.6. NWC from 1962 to 1967

References for Chapter 9

1. John Spanier, *American Foreign Policy Since World War II,* 12th ed., rev. (Washington, D. C.: CQ Press, A Division of Congressional Quarterly, Inc., 1992), 90.

2. Jeffry Porro, ed., *The Nuclear Age Reader* (New York: McGraw-Hill, Inc., 1989), 81–87.

3. Spanier, *American Foreign Policy Since World War II,* 90.

4. Robert Andrews, *The Columbia Dictionary of Quotations* (New York: Columbia University Press, 1993), 160.

5. Porro, *The Nuclear Age Reader,* 94-98; and Spanier, *American Foreign Policy Since World War II,* 113.

6. Spanier, *American Foreign Policy Since World War II,* 110–112, 120–122.

7. Porro, *The Nuclear Age Reader,* 94; and Spanier, *American Foreign Policy Since World War II,* 121.

8. Kenneth L. Hill, *Cold War Chronology: Soviet-American Relations, 1945-1991* (Washington, D.C.: Congressional Quarterly, Inc., 1993), 116–117.

9. Ibid., 119.

10. John Bartlett, *Familiar Quotations,* 15th ed., rev. and enl. (Boston: Little Brown and Company, 1980), 890.

11. Spanier, *American Foreign Policy Since World War II,* 126–128.

12. Ibid., 122.

13. Stephen I. Schwartz, ed., *Atomic Audit: The Costs and Consequences of U.S. Nuclear Weapons Since 1940* (Washington, D. C.: Brookings Institution Press, 1998), 319.

14. Ibid., 312–320.

15. Spanier, *American Foreign Policy Since World War II,* 122–123.

16. John Lewis Gaddis, *We Now Know: Rethinking Cold War History* (Oxford: Clarendon Press, 1997), 149.

17. Spanier, *American Foreign Policy Since World War II,* 122–124.

18. Porro, *The Nuclear Age Reader,* 173.

19. Spanier, *American Foreign Policy Since World War II,* 128-130; and Porro, *The Nuclear Age Reader,* 173.

20. U.S. Department of Energy, Office of Environmental Management, *Linking Legacies*, DOE/EM-0319 (Washington, D.C.: U. S. Department of Energy, 1997), 26.

21. Ibid., 142–143.

22. Ibid., 143.

23. Ibid., 26.

24. Ibid., 27, 198; and Ann Arnold Lemert, *First You Take a Pick and Shovel: The Story of the Mason Companies* (Lexington, KY: The John Bradford Press, 1979), 183, and Carr, B. H., *Pantex History: 1942 to 1992* (Amarillo: Pantex Plant Report, 1992), 20-21.

25. U.S. Department of Energy, *Linking Legacies*, 15, 18, 158.

26. Ibid., 26, 192.

CHAPTER TEN

Safety and Security Improvements

Permissive Action Link

As the stockpile grew, there was increasing concern that nuclear weapons might be used without approval from the President. In response to this concern, the NWC laboratories studied ways to improve the nuclear weapon command and control system. The result was a Permissive Action Link (PAL).

PAL is a system that prevents a nuclear weapon from being armed until a prescribed code or combination is inserted. A typical system, as shown below, includes a motor-driven electrical switch that is installed inside a nuclear weapon. It is operated remotely by electrical signals from a ground or aircraft controller.

Figure 10.1. Permissive Action Link

The weapon-arming signal is blocked until this switch is closed. With this design, a nuclear weapon cannot be armed until the President's order passes through command channels to an officer controlling the weapon system, who then enters the code.

PAL systems are designed to ensure that a weapon can be used when it is authorized and ensure against unauthorized use. They must be resistant to bypass by an adversary using either sophisticated techniques or brute force. Consequently, PAL systems are built around very robust designs.

> *Herman Kahn from the RAND Corporation, a leading strategic think tank of the 1950s, applied a totally rational and dispassionate analysis to nuclear war. In 1961, he wrote a book entitled* On Thermonuclear War *in which he made statements such as, "better 20 million dead than 40 million dead," and introduced the concept of a "doomsday machine." Kahn is often cited as providing the inspiration for Stanley Kubrick's hilarious and frightening classic film* Dr. Strangelove. *In this film, a deranged American military commander launches a preemptive nuclear strike against the Soviet Union without Presidential authority. PAL systems were developed to prevent such an occurrence. Three other individuals are occasionally cited as the model for Dr. Strangelove: Werner von Braun, the rocket scientist; Henry Kissinger, the former Secretary of State; and Edward Teller, the "father" of the hydrogen bomb.*[1]

There are several categories of PAL, which are designated as CAT A, CAT D, etc. These categories include different features and range from simple mechanical locks to very complex electromechanical systems with features to prevent bypass. For example, current PAL systems contain a limited try feature to prevent code guessing. The system will "lockout" after a specified number of tries.

The first PAL hardware was delivered to the Air Force in 1961 for installation in the W49/Jupiter system. In June 1962, the Kennedy Administration issued a memorandum mandating PALs for all land-based nuclear weapons in Europe.[2] PAL devices are built at the Kansas City Plant.

Nuclear Weapon Accidents

There have been 32 accidents involving nuclear weapons belonging to the United States. None of these accidents resulted in even a partial nuclear detonation in spite of the very severe stresses imposed upon the involved weapons. Only two accidents resulted in a widespread dispersal of nuclear materials.[3]

The first of these accidents occurred on January 17, 1966, when a B-52 collided with a KC-135 tanker during a routine refueling operation over Palomares, Spain. Three of the seven crew members of the B-52 were killed along with all four of the crew on the KC-135. The B-52 was carrying four B28 nuclear bombs, which fell over 28,000 feet.

One bomb fell into the sea. After an extensive underwater search, it was found five miles off the coast at a depth of 2,500 feet. This bomb was recovered on April 7, 1966. It was dented but intact, and there was no radiation leakage.

Figure 10.2. Bomb Hoisted Aboard the U.S.S. Petrel

Three bombs landed on the ground. A small parachute deployed on one bomb and it remained relatively intact. Parachutes did not deploy on the other two bombs. Their high-explosive materials detonated on impact with the ground and caused the release of some radioactive materials. Approximately 1400 tons of slightly contaminated soil and vegetation were removed to the U.S. for storage at the Savannah River Site.

The two bombs that did not detonate and were recovered may be seen at the National Museum of Nuclear Science and History in Albuquerque, New Mexico.

The second accident occurred on January 21, 1968, when a B-52 that was carrying four nuclear bombs caught fire and crashed near Thule, Greenland. One of the seven crew members was killed. The high explosives in all four of the bombs detonated. Some radioactive contamination occurred in the area of the crash, which was on sea ice.

An Air Force officer allegedly joked that he hoped it would burn through the ice because it would then be the Navy's problem.

Approximately 237,000 cubic feet of contaminated ice, snow, and water with crash debris were removed to the U.S. for storage. The contaminated ice, snow, and water were sent to the Savannah River Site. The crash debris contained classified materials and was sent to Pantex. In 1984, this debris was transferred to the Nevada Test Site.[4]

Neither of these accidents resulted in a nuclear detonation because the weapons were designed to be one-point safe; that is, if the high explosive is initiated at any one point, there will be no significant nuclear yield. As discussed in Chapter Two, a nuclear weapon has a plutonium "pit" surrounded by high-explosive lenses, which must be initiated simultaneously in order to get a nuclear detonation. These two accidents caused the lenses to explode, but not simultaneously.[5]

Weapon Safety Improvements

Although the existing safing systems had proved adequate, these incidents spurred Sandia to improve the nuclear detonation safing concept. In this new concept, a "strong link" in conjunction with an exclusion barrier isolates a weapon firing set and detonators from all electrical signals. The "strong link" requires a unique set of coded signals in order to activate. Only then can the firing signals pass through the "strong link" and the exclusion barrier to the firing set and detonators.

This concept also includes a "weak link" in which components vital to arming a weapon have been designed to fail during accidents and fires before the "strong links" can be destroyed. One example of a weak link is a mylar capacitor in a weapon fireset. If the weapon were to experience an excessively high temperature (e.g., in a fuel fire) the mylar would melt and prevent a weapon firing signal from going to the detonators.[6]

In 1977, the fifth modification to the B61 bomb was fielded. It was the first weapon to incorporate the weak link/strong link/ exclusion barrier/unique-signal design. This concept became known as enhanced nuclear detonation safety (ENDS).[7]

Sandia applied these safety improvements to all of its subsequent designs. Sandia also initiated a stockpile improvement program to install ENDS in older weapons. These efforts continued until the end of the cold war when the older weapons began to be dismantled.

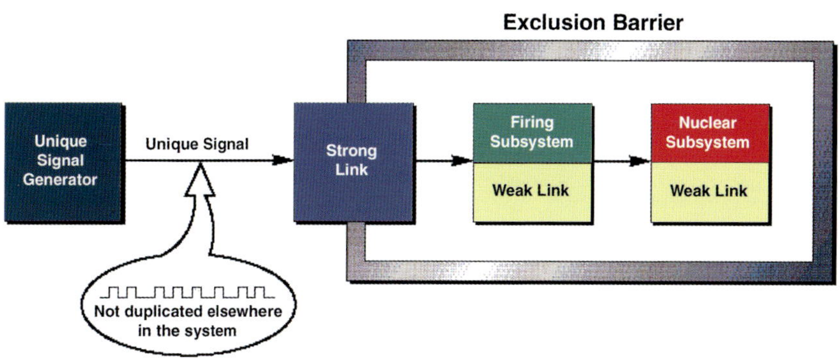

Figure 10.3. Enhanced Nuclear Detonation Safety

Strong links were built at the Kansas City and Mound Plants. Weak links were built in the Kansas City and Pinellas Plants. Exclusion barriers were built in the Kansas City Plant.

NWC from 1975 to 1979

Another step toward consolidation was taken in 1975 when the high explosive and weapon assembly work at the Burlington Plant was transferred to the Pantex Plant and the Burlington Plant was closed. With the closure of Burlington, the last bit of redundancy among the production plants was eliminated.

At the end of December 1979, the three design laboratories; LASL, Sandia, and UCRL, became national laboratories; specifically, Los Alamos National Laboratory (LANL), Sandia National Laboratories (SNL), and Lawrence Livermore National Laboratory (LLNL). This change acknowledged that they were more than weapons laboratories and were expected to engage in broad, multiprogram research.[8]

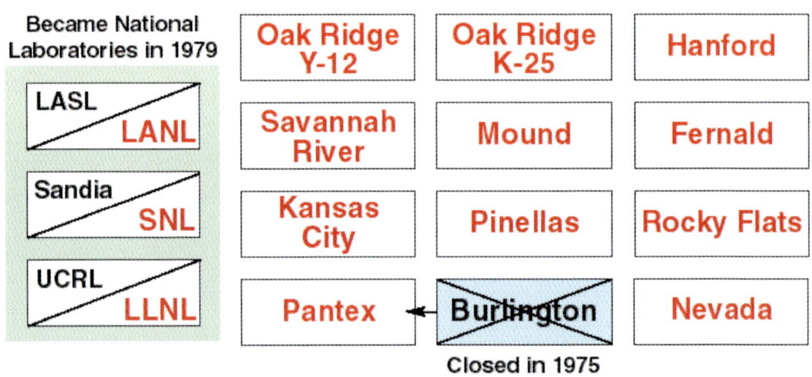

Figure 10.4. NWC from 1975 to 1979

U.S. Government Organizations

On January 1, 1947, the AEC took over the nation's atomic energy program from the Army's Manhattan Engineering District. The headquarters for the AEC was located in Germantown, MD. The AEC assigned the mission for nuclear weapons research, testing, production, and storage to a new organization called the Office of Santa Fe Directed Operations, which was located in Los Alamos.

Section 12a (4) of the Atomic Energy Act authorized the AEC to employ personnel and fix compensation without regard to Civil Service laws. The Commissioners felt their success was "uniquely dependent upon the quality of its staff," and that an ordinary personnel system using routine techniques could not find the people they required. The AEC thus developed an independent personnel system that met its special needs but conformed to Civil Service standards and procedures on all other points. As a result, AEC salaries were considerably above the rates paid for comparable positions under the Civil Service.[9]

On July 2, 1947, this new office took over direct field operation of the weapons program. Its name was later changed to the Santa Fe Operations Office. All weapon programs were managed by this office even though some of the NWC sites were under the administrative direction of other operations offices (e.g., the Y-12 Plant under the Oak Ridge Operations Office).

In 1947, the AEC assigned the Santa Fe Operations Office to manage and conduct nuclear testing in the Pacific Ocean and at the Nevada Proving Ground (the name was later changed to the Nevada Test Site).[10]

Most of the air-drop devices tested in Nevada were flown out of Kirtland Air Force Base in Albuquerque, New Mexico.

During 1950 and 1951, Los Alamos was increasing its staff to support the development of fusion weapons. There was a serious shortage of housing for the new scientists and technicians. Consequently, in July/October, 1951, the Santa Fe Operations Office moved to a former girls' school in Albuquerque. In April 1956, its name was changed to the Albuquerque Operations Office. Over time, the abbreviations for this office changed from ALOO to ALO to AL. In 1958, AL moved into four surplus barracks buildings on Sandia Base, which subsequently became a part of Kirtland Air Force Base.

On March 6, 1962, the Nevada Operations Office was established to assume responsibility for nuclear testing programs from AL.

On January 19, 1975, the AEC was replaced by two new Federal agencies: (1) the Nuclear Regulatory Commission, which was charged with regulating the civilian use of atomic energy, and (2) the Energy Research and Development Administration (ERDA), which became the managing agency for the NWC.

On October 1, 1977, ERDA was replaced by the Department of Energy (DOE). The DOE headquarters was expanded to include the Forrestal Building in Washington, D.C.

Figure 10.5. AEC, ERDA, and DOE Logos

The DOE managed the NWC at three levels. The involved organizations and their responsibilities, in brief, were as follows:[11]

- **DOE Headquarters (DOE/HQ)** was divided between two locations — the Forrestal Building in Washington, D.C., and a building in Germantown, Maryland. DOE Headquarters provided the NWC with overall program policy and direction. They also provided liaison with other Washington, D.C., area organizations such as Congress, the Office of Management and Budget, the Department of Defense, and other federal agencies.

  For weapon programs, DOE/HQ translated the annual Nuclear Weapons Stockpile Memorandum, as signed by the President, into the Production and Planning Directive (P&PD). In essence, these documents define the quantity and type of weapons that should be in the stockpile at the end of each fiscal year. The P&PD authorizes the production and retirement of nuclear weapons and components.

- **Operations Offices:** There were five operations offices under DOE Headquarters that had responsibilities for activities in the NWC. The operations offices served as the contracting agency for the NWC sites. They executed programs on behalf of the offices in DOE Headquarters.

  Four of the operations offices were each associated with a single NWC site:

  - Nevada Operations Office (NV) for the Nevada Test Site (NTS)
  - Oakland Operations Office (OAK) for LLNL
  - Oak Ridge Operations Office (OR) for the Y-12 Plant
  - Savannah River Operations Office (SR) for the Savannah River Site (SRS)

  The Albuquerque Operations Office (AL) also had the responsibility to serve as the field program integrator for stockpile management. AL took the P&PD and created detailed weapon program management documents (e.g., monthly production schedules by component for each NWC site). In addition, AL managed four NWC sites: LANL, SNL, the Kansas City Plant, and the Pantex Plant.

- **Area Offices:** An area office was collocated with each of the four sites under AL:

  - Office of Los Alamos Site Operations (OLASO) at LANL
  - Office of Kirtland Site Operations (OKSO) at SNL
  - Office of Kansas City Site Operations (OKCSO) at the Kansas City Plant (KC)
  - Office of Amarillo Site Operations (OASO) at the Pantex Plant (PX)

These offices provided management oversight of contractor operations. They also ensured day-to-day implementation, verification, and reporting of activities at the sites.

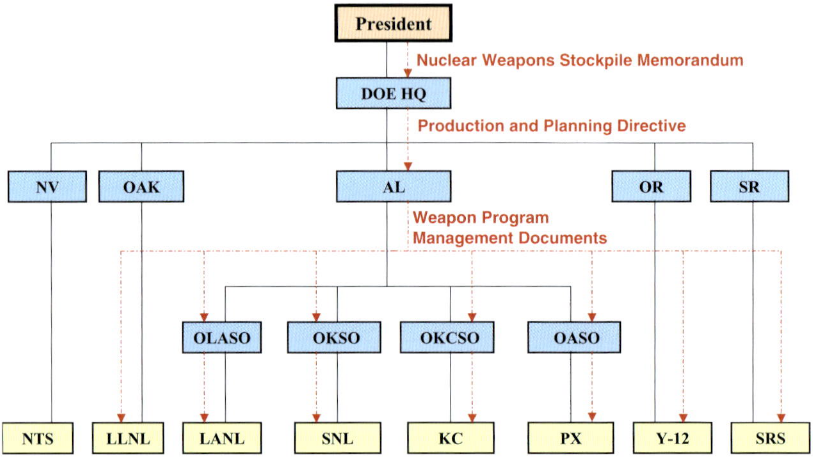

Figure 10.6. DOE Organization for Weapon Program Management

Environment, Safety, and Health Concerns

On January 1, 1970, the National Environmental Policy Act (NEPA) was signed into law. This act reflected a growing environmental consciousness in the U.S. and has been heralded as the Magna Carta of the nation's environmental movement.[12] Additional details on NEPA and its implementing regulations and processes are provided in Appendix B.

By the 1980s, the public had become much more sensitive to environment, safety, and health (ES&H) problems. These problems included the accident at Three Mile Island in the U.S. in 1979 and the much more serious accident at Chernobyl in the Soviet Union in 1986. Although these accidents involved reactors used for the generation of electrical power, they contributed to the apprehension by the general public towards all nuclear operations including those in the NWC.

In January 1989, George H. W. Bush began his term as President. He appointed James T. Watkins as the Secretary of Energy. By this time, it was evident that some of the sites in the NWC had significant environmental problems. Like most industrial and manufacturing operations, the NWC generated waste, pollution, and contamination. The problems in the NWC were complicated because of the radiation hazards and the large number of contaminated facilities such as reactors, chemical plants for extracting nuclear materials, and evaporation ponds.

Further, as the Cold War was ending, there was a growing belief that the NWC had placed too much emphasis on production at the expense of the environment. Although it could be argued that this claim was "Monday morning quarterbacking," there was no denying that the NWC had some serious environmental problems. As a result, in 1989, Secretary Watkins established the Office of Environmental Management within the DOE to deal with these problems.[13]

NWC from 1982 to 1989

In 1982, the heavy water plant at Savannah River was shut down. A stockpile of heavy water was stored at the Y-12 plant. If needed, deuterium (which is used for gas boosting) can be extracted from this heavy water using an electrolytic process.[14]

In 1984, the DOE purchased Precision Forge in Oxnard, California, and placed this facility under the management of Rocky Flats. This facility produced very specialized high-energy-rate forgings (HERFs) that have a unique grain structure and are required for the production of reservoirs. Precision Forge was renamed as the Oxnard Facility.[15]

The DOE did not want to purchase this facility but felt there was no alternative. Precision Forge was going out of business and the DOE had been unable to find an alternate source for HERFs.

In 1986, the "N" reactor at Hanford was shut down. This was the last of the nine reactors that had been built at that site. The need for new plutonium had declined and could be satisfied easily by the reactors at Savannah River.[16]

"N" reactor began operating in 1963. The original eight reactors at Hanford had been shut down between 1964 and 1971 because of irreversible radiation damage to their graphite cores.

In 1987, the K-25 Plant was shut down. The DOE no longer needed the enriched uranium produced at this plant.[17]

Figure 10.7. NWC from 1982 to 1989

In 1988, the last three operating reactors at Savannah River, which produced plutonium and tritium, were shut down for environmental and safety upgrades. With the exception of two brief restarts (in 1989 and 1992), production was never resumed.[18]

The NWC did not need any new plutonium because it has a very long half-life (24,000 years) and can be recycled from retired weapons. Tritium can also be recycled. However, because of its relatively short half-life (12.3 years), the NWC would need a new supply of tritium in the not-too-distant future.

> *Five reactors had been built at Savannah River (R, C, P, L, and K). "R" was shut down in 1964. "C" was shut down in 1986. The other three operated until 1988.*

In 1989, Fernald was shut down for environmental and safety upgrades. Production was never resumed.[19] Since the reactors at Hanford and Savannah River were closed, there was no longer a need for feed materials.

In 1989, nuclear operations at the Rocky Flats Plant were shut down in order to bring it in line with environmental regulations. These operations were never restarted.[20] Nonnuclear operations, such as machining for the production of reservoirs, were allowed to continue.

References for Chapter 10

1. Herman Kahn, *On Thermonuclear War* (Princeton, NJ: Princeton University Press, 1961), 238, and Peter Goodchild, *Edward Teller: The Real Dr. Strangelove* (Cambridge: Harvard University Press, 2004), xxi-xxii.

2. Leland Johnson, *Sandia National Laboratories: A History of Exceptional Service in the National Interest*, SAND97-1029 (Albuquerque: Sandia National Laboratories, 1997), 107-108.

3. Randall C. Maydew, *America's Lost H-Bomb* (Manhattan, KS: Sunflower University Press, 1997), 116-117.

4. Ibid., 137-139; Derek Scammell, Public Affairs Officer, U. S. Department of Energy, Nevada Operations Office, fax to author, 17 January 2001; and Steve Mentrup, Westinghouse Corp., Savannah River Site, telephone interview by author, 1 February 2001.

5. Ibid., 23.

6. David W. Plummer and William H. Greenwood, *The History of Nuclear Weapon Safety Devices*, SAND98-1184C (Albuquerque: Sandia National Laboratories, 1998), 1-5.

7. Johnson, *A History of Exceptional Service in the National Interest*, 146-147.

8. Ibid., 225, 340.

9. Richard G. Hewlett and Francis Duncan, *Atomic Shield*, 1947/1952 (University Park, PA and London: The Pennsylvania State University Press, 1969), 21-22.

10. U.S. Atomic Energy Commission, Albuquerque Operations Office, *The Story of Albuquerque Operations*, AL Pamphlet 3100-2 (Albuquerque: Atomic Energy Commission, March 1973), 1-2; and U.S. Energy Research and Development Administration, Albuquerque Operations Office, *The Story of Albuquerque Operations*, AL Pamphlet 3100-2 (Albuquerque: Energy Research and Development Administration, June 1975), 1-2.

11. Paul H. Richanbach, David R. Graham, James P. Bell, and James D. Silk, *The Organization and Management of the Nuclear Weapons Program (the 120-Day Study)*, Institute for Defense Analyses Report, ADA-323402 (Alexandria, VA: U.S. Department of Commerce, National Technical Information Service, March 1997), I-4 to I-7.

12. Thomas F.P. Sullivan, ed., *Environmental Law Handbook* (Rockville, MD: Government Institutes, Inc., 1997), 404.

13. U.S. Department of Energy, Office of Environmental Management, *Closing the Circle on the Splitting of the Atom*, DOE/EM-0266 (Washington, D.C.: U.S. Department of Energy, 1995), 4-5.

14. U.S. Department of Energy, Office of Environmental Management, Linking Legacies, DOE/EM-0319 (Washington, D.C.: U. S. Department of Energy, 1997), 26.

15. Ibid., 193-194.

16. Ibid., 167-168.

17. Ibid., 142-143.

18. Ibid., 23, 158, 167.

19. Ibid., 158.

20. Ibid., 186.

CHAPTER ELEVEN

Ending the Cold War

Negotiate from Strength

In January 1969, Richard M. Nixon began his first term as President, and he adopted a new, less ideological foreign policy toward the Soviet Union. His objective was to encourage the Soviet Union to become a part of a stable international system. In particular, Nixon wanted the Soviet Union to join the U.S. in limiting the nuclear arms race and reduce its support for revolutions in the Third World (i.e., the underdeveloped nations in Africa, Asia, and Latin America, which were part of neither the First World of industrialized nations led by the United States nor the Second World led by the Soviet Union). This policy became known as détente.

The high point for détente came in 1972 when the Strategic Arms Limitation Talks (SALT I) agreement and the Anti-Ballistic Missile Treaty were signed. (Additional details on Nuclear Weapon Treaties are provided in Appendix D.) In some circles, there was a feeling that the Cold War was over.

Figure 11.1. President Reagon

Unfortunately, the period of détente was relatively short-lived. Although the U.S. and the Soviet Union had some common interests, most notably on nuclear arms control, they differed sharply in their interests in the Third World.[1]

In January 1981, Ronald Reagan began the first of his

two terms as President. He believed that the Soviet Union had taken advantage of the U.S. during détente to advance its strategic interests. Several Soviet policies — including continued adventurism in the Third World, the decision to deploy mobile SS-20 intermediate-range ballistic missiles capable of targeting bases and cities in Western Europe, and the 1979 invasion of Afghanistan — soured U.S. decision makers on détente.[2]

Also, for several years the U.S. defense budgets had declined while the Soviet's defense budgets had increased. Reagan once asked, "What arms race? We stopped, they raced."[3]

Reagan was suspicious of previous nuclear weapon limitation agreements. He felt that the U.S. should aim for deep reductions, not just limitations. Toward that end, he changed the name of the Strategic Arms *Limitation* Talks (SALT) to Strategic Arms *Reduction* Talks (START). Reagan also felt that the U.S. should negotiate from a position of strength.[4]

During the Reagan era, the U.S. fielded several new nuclear weapon systems, including:

- Air-Launched Cruise Missile (W80 warhead)
- Modern strategic bomb (B83)

Figure 11.2. Trident II Missile breaks the water after a submarine launch

- Ground-Launched Cruise Missile (W84 warhead)
- Intermediate-range missile, called the Pershing II (W85 warhead)
- Land-based intercontinental ballistic missile, called the Peacekeeper (W87 warhead)
- Sea-launched intercontinental ballistic missile for the Trident submarine (W88 warhead).

Cold War Ends: 1987 to 1991

By 1987, the Soviet Union was facing economic collapse. As a result, Soviet Union President Mikhail Gorbachev started a new détente with the U.S.

Events kept going downhill for the Soviets, and by 1989 – 1990, communism had effectively collapsed in Europe. During this period, Poland, Hungary, and Czechoslovakia rejected communism at the polls.

In May 1989, Hungary began dismantling the 150-mile-long barbed wire fence along its border with Austria. This action led to a series of events that contributed to the collapse of the Socialist Unity (Communist) Party in East Germany. Tens of thousands of East Germans took advantage of their right to travel to Hungary and crossed the border into Austria on their way to West Germany.[5]

Figure 11.3. Berlin Wall Being Destroyed

In November 1989, the Berlin Wall was torn down. The people of Berlin took great joy in attacking this hated symbol of communist repression.

In October 1990, the German Democratic Republic (i.e., the Communist government of East Germany) was abolished, and Germany was reunited. This reunited Germany was a member of NATO.[6]

By 1991, all of the republics in the Soviet Union were pressing for their independence. On September 6, 1991, the Soviet Union recognized the independence of the three Baltic states — Lithuania, Latvia, and Estonia.

On December 21, eleven additional republics declared their independence.

On December 25, 1991, the Soviet Union formally disintegrated. The red hammer-and-sickle Soviet flag atop the Kremlin was replaced with the white, red, and blue flag of pre-revolutionary Russia. The Cold War was over. It ended with a whimper instead of a bang.[7]

Stockpile Reductions

As the Cold War was ending, the U.S. and the Soviet Union were able to make some dramatic reductions in their nuclear weapons stockpiles.

In December 1987, the United States and the Soviet Union signed the Intermediate-Range Nuclear Forces (INF) Treaty. This treaty eliminated an entire category of nuclear weapons — specifically, land-based missiles with ranges from 300 to 3400 miles.

> *Pershing II was a two-stage, solid-propellant missile equipped with the W85 nuclear warhead. It was first deployed in December 1983 with the U.S. Army's 56th Field Artillery Command in the Federal Republic of Germany. Its 1200 mile range and pinpoint accuracy were major factors in motivating the Soviet Union to the INF Treaty negotiations. On September 8, 1988, in a speech at the Longhorn Army Ammunition Plant, Vice President George H. W. Bush said, "The Pershing Missile System strengthened deterrence and was concrete evidence of United States resolve. If we had not deployed [Pershing] there would not be an INF Treaty today."*[8]

In July 1991, Presidents George H. W. Bush and Mikhail Gorbachev signed the Strategic Arms Reduction Treaty (START). This treaty reduced the number of strategic nuclear warheads on each side to 6000.[9]

In January 1992, President Bush, in his State-of-the-Union Address, announced further stockpile reduction initiatives. These initiatives reduced the proposed production rate for new nuclear weapons by approximately 50%. At that time, Bush was trying to provide political support for Gorbachev against the hard-liners who feared the U.S. and opposed stockpile reductions.

Figure 11.4. Presidents Bush and Gorbachev

In June 1992, Presidents Bush and Gorbachev signed an agreement that effectively eliminated all new weapons production. Later in 1992, President Bush and the military services canceled phase 3 engineering for the W82, W89, B90, and W91 weapons. This was the first time that the NWC had no active nuclear weapon development programs.

In January 1993, Presidents Bush and Yeltsin signed the START II protocol that formalized their agreement of June 1992. START II would reduce the number of deployed strategic warheads to no more than 3500 for each side. The U.S. Senate ratified START II in January 1996. It was not ratified by the Russian Duma (parliament) until April 1996 and then only with some modifications. At the end of 2000, the U.S. Senate had not approved these modifications, and START II remained a protocol rather than a treaty.

It is important to note that START I and START II only control the number of warheads that can be loaded on treaty-specified and -verified strategic missiles and bombers. These treaties do not control the total stockpile size or the composition of strategic and nonstrategic nuclear weapons of either side. The U.S. stockpile will be larger than 6000 under START I and 3500 under START II because the stockpile also includes weapons for nonstrategic nuclear forces, DoD operational spares, and spares to replace weapons attrited by DOE surveillance testing.[10]

Additional details on Nuclear Weapon Treaties are provided in Appendix D.

Nonnuclear Reconfiguration Program

The end of the Cold War and the succeeding arms agreements have eliminated all new production requirements and will result in major reductions in the nuclear weapons stockpile.

The DOE responded to these changes by initiating a new round of studies aimed at reconfiguring the NWC to be smaller, less diverse, and less costly to operate. In January 1991, the DOE Secretary issued the Nuclear Weapons Complex Reconfiguration Study, which concluded that the NWC should be smaller and less expensive to operate. It also said that alternatives should be evaluated in a Programmatic Environmental Impact Statement (PEIS), which is a type of document required by the National Environmental Policy Act (NEPA).

Additional details on NEPA and the documents used to comply with this Act are provided in Appendix B.

In April 1991, the DOE's Assistant Secretary for Defense Programs, tasked the Albuquerque Operations Office (AL) to develop a Nonnuclear Consolidation Plan (NCP). The NCP recommended closing the Mound Plant, the Pinellas Plant, and the nonnuclear portion of the Rocky Flats Plant. (As discussed in Chapter Ten, nuclear operations at the Rocky Flats Plant were shut down in 1989.)

In December 1991, the DOE Secretary announced his decision to pursue the recommendations contained in the NCP. He further decided to remove Nonnuclear Reconfiguration from the PEIS and, instead, to conduct an Environmental Assessment (EA). DOE headquarters then tasked DOE/AL to manage the detailed planning for this effort, and they established a Nonnuclear Reconfiguration Program Office.

In September 1993, the EA was completed, and a Finding of No Significant Impact (FONSI) was issued. DOE then began to implement all elements of the Nonnuclear Reconfiguration Program. Most of the activities at the Mound, Pinellas, and Rocky Flats plants were transferred to the Kansas City Plant with a few exceptions as follows:

- Tritium activities went from Mound to Savannah River;
- High-power detonators went from Mound to LANL;
- Low-power explosive devices went from Mound to SNL;
- Neutron generators went from Pinellas to SNL, except for neutron tube target loading, which went to LANL; and
- Beryllium and pit support functions went from Rocky Flats to LANL.

Mound, Pinellas and Rocky Flats completed their production assignments on September 30, 1994. This left Kansas City as the only *dedicated* nonnuclear manufacturing plant in the NWC.

A more complete summary of the Nonnuclear Reconfiguration Program is provided in Appendix C.

In addition, SNL was given the mission to procure several products under the Manufacturing Development Engineering (MDE) program. Under this program, SNL procured weapon materials and components directly from private industry without going through the plants. This resulted in cost savings by eliminating the need to maintain MDE technologies at the plants. In 2001, SNL dropped the name MDE in favor of Concurrent Design and Manufacturing (CDM).

> *From 1952 to 1969 SNL had a Manufacturing Development Engineering Department that procured weapon materials and components. As the NWC grew, this function was delegated to the plants. The term MDE came back into use in 1990, when a team was working on the Nuclear Weapons Complex Reconfiguration Study. An SNL member of this team (Del Olson) mentioned that they used to procure weapon materials and components in the "MDE" organization and the term stuck.*

Figure 11.5 shows the specific activities that were transferred during the Nonnuclear Reconfiguration Program in greater detail. This program addressed 26 activities. Fourteen of these activities went to Kansas City, six to LANL, two to Savannah River, and four to SNL in Albuquerque.

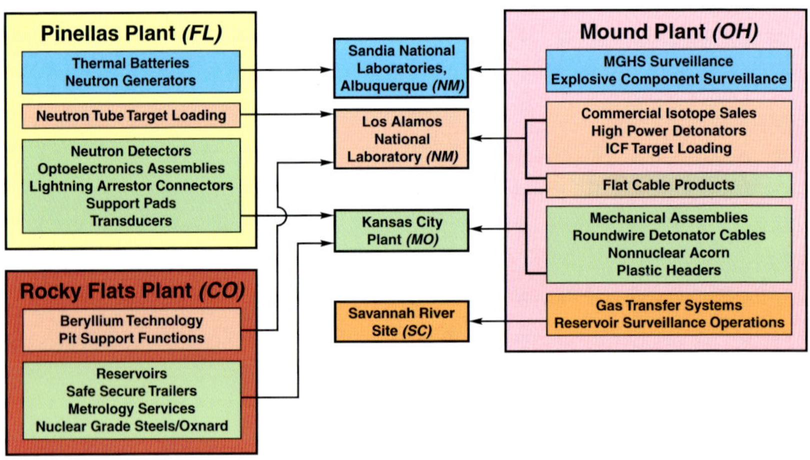

Figure 11.5. Nonnuclear Reconfiguration

In February 2006, Neutron Tube Target Loading was transferred from LANL to SNL. The Oxnard Facility, which had operated under Rocky Flats, was privatized in 1996.[11]

NWC in 1994

Between 1942 and 1994, the U.S. government opened 27 design or production sites plus the Nevada Test Site as a part of the NWC. By the end of 1994, 20 of these sites had been closed.

The U.S. government also opened 21 other test sites and five prototype, test, and research reactors. By the end of 1994, 19 of the test sites and all of the reactors had been closed.

Figure 11.6 shows the NWC after nonnuclear reconfiguration in 1994. The NWC was left with only eight major sites: three laboratories, four production plants, and the Nevada Test Site.

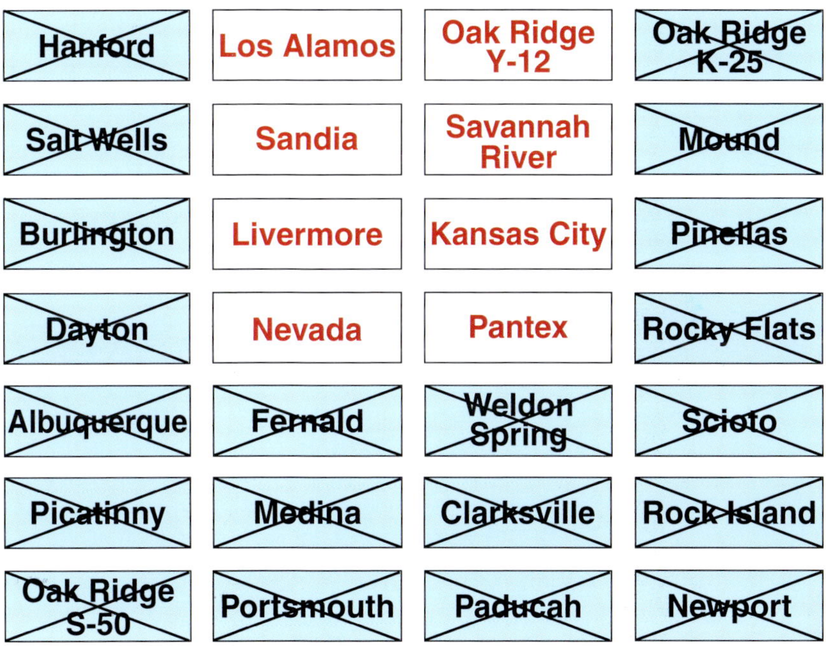

Figure 11.6. NWC in 1994

Sandia includes facilities in Albuquerque, New Mexico, and Livermore, California. Also, two of the test sites, Tonopah and Kauai, are operated under Sandia and are not shown separately.

While the complex is still larger than in the early days of the Manhattan Project, it is much smaller than it was at the height of the Cold War.

NWC Site Missions

The Defense Programs missions of the eight remaining sites in the NWC are as follows.[12]

PRODUCTION SITES

Kansas City Plant:

- Produce, procure non-nuclear components (electrical, electronic, mechanical).
- Conduct surveillance testing on and repair non-nuclear components.

Pantex Plant:

- Assemble, maintain, and conduct surveillance on warheads.
- Disassemble nuclear warheads being retired.
- Fabricate chemical high-explosive components.
- Store plutonium components from dismantled warheads.
- Establish capability for non-intrusive modification pit reuse.

Y-12 Plant:

- Maintain capability to produce secondaries and cases.
- Conduct surveillance on and dismantle secondaries.
- Store and process uranium and lithium materials and parts.
- Provide production support to weapons laboratories.

Savannah River/Tritium Operations:

- Recycle (unload/purify/load) tritium from dismantled warheads.
- Conduct surveillance on and reclaim returned tritium reservoirs.
- Support tritium source projects.

LABORATORIES AND THE NEVADA TEST SITE

Sandia National Laboratories:

- Conduct research and engineering activities.
- Conduct experiments on nuclear weapons effects.
- Design non-nuclear components and perform related systems engineering.
- Manufacture selected non-nuclear components.
- Provide safety and reliability assessments of the stockpile.

Lawrence Livermore National Laboratory:

- Conduct research and development (R&D) in basic sciences, mathematics, and computing.
- Conduct experiments on physics of nuclear weapons.
- Maintain capability to design nuclear explosive packages.
- Design and test advanced technology concepts.
- Provide safety and reliability assessments of the stockpile.

Los Alamos National Laboratory:

- Conduct R&D in basic sciences, mathematics, and computing.
- Conduct experiments on physics of nuclear weapons.
- Maintain capability to design nuclear explosive packages.
- Design and test advanced technology concepts.
- Provide safety and reliability assessments of the stockpile.
- Manufacture and conduct surveillance on selected non-nuclear components.
- Conduct pit surveillance and intrusive modification for reuse; fabricate pits.

Nevada Test Site:

- Maintain capability to conduct underground nuclear tests, and evaluate effects.
- Conduct experiments on physics of nuclear weapons.
- Support emergency response and radiation-sensing activities.

References for Chapter 11

1. John Spanier, *American Foreign Policy Since World War II*, 12th ed., rev. (Washington: CQ Press, A Division of Congressional Quarterly, Inc., 1992), 135-136, and Jeffry Porro, ed., *The Nuclear Age Reader* (New York: McGraw-Hill, Inc., 1989), 216.

2. Stephen I. Schwartz, ed., *Atomic Audit: The Costs and Consequences of U.S. Nuclear Weapons Since 1940* (Washington, D.C.: Brookings Institution Press, 1998), 71.

3. Spanier, *American Foreign Policy Since World War II*, 272.

4. Ibid., 266 and 278.

5. Thomas S. Arms, *Encyclopedia of the Cold War* (New York: Facts on File, Inc., 1994), 153-154, 293-294, 465.

6. Spanier, *American Foreign Policy Since World War II*, 354, 355, and 361.

7. Ibid., 372-374, and Arms, *Encyclopedia of the Cold War*, 43-45 and 137-138.

8. Peter Applebome, "First U.S. Missiles Destroyed as Part of Nuclear Treaty with Soviets," *New York Times* 9 September 1988, A-13.

9. U.S. Department of Energy, *Final Programmatic Impact Statement for Stockpile Stewardship and Management: Summary*, DOE/EIS-0236 (Washington, D.C.: U.S. Department of Energy, September 1996), S-13.

10. Ibid.

11. U.S. Department of Energy, Office of Environmental Management, *Linking Legacies*, DOE/EM-0319 (Washington, D.C.: U.S. Department of Energy, 1997), 194.

12. Paul H. Richanbach, David R. Graham, James P. Bell, and James D. Silk, *The Organization and Management of the Nuclear Weapons Program*, (the 120-Day Study), Institute for Defense Analyses Report, ADA-323402 (Alexandria: U.S. Department of Commerce, National Technical Information Service, March 1997), I-3.

CHAPTER TWELVE

Maintaining Deterrence

The Challenge

Since the Nonnuclear Reconfiguration Program was completed, U.S. national security policies have changed in ways that required further changes in the Nuclear Weapons Complex (NWC). Most notably, in 1992, the U.S. declared a moratorium on underground nuclear testing.

In August 1995, President Clinton extended this moratorium and decided to pursue a "zero-yield" Comprehensive Test Ban Treaty. He signed this treaty on September 24, 1996, but it was rejected by the U.S. Senate in 1999. Nevertheless, the U.S. has been complying with this moratorium.

The challenge now is to maintain a safe, secure, and reliable nuclear weapons stockpile with no new-design weapons, zero-yield nuclear testing, and reduced NWC operating costs. In response to this challenge, the DOE analyzed a series of alternatives in three Programmatic Environmental Impact Statements (PEIS). As explained in Appendix B, the conclusions reached in a PEIS are documented in a Record of Decision (ROD).

Stockpile Stewardship and Management

On December 19, 1996, the DOE Secretary issued a ROD for the PEIS on Stockpile Stewardship and Management.[1]

Stockpile Stewardship includes the science and technology aspects of assessing and certifying the safety and reliability of the stockpile in the absence of nuclear testing under the Comprehensive Test Ban Treaty. Under Stockpile Stewardship, the DOE decided to construct and operate three enhanced experimental facilities:

- National Ignition Facility at LLNL,
- Contained Firing Facility at LLNL, and
- Atlas Facility at LANL (subsequently transferred to the NTS).

Stockpile Management includes the maintenance, surveillance, fabrication, or repair of replacement weapons and components and dismantlement of weapons to U.S. security requirements. Under Stockpile Management, the DOE decided to:

- Downsize the plants at Kansas City, Y-12, and Pantex and
- Reestablish a plutonium pit production capability at LANL.

None of the remaining sites in the NWC are targeted for closure in the foreseeable future.

In 1994, DOE Secretary Hazel O'Leary formed the Task Force on Alternate Futures, which was chaired by Robert Galvin of Motorola. This task force came to be known as the Galvin Commission. In 1995, the Galvin Commission recommended transferring LLNL's defense programs mission to LANL. No action has been taken to implement this recommendation.[2]

Storage and Disposition of Weapons-Usable Fissile Material

In July 1996, the DOE issued an ROD for an EIS on the Disposition of Surplus Highly Enriched Uranium. In January 1997, the DOE issued an ROD for a PEIS on the Storage and Disposition of Weapons-Usable Fissile Material. The essence of these RODs is described below:[3]

Storage

The DOE's objective is to reduce the number of locations where the various forms of plutonium and highly-enriched uranium are stored. Toward that end it will:

- Consolidate storage of plutonium pits at Pantex; pits at Rocky Flats will be sent to Pantex.
- Send surplus nonpit plutonium materials from Rocky Flats to the Savannah River Site for storage pending disposition.
- Continue storage of surplus plutonium currently onsite at Hanford, LANL, and the Idaho National Engineering Laboratory (INEL) pending disposition.
- Store surplus and nonsurplus highly-enriched uranium (HEU) at the Y-12 plant.

Disposition

The DOE's objective is to convert surplus fissile materials into forms that are unsuitable for use in nuclear weapons. Toward that end it will:

- Immobilize some surplus plutonium in glass or ceramic material for disposal in a geologic repository.
- Convert some surplus plutonium into mixed oxide (MOX), which is a blend of uranium dioxide and plutonium dioxide, for use as fuel in commercial reactors.
- Downblend surplus HEU into low-enriched uranium for use as fuel in commercial reactors.

Tritium Supply and Recycling

In December 1995, the DOE issued an ROD for a PEIS on Tritium Supply and Recycling.[4] The DOE decided to:

- Not build a new production reactor.
- Pursue two alternatives for tritium production:
  - Accelerator Production of Tritium (APT) and
  - Commercial Light Water Reactor (CLWR). This alternative included a Tritium Extraction Facility (TEF) at the SRS.
- Develop EISs for these alternatives.

In December 1998, the DOE Secretary announced his preference for the CLWR as the primary tritium supply source. He also announced that the DOE will finalize the draft Environmental Impact Statements (EISs) for all three facilities (APT, CLWR, and TEF).

In May 1999, the DOE Secretary issued a consolidated ROD for the three EISs with the following conclusions:[5]

- Produce tritium in one or more of three commercial reactors operated by the Tennessee Valley Authority (TVA): Watts Bar #1 and Sequoyah #1 and #2.
- Construct TEF at the Savannah River Site. (Construction began in 2000 and is scheduled for completion in 2007.)
- Continue work on APT as a backup. (Congress terminated APT in 2002.)

In conjunction with this ROD, the DOE established an interagency agreement with the TVA. In accordance with this draft agreement, TVA will:

- Begin irradiating lithium-6 targets in 2003.
- Begin extracting tritium from these targets in 2005 in order to support the stockpile under START I.

Projections in 2005 showed that new tritium would not be needed until 2011.

Stockpile Life Extension Program

The DOE's policies and procedures for the design, development, production, modification, repair, stockpile support, retirement, and disposal of nuclear weapons are contained in DOE/NNSA Directive 56XB, the *Development and Production Manual*. This manual defines the seven phases in a weapon program.[6]

- Phase 1 – Weapon Conception
- Phase 2 – Program Feasibility Study
- Phase 3 – Development Engineering

- Phase 4 – Production Engineering
- Phase 5 – First Production
- Phase 6 – Quantity Production and Stockpile
- Phase 7 – Dismantlement

The *Development and Production Manual* describes the processes to be employed in each of these phases along with the responsibilities of each involved organization. Phase 6 includes activities required to support existing weapons, such as stockpile evaluation tests and the replacement of limited-life components.

Additional information on the *Development and Production Manual* and the seven weapon phases is provided in Appendix A.

Current U.S. policy dictates no new weapon development. Consequently, all U.S. nuclear weapon programs are in either Phase 6 or Phase 7. Because weapon materials and components degrade over time, some actions must be taken to extend the life of the stockpile.

In 1996, the DOE established a Stockpile Life Extension Program (SLEP). This program defines a process to evaluate weapon program needs and to plan and schedule the specific refurbishment actions to be conducted on each weapon system. The SLEP results in an integrated plan for the entire NWC.

In April 1999, DOE/AL revised the Development and Production Manual to add Phase 6.X, entitled "Stockpile Life Extension," to the existing seven-phase program. It is an expanded subset of Phase 6 and accordingly has been called the "6.X" process. It describes how existing weapons are to be removed from the stockpile, refurbished as necessary, and returned to the stockpile. The 6.X process incorporates SLEP into the overall weapons management system.

In many ways, extending the life of an old system is more difficult than building a new one. Imagine trying to keep a Model "T" Ford on the road today. Many replacement parts and materials are no longer in production or available from suppliers. Consequently, they must either be produced as specialty items, which is usually very difficult and expensive, or be replaced with more modern substitutes. Similar problems exist with nuclear weapons. Extending the life of the stockpile presents a great challenge for the future.

National Nuclear Security Administration

When the DOE was created in 1977, it brought together two very different programmatic traditions. One tradition consisted of the Federal Government's activities in the field of nuclear weapons, which began with the Manhattan Project. It was characterized by a bureaucratically centralized and security-oriented organization with close ties to the military.

The other tradition consisted of a loosely knit amalgamation of agencies, offices, and commissions that were scattered throughout the Federal Government. These organizations dealt with various aspects of federal energy policy and programs including research, development, regulation, pricing, and conservation. Although the Federal Government had been involved in these programs for decades, the involved organizations had seldom coordinated their activities or policies.[7]

The melding of these two traditions into one massive agency has long been an uneasy union. As stated by Vic Reis, a former DOE Assistant Secretary for Defense Programs, "the price of gasoline, quarks, nuclear cleanup and nuclear weapons just don't come together naturally."[8]

Several high-level studies have been critical of the oversight and management at the DOE. In 1995, the Secretary of Energy's Task Force on Alternative Futures for the DOE National Laboratories, commonly called the Galvin Commission, found that the GOCO (government-owned, contractor-operated) concept, the model on which the laboratories have operated for the last fifty years, had been irretrievably weakened through unrestrained growth in DOE micromanagement, rule-making, and excessive oversight. This report was very direct in its criticism of "excessive oversight and micromanaging" by the DOE:

> *The net effect is that thousands of people are engaged on the government payroll to oversee and prescribe tens of thousands of how-to functions. The laboratories must staff up or reallocate the resources of its people to be responsive to such myriads of directives; more and more of the science-intended resources are having to be redirected to the phenomenon of accountability versus producing science and technology benefits.*[9]

In 1997, the Institute for Defense Analyses echoed these concerns in its study for Congress (commissioned by the National Defense Authorization Act for Fiscal Year 1997), commonly known as the "120-Day Study":

> *The current system can best be described as one in which everybody reviews everything until everyone is satisfied. The "process" is ad hoc, and almost defies description. . . . There is no consensus among all these reviewers and checkers and checkers of checkers regarding the desired end-state for a facility. Consequently, each of the organizations that reviews a document, decision, or process does so from its own perspective and insists that the facility meet its priority requirements for safety.*[10]

In 1999, The Commission on Maintaining United States Nuclear Weapons Expertise (established via the National Defense Authorization Acts of 1997 and 1998), commonly called the "Chiles Commission," expressed similar concerns:

> *Reorganization of DOE is needed to eliminate excessive oversight and overlapping, unclear government roles. The Assistant Secretary for Defense Programs (ASDP) should be given direct line management authority over all aspects of the nuclear weapons complex, including corresponding elements of the DOE field structure.*[11]

In October 1999, President Clinton signed the National Defense Authorization Act for Fiscal Year 2000, which included a requirement to establish a new semiautonomous National Nuclear Security Administration (NNSA) within the DOE.

The intent of this act is to isolate the nuclear weapons, nonproliferation and verification, and naval reactors programs from the rest of the DOE. It is an attempt to break as many bureaucratic lines as possible in order that the new agency can get on with its mission while achieving high levels of security and safety in a fashion that is integrated with its program responsibilities.

The NNSA was established on March 1, 2000. General John Gordon was sworn in as the Undersecretary for Nuclear Security/ Administrator for NNSA on July 12, 2000.

National Nuclear Security Administration

Figure 12.1. NNSA Logo

NNSA Reorganization

On December 20, 2002, NNSA Administrator John Gordon announced a major reorganization to eliminate a layer in NNSA's field management and streamline the operation of the nuclear weapons complex. There are four key elements of this reorganization:

- Eliminated three Operations Offices: Albuquerque, Nevada and Oakland
- Eliminated the four Area Offices that were under AL: Kirtland, Los Alamos, Kansas City, and Amarillo
- Established eight Site Offices: Nevada (NSO), Livermore (LSO), Los Alamos (LASO), Sandia (SSO), Kansas City (KCSO), Pantex (PSO), Y-12 (YSO), and Savannah River (SRSO)
- Established the NNSA Service Center in Albuquerque.

This reorganization is shown in Figure 12.2. The new NNSA is comprised of three basic units with missions as follows:

(1) **Headquarters** provides high-level guidance, sets requirements, defines policy and corporate processes, integrates overall program plans, develops and defends corporate budgets, assists the field in

evaluating contractors, evaluates field oversight programs, and works with other governmental customers and stakeholders.

It is important to note that DOE/NNSA Weapon Project Officers have the primary responsibility for managing nuclear weapon programs. These individuals had previously served under AL and are now under NNSA Headquarters.

(2) **Site Offices** provide operations oversight and contract administration for each NNSA site. They are responsible for:

- safe and secure operation of facilities under the purview of NNSA
- supporting NNSA programs to ensure their success in accordance with expectations
- ensuring the long term viability of the site to support NNSA programs and projects

(3) The **Service Center** provides administratve and technical services for Headquarters and the Site Offices.

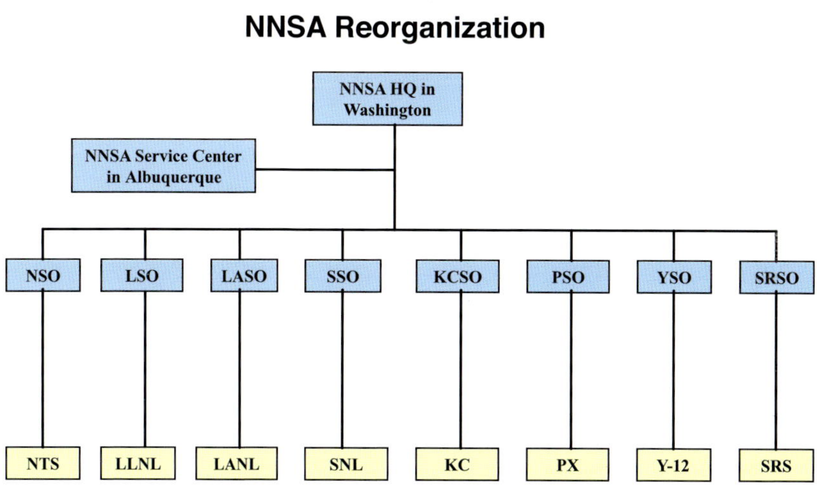

Figure 12.2. NNSA Reorganization

In 2011, the NNSA Service Center in Albuquerque was replaced by the Albuquerque Complex.

On October 9, 2008, Thomas D'Agostino of the NNSA changed the name Nuclear Weapons Complex to Nuclear Security Enterprise (NSE). This change was concurrent with his approval of the *Final Environmental Impact Statement Study for Complex Transformation*. The NNSA plans to transform the NWC to a 21st century NSE that is smaller, safer, more secure, and less expensive to operate.

On August 23, 2010, he changed the name Nevada Test Site to Nevada National Security Site (NNSS).

Summary

The NWC has evolved as required to meet the nation's security objectives. The NWC has met these objectives by:

- building the weapons that ended World War II,
- building a stockpile of weapons that served as a deterrent to the Soviet Union during the Cold War,
- incorporating new technologies into the stockpile,
- safely downsizing the stockpile and dismantling the excess nuclear weapons after the Cold War was over, and
- ensuring that the remaining stockpile is safe and reliable.

The NWC has done a wonderful job for over 50 years. But the job is not done. The mission for national security is ongoing. Many great challenges lie ahead that must be met by a new generation of people with fresh ideas using the latest technologies.

All past and present members of the NWC have good reason to be proud of their service to the nation. New members should recognize that they are standing on the shoulders of giants.

References for Chapter 12

1. U.S. Department of Energy, *Record of Decision: Programmatic Environmental Impact Statement for Stockpile Stewardship and Management* (Washington, D.C.: U.S. Department of Energy, December 1996).

2. Leland Johnson, *Sandia National Laboratories: A History of Exceptional Service in the National Interest*, SAND97-1029 (Albuquerque: Sandia National Laboratories, 1997), 368.

3. U.S. Department of Energy, *Record of Decision for the Disposition of Surplus Highly Enriched Uranium Final Environmental Impact Statement* (Washington, D.C.: U.S. Department of Energy, July 1996); and U.S. Department of Energy, *Record of Decision for the Storage and Disposition of Weapons-Usable Fissile Materials* (Washington, D.C.: U.S. Department of Energy, January 1997).

4. U.S. Department of Energy, *Record of Decision for the Final Programmatic Environmental Impact Statement for Tritium Supply and Recycling* (Washington, D.C.: U.S. Department of Energy, October 1995).

5. U.S. Department of Energy, *Record of Decision: Tritium Supply and Recycling Programmatic Environmental Impact Statement* (Washington, D.C.: U.S. Department of Energy, May 1999).

6. U.S. Department of Energy, Albuquerque Operations Office, *AL Supplemental Directive 56XB, Nuclear Weapons Development and Production,* and its Appendix, the *Development and Production Manual* (Albuquerque: Albuquerque Operations Office, Change 29, April 23, 1999), Chapter 3.1, Phases 1, 2, and 2A, and Chapter 3.2, Phases 3 Through 7.

7. Terrence R. Fehner and Jack M. Holl, *Department of Energy 1977-1994: A Summary History*, DOE/HR-0098 (Washington, D.C.: U.S. Department of Energy, History Division, Executive Secretariat, Human Resources and Administration, 1994), 2.

8. John Fleck and Ian Hoffman, "New DOE Agency Debated," *Albuquerque Journal,* 28 November 1999, A1.

9. Secretary of Energy Advisory Board, Task Force on Alternative Futures for the Department of Energy National Laboratories (the Galvin Commission), *Alternative Futures for the Department of Energy National Laboratories,* vol. 1 (Washington, D.C.: U.S. Department of Energy, February 1995), A-1.

10. Paul H. Richanbach, David R. Graham, James P. Bell, and James D. Silk, *The Organization and Management of the Nuclear Weapons Program,* (the 120-Day Study), Institute for Defense Analyses Report, ADA-323402 (Alexandria, VA: U.S. Department of Commerce, National Technical Information Service, March 1997), ES-1.

11. Commission on Maintaining United States Nuclear Weapons Expertise (the Chiles Commission), Report to the Congress and Secretary of Energy (Washington, D.C.: General Services Administration, March 1999), iii-v

EPILOGUE

As mentioned in the preface, this book parallels my presentations on the history of the NWC. I usually left time for questions at the end of these presentations. Many of the questions went outside the scope of these presentations, and some of them solicited my opinion — not just facts — on various subjects. This epilogue is built around twelve of the most interesting and challenging questions.

1. What caused the Cold War and who started it?

The stage for conflict between the United States and the Soviet Union was set at the end of World War II. As the two primary victors, they had opposing visions for the postwar world — democratic capitalism versus authoritarian communism. The World War II allies' failure to agree on a postwar political structure for Germany served as a focal point for this conflict. However, a conflict so long and severe as the Cold War was not inevitable.[1]

John Lewis Gaddis is considered by many to be the preeminent American authority on the United States and the Cold War. In his book *We Now Know: Rethinking Cold War History*, Gaddis states that, "...as long as Stalin was running the Soviet Union a Cold War was unavoidable." He goes on to say, "...the answer is authoritarianism in general, and Stalin in particular."[2]

Stalin operated in an authoritarian system. Unlike in a democracy, where the leader has to share power, Stalin had no effective restraints on his actions. He was ruthless and waged cold war within his alliances, within his country, within his party, and within his personal entourage. His policies before World War II resulted in the deaths of between 17 and 22 million of his own countrymen. It took many years after Stalin's death in 1953 for this authoritarian system to be dismantled. In 1956, Khrushchev condemned Stalin for inhumanity and massive crimes against the Soviet people.[3]

The U.S. really tried to avoid a conflict after World War II as evidenced by the Baruch Plan in 1946. If the Soviet Union had

had a more moderate leader from 1945 to 1953, the Cold War might have been avoided.

2. Why did the Cold War last so long?

World War I took four years to fight; World War II required six. The Cold War dragged on for 45 years. Nuclear weapons created constraints against escalation that had never before existed. As a result, crises that would have caused major wars in the past were not allowed to escalate to that level during the Cold War.

Nuclear weapons also enabled the Soviet Union to remain a military superpower long after it had entered into its terminal decline. The West did not dare to push it too far. Consequently, there was a trade-off: we avoided destruction, but at the price of duration. The Cold War went on much longer than it might have if nuclear weapons had not been available.[4]

3. How much did the U.S. spend on nuclear weapons?

Costs are often very difficult to compile, especially when they involve a multitude of agencies over a long period of time. Different accounting systems, incomplete source data, varying assumptions as to which costs should properly be assigned to a project can all contribute to controversy. A proper compilation must include much more than just the costs to build the bombs and warheads, which is a relatively small portion of the total.

From 1940 through 1996, the U.S. spent almost $5.5 trillion (in 1996 dollars) on nuclear weapons and related programs.[5] This total can be subdivided as follows:

Activity	Cost
Building the bombs and warheads, which includes the production of fissionable materials, weapons research, development, testing, and manufacturing. This figure includes approximately $26 billion in 1996 dollars — $2.2 billion in actual year dollars — for the Manhattan Project.[6]	$0.41 trillion

Activity	Cost
Deploying nuclear weapons, which includes the costs for delivery systems (e.g., airplanes and missiles), military infrastructure to deploy the weapons, maintenance of the weapons, and command and control systems.[7]	$3.24 trillion
Targeting and controlling the bomb, which includes spy satellites and other intelligence-related activities.[8]	$0.83 trillion
Defending against the bomb, which includes programs for strategic air and missile defense, antisatellite and antisubmarine warfare, and civil defense.[9]	$0.94 trillion
A variety of activities such as nuclear weapon dismantlement, nuclear waste management, and environmental remediation.[10]	$0.06 trillion

4. Was this expenditure worth the cost?

The answer to this question depends on a person's point of view. To the U.S. servicemen who were preparing for the invasion of Japan in 1945, and to most citizens of Western Europe who were protected from communist aggression during the Cold War by the U.S. nuclear umbrella, the answer is a resounding "yes." To others who have never faced a direct threat of living under communism or to those who have suffered damage to their health from environmental contamination that stemmed from nuclear weapon production or testing, the answer can be an equally resounding "no." Obviously, this question cannot be answered to everyone's satisfaction.

The expenditure of a huge figure like $5.5 trillion is difficult to fathom and can best be interpreted in relation to other financial yardsticks. As one perspective, this figure represents approximately 29 percent of all military spending during the 1940 through 1996 period. It is interesting to note that, in 1948, President Truman decided to place increased reliance on nuclear weapons in order to save money. His successors followed suit. In general, the costs for national defense would have been much higher without nuclear weapons.[11]

The bottom line is that nuclear weapons prevented another world war. From that perspective, I feel that this expenditure was very definitely worth the cost.

5. What impact has the production of nuclear weapons caused to the environment?

The production of nuclear weapons has resulted in significant contamination at some sites in the NWC. The largest portion of this contamination resulted from the production of fissile materials, i.e., plutonium and HEU. The assembly of weapons from these fissile materials added relatively little contamination. Fissile materials production encompasses seven steps: (1) uranium mining, (2) milling, (3) refining, (4) uranium enrichment, (5) fuel and target fabrication, (6) reactor operations, and (7) chemical separations. The last step accounted for most of the waste and contamination.

Chemical separations involve dissolving spent nuclear fuel rods and targets in acid and separating out the plutonium and uranium using a chemical process. Waste generated by chemical separations processes accounted for more than 85 percent of the radioactivity generated in the nuclear weapons production process. Most of the contamination from the production of plutonium and HEU exists at the Hanford and Savannah River sites and the three gaseous diffusion plants, K-25, Portsmouth, and Paducah.[12]

In 1989, the Secretary of Energy created the Office of Environmental Restoration and Waste Management (later renamed the Office of Environmental Management) to focus on these problems. This office is coordinating activities throughout the DOE to mitigate the risks and hazards posed by the legacy of nuclear weapons production. All of the identified waste and contamination situations are being addressed.[13]

6. What affect has the testing of nuclear weapons had on human health?

Everyone in the world has been exposed to some degree of radiation above normal background because of the hundreds of above-ground nuclear weapons tests that were conducted between 1945 and 1980. The radioactive debris from these tests went into the atmosphere and circled the globe.

Many different isotopes are formed during a nuclear explosion, but only the relatively long-lived isotopes are deposited as fallout, in particular, strontium-90, carbon-14, and cesium-137. Strontium-90 presents the greatest hazard because it is chemically similar to calcium and may become concentrated in the human body, especially in the bones of growing children. Strontium-90 has a half-life of twenty-eight years.

Hundreds of downwind residents in the vicinity of the test sites received significant radiation exposures from fallout during the above-ground testing period. Also, approximately 205,000 military men participated in the atmospheric testing program in Nevada or the Pacific Proving Ground and were exposed. The highest exposures were received by sampler pilots. These pilots flew into the radioactive cloud above a nuclear detonation to obtain samples of the radioactive debris, which collected on special filter paper attached to the wings.

Above-ground testing was stopped before it became a significant threat to the average person. The U.S. and the Soviet Union ceased above-ground testing after signing the Limited Test Ban Treaty in 1963. The last above-ground test was conducted by China in 1980. Underground tests present no significant threat to human health.[14]

7. Is it true that the U.S. conducted some unethical medical experiments with radioactive materials?

Experiments were conducted during the Manhattan Project and subsequently by the AEC to determine the health effects of radioactive materials on human beings. In 1947, the Chairman of the AEC, Carol Wilson, issued a directive that no radiation experiment should be carried out unless it held therapeutic promise for the patient. Unfortunately, this directive was not always followed.

A fuzzy line existed between bona fide treatment and full–blown experimentation. Researchers occasionally slipped over the line, rationalizing that their experiments were harmless, the procedure was no more harmful than some other accepted medical treatment, or the knowledge gained from the experiment would benefit mankind.

Most of the experiments were the so-called tracer studies, which involved administering radioactive materials in quantities so small that they probably caused no harm. Many of these experiments increased scientific understanding and led to new diagnostic tools, while others were of questionable scientific value. One study involved injecting eighteen people with plutonium and is a prime example of bad science.[15]

On December 7, 1993, DOE Secretary Hazel O'Leary held a press conference during which she acknowledged that the DOE had conducted human radiation experiments. President Clinton then established an Advisory Committee on Human Radiation Experiments to investigate the studies. The committee found that many of the studies were unethical, that the doctors routinely violated their patients' trust, and that subjects were not fully informed. With few exceptions, though, the panel declared no one was harmed, no one was to blame, and no one needed medical monitoring.

President Clinton formally accepted the Advisory Committee's final report in a quiet ceremony at the White House on October 3, 1995. He said, "while most of the tests were ethical by any standards, some were unethical, not only by today's standards, but by the standards of the time in which they were conducted. They failed both the test of our national values and the test of humanity. ...So today, on behalf of another generation of American leaders and another generation of American citizens, the United States of America offers a sincere apology to those of our citizens who were subjected to these experiments, to their families and to their communities."[16]

8. Why are some people so opposed to nuclear weapons and the NWC?

Hugh Gusterson is an anthropologist and has addressed this question quite well in his book *Nuclear Rites: A Weapons Laboratory at the End of the Cold War.* Gusterson had been an anti-nuclear activist in the early 1980s. As time went on, he began to see some logic in the pro-nuclear arguments. Similarly, he began to see weaknesses in the anti-nuclear position. In 1987, he began a study of the Lawrence Livermore Laboratory to learn why reasonable people could review identical information and come to such different viewpoints.

He found these people had much in common. For example, they were all well-educated and wanted to avoid nuclear war. They differed on the question of how best to reduce the risk of war. Gusterson believes that the perception of risk is inherently social and is always colored by ideology. The weapon scientists tended to be middle-class white men while the antinuclear activists were more likely to be female or students who worked in the welfare or creative professions. Consequently, they had very different viewpoints of the good society.

The pro-nuclear viewpoint is largely based on the belief that nuclear weapons are a deterrent to war and thus serve the cause of peace. From this perspective, the real problem is the anarchic international system with its tendency to generate conventional wars. Until this system improves, having a nuclear deterrent is our best hope for peace.

The anti-nuclear viewpoint generally sees nuclear weapons as the greatest possible threat to humanity. They feel that possessing nuclear weapons is madness and that our enemies have such weapons at least in part because we have them. They also feel that nations cannot have arsenals indefinitely without using them.[17]

Freeman Dyson is an internationally acclaimed scientist; he has also addressed this question. His view is similar to Gusterson's. In his book, *Weapons and Hope,* Dyson examines the reasons why people have such divergent views of nuclear weapons. He feels that people live in two different worlds, which he calls warriors and victims. The warriors accept the world with all of its imperfections as a given and then work to preserve it. By contrast, the victims worry about the world and want to rebuild it from its foundations. Since they have such divergent views of the world, it is very difficult for them to communicate with each other.[18]

9. The NWC had a high workload in the 1980s. Why were so many nuclear sites closed during this period?

There are three reasons. First, the U. S. had little need for any additional fissile materials (Pu–239 and HEU). These materials were being recycled from retired weapons.

Second, the nation had become more conscious of environmental concerns as evidenced by the National Environmental Policy Act of 1970 and a subsequent series of related laws. As a result, public opinion had become hostile to many sites in the NWC.

Third, the general public had become frightened of anything nuclear because of accidents at the nuclear power plants at Three Mile Island in Harrisburg, Pennsylvania, in 1979 and Chernobyl in the Soviet Union in 1986. Although there were no significant radioactive emissions or personnel injuries from the Three Mile Island accident, it provoked wide demonstrations against nuclear power. Coincidentally, just two weeks before this accident, the movie *China Syndrome* had been released. This film, which starred Jane Fonda, Jack Lemon, and Michael Douglas, revolved around efforts by utility executives to suppress news of an accident that almost resulted in a core meltdown at a fictional nuclear power plant near Los Angeles.[19]

By contrast, the accident at Chernobyl was a disaster. This plant did not have a containment vessel as required for all plants in the U.S. As a result, the accident caused hundreds of deaths and widespread radiation contamination.

Unfortunately, the average non-technically-trained person often fails to make an adequate distinction between nuclear power plants and the NWC sites. In my opinion, political pressure in the wake of these events was a major factor in the DOE's decisions to cease nuclear operations at Hanford, Fernald, K-25, Savannah River, and Rocky Flats during the 1980s.

10. Was the U.S. justified in dropping atomic bombs on Japan in World War II?

At Hiroshima, approximately 70,000 people were killed and 130,000 wounded. By the end of 1945, the death toll had grown to 140,000 due to radiation sickness and other injuries, and reached 200,000 after five years. At Nagasaki, approximately 40,000 were killed and 60,000 wounded. By the end of 1945 the death toll had grown to 70,000 and reached 140,000 after five years. By comparison, approximately 100,000 people died on March 9, 1945, in a firebombing raid on Tokyo.[20]

After the war, President Truman said that an invasion would have cost between two hundred and fifty thousand and one million American casualties. Similarly, British Prime Minister Winston Churchill claimed that an invasion would have cost one million American and five hundred thousand British lives.[21] In addition, the number of Japanese lives lost would have been many times greater. The exact number will never be known, but if the Japanese defended their homeland with the same determination they exhibited at Guadalcanal, Guam, and Iwo Jima, the loss of life would have been huge.

The two atomic bombs shocked Japan into surrendering and thus saved millions of lives. From this standpoint, the U.S. was justified in dropping the bombs.

11. What was the greatest danger during the Cold War?

Most people feel that the Cuban Missile Crisis was the period of greatest danger during the Cold War. I disagree. Soviet President Khrushchev was not a madman and did not have a death wish for his nation. Had he allowed a nuclear attack against the U.S., the Soviet Union would have been destroyed in retaliation. Although there was a great deal of saber rattling, I think the threat was more bluster than real.

In my opinion, the greatest threat was McCarthyism, that is, the period from 1948 to 1954 when intellectual freedom and judicial honesty were suppressed in the name of national security. McCarthyism was an internal threat. The other threats were external. When citizens lose their rights as defined in our Constitution, then the very foundation of our democracy is threatened. As evidenced by the fall of ancient Rome and more recently by the collapse of the Soviet Union, nations are most vulnerable when they rot from within.

This danger is never very remote as demonstrated by the government's treatment of Dr. Wen Ho Lee, a former employee of LANL. Dr. Lee was indicted in December 1999 for mishandling classified information, which is a violation under the statutes of the Atomic Energy Act of 1954. He was never accused of espionage. Mishandling classified information is normally handled as an administrative matter. Until this case, no one had ever been criminally prosecuted for mishandling classified information.

Dr. Lee was arrested and placed into solitary confinement. In our democracy, every citizen is supposed to be presumed innocent until proven guilty. After nine months in solitary confinement, on September 13, 2000, Federal Judge James Parker released Dr. Lee on bail and took the extraordinary step of apologizing to him. Judge Parker said, "it is only the top decision makers in the Executive Branch, especially the Department of Justice and the Department of Energy and locally, during December, who have caused embarrassment by the way this case was handled. They did not embarrass me alone. They have embarrassed our entire nation and each of us who is a citizen of it." He went on to say, "I sincerely apologize to you, Dr. Lee, for the unfair manner you were held in custody by the Executive Branch." [22]

The Lee case shows that the rights of citizens can still be threatened under the name of national security. We cannot let our nation revert back to the excesses of the McCarthy period. As expressed by Thomas Jefferson, "eternal vigilance is the price of liberty."

12. All things considered, have nuclear weapons been a force for good or for evil?

Debates over the value of nuclear weapons as a deterrent to aggression often generate more heat than light. A perspective on war in general was offered by Will and Ariel Durant, who are among the most famous historians of the twentieth century. In 1967, after over forty years of labor, they completed the last of ten monumental volumes that comprise *The Story of Civilization.* At that point, they decided to review their works to see what, if any, messages they revealed. In 1968, their reflections were published as *The Lessons of History.* One chapter in this book is entitled "History and War." Some excerpts:

> *War is one of the constants of history, and has not diminished with civilization or democracy. In the last 3,421 years of recorded history only 268 have seen no war. We have acknowledged war as at present the ultimate form of competition and natural selection in the human species.*
>
> *The causes of war are the same as the causes of competition among individuals: acquisitiveness, pugnacity, and pride; the desire for food, land, materials, fuel, mastery. The state has our instincts without our restraints. The individual submits to restraints laid upon him by morals and laws, and agrees to replace combat with conference, because the state guarantees him basic protection in his life, property and legal rights. The state itself acknowledges no substantial restraints, either because it is strong enough to defy interference with its will or because there is no superstate to offer it basic protection, and no international law or moral code wielding effective force.*[23]

Nuclear weapons have placed a restraint upon the state and thus serve to preserve peace.

Another perspective was offered by General Groves after World War II.

> *In answer to the question, Was the development of the atomic bomb by the United States necessary? I reply unequivocally, Yes. To the question, Is atomic energy a force for good or evil? I can only say, As mankind wills it.*[24]

A more recent perspective was offered by Dr. Paul Robinson, the former President of SNL. On November 2, 2000, leaders of nuclear weapons activities in the original four nuclear powers — the U.S., Russia, France and the United Kingdom — spent a day together at SNL sharing ideas on the history and future of humankind's most destructive invention. Paul Robinson gave the opening remarks. He noted that 2.5 percent of the world's population was killed in World War I and 3 percent in World War II. Until then this was the bloodiest century in history. But over the next 50 years, the death rate from such conflict declined to two tenths of one percent.

> *It has defied the laws of every historical pattern. I would suggest that nuclear deterrence is the countervailing force to man's spirit of aggression.*[25]

References for Epilogue

1. Thomas S. Arms, *Encyclopedia of the Cold War* (New York: Facts on File, Inc., 1994), x.

2. John Lewis Gaddis, *We Now Know: Rethinking Cold War History* (Oxford: Clarendon Press, 1997), 292-294.

3. Ibid., 8, 129, 208, 293.

4. Ibid., 281-282, 291-292.

5. Stephen I. Schwartz, ed., *Atomic Audit: The Costs and Consequences of U.S. Nuclear Weapons Since 1940* (Washington, D.C.: Brookings Institution Press, 1998), 3-4.

6. Ibid., 32-33, 63.

7. Ibid., 102-106.

8. Ibid., 197-198.

9. Ibid., 269-270.

10. Ibid., 3, 326-328, 354-356.

11. Ibid., 3, 13.

12. U.S. Department of Energy, Office of Environmental Management, *Linking Legacies*, DOE/EM-0319 (Washington, D.C.: U. S. Department of Energy, 1997), 6, 62, 136-143, 172-181.

13. Ibid., 1.

14. Eileen Welsome, *The Plutonium Files* (New York: The Dial Press, Random House, Inc., 1999), 247, 251, 277, 303.

15. Ibid., 214, 413, 482.

16. Ibid., 424-425, 447, 463, 460-470.

17. Hugh Gusterson, *Nuclear Rites: A Weapons Laboratory at the End of the Cold War* (Berkeley and Los Angeles: University of California Press, 1996), 2, 8-11, 219-221, 234.

18. Freeman Dyson, *Weapons and Hope* (New York: Harper and Row, 1984), 3-9; and Jeffry Porro, ed., *The Nuclear Age Reader* (New York: McGraw-Hill, Inc., 1989), 488-490.

19. Wellsome, *The Plutonium Files*, 412.

20. Richard Rhodes, *The Making of the Atomic Bomb*, (New York: Simon and Schuster, 1986), 733-734, 741-742.

21. John Ray Skates, *The Invasion of Japan: Alternative to the Bomb* (Columbia: University of South Carolina Press, 1994), 77.

22. "Parker Tells Scientist He Was Punished Harshly," *Albuquerque Journal*, 16 September 2000, B6.

23. Will Durant and Ariel Durant, *The Lessons of History* (New York: Simon and Schuster, 1968), 81-86.

24. Leslie R. Groves, *Now It Can Be Told* (New York: Harper, 1962), 415.

25. *SNL Daily News*, November 19, 1999, 1 and 4.

APPENDIX A

AEC – DoD Agreements

Missiles and Rockets Agreement

As the stockpile began to grow in the late 1940s, some conflicts surfaced between the AEC and the DoD over portions of their responsibilities for nuclear weapon design and production. The Atomic Energy Act of 1946 gave the AEC the authority "to conduct experiments and do research and development work in the military application of atomic energy and engage in the production of atomic bomb parts or other military weapons utilizing fissionable material." This act provided no further details about the interface with the DoD. Compounding the problem, the DoD had no clearly defined system for communicating its requirements.[1]

The two agencies began a long and complicated negotiation process. As an outgrowth of this process some important definitions evolved such as "warhead" and "warhead installation." In a memorandum dated May 9, 1952, the Military Liaison Committee (MLC) added a definition for the term "adaption kit" as follows:

> *The adaption kit is defined as those items peculiar to the warhead installation less the warhead; namely, the arming and fuzing systems, power supply and all hardware, adaptors, etc., required by a particular installation.*

Deeper reflection by persons involved in arming and fuzing responsibility issues suggested that this addition was a move by the DoD to facilitate assignment of such responsibilities to its own agencies.[2]

On January 16, 1953, Gordon Dean, Chairman of the AEC, wrote to Robert LeBaron, Chairman of the MLC to inform him that the AEC had reviewed the proposed agreement, along with the changes submitted by the MLC, and had accepted all of them. This memorandum has come to be known as the "Missiles and Rockets Agreement." In brief, the division of responsibilities would be as follows:

a. The AEC would be responsible for the warhead including the nuclear components, detonators, and firing unit.

b. The DOD would be responsible for all rocket or guided missile parts including the fuze.

c. Responsibility for the large gray area of the "adaption kit" was not defined clearly. It suggests that this question is not involved primarily in a division of responsibilities and that "the solution of this problem be attained separately by such means as basic requirements and coordination during development, manufacturing, and stockpiling operations."

On August 7, 1953, the MLC recommended that those elements of missiles not included in the atomic warhead be developed and procured by the DoD. In the years thereafter, beginning with the W31/Honest John program in 1955, the U.S. Army gave the responsibility for all of its "adaption kits" to Picatinny Arsenal. Similarly, beginning with the W49/MK1 Atlas Reentry Vehicle, the U.S. Air Force gave this work to its missile contractors such as AVCO and General Electric.

The U. S. Navy took a different approach and, beginning with the W68/MK 3 Reentry Body/Poseidon in 1967, gave all of this work for the fleet ballistic missile programs to the AEC.[3]

1953 AEC – DoD Agreement

On March 21, 1953, a document was issued entitled "An Agreement Between the AEC and the DoD for the Development, Production, and Standardization of Atomic Weapons."

The key features of this agreement are as follows:

a. The development and production of atomic weapons will be the complementary responsibilities of the AEC and the DoD.

This statement was of great importance to the AEC. The prevailing attitude within the DoD had been that the DoD was the "buyer" and the AEC was the "contractor." Without this statement, the AEC's nuclear weapon program could have become subordinate to the DoD.[4]

b. The development and production of nuclear systems are primary functions of the AEC.

c. The division of responsibilities for the development and production of atomic weapons, exclusive of the nuclear systems, will be by joint agreement on each weapon system or by classes of weapons between the AEC and the DoD.

d. The determination of military characteristics, suitability, and acceptability (standardization) is a primary function of the DoD.

e. The functions to be performed by the AEC and DoD would be defined in six phases. A seventh phase that addressed retirement was added later.

These seven phases are still in use today. This information is promulgated throughout the NWC via DOE/NNSA Directive 56XB, Nuclear Weapons Development and Production, and its appendix, the *Development and Production Manual*, Chapters 3.1 and 3.2 as follows:

Phase 1 – Weapon Conception: consists of studies conducted by the DoD and the DOE, either jointly or independently, to decide whether a weapon concept warrants a formal program study.

Phase 2 – Program Feasibility Study: consists of studies to determine the feasibility of the proposed weapon program. During this period, the Military Characteristics and Stockpile to Target Sequence are refined, and the warhead/carrier interfaces are defined by the DOE and the DoD.

Phase 2A – Design Definition and Cost Study: begins when a weapon program is deemed sufficiently feasible to merit complete definition of the design and a thorough cost analysis.

Phase 3 – Development Engineering: the period for defining a tested, manufacturable nuclear weapons design, including training and testing weapons, special equipment, and acceptance equipment.

Phase 4 – Production Engineering: the period when production agencies proceed with adapting a development design into a manufacturing system. This includes product engineering, process engineering, tooling, prototype procurement and inspection, and test and handling procedures.

Phase 5 – First Production: the period when manufacture of the weapon according to product specifications is initiated, and quality control and inspection procedures are implemented. This culminates in an authorization that releases material for specified uses.

Phase 6 – Quantity Production and Stockpile: the period when production facilities will produce weapons at the level required to meet stockpile needs.

Phase 7 – Dismantlement: a program is initiated for the physical elimination of a nuclear weapon or major assembly from the stockpile.

References for Appendix A

1. Necah Stewart Furman, *Sandia National Laboratories, The Postwar Decade* (Albuquerque: University of New Mexico Press, 1990), 533.

2. Captain R.P. Hunter, USN Executive Secretary DOD/MLC, to Director AEC/DMA, SRD Memo, "Definition of Terms Warhead, Warhead Installation, and Adaption Kit," 9 May 1952.

3. W.L. Stevens, Sandia National Laboratories, Memorandum, "Early AEC/DOD Agreements on Nuclear Weapon Program Responsibilities," 24 October 1984, 25 and 26.

4. Ibid., enclosure 2, page 4.

APPENDIX B

National Environmental Policy Act

The National Environmental Policy Act (NEPA) has been heralded as the Magna Carta of the country's environmental movement. It was signed into law on January 1, 1970, to address the need for an environmental policy to guide the growing environmental consciousness and to shape a national response. The essential purpose of NEPA is to ensure that environmental factors are given the same consideration as other factors in decisions by the federal agencies.[1]

A Council on Environmental Quality (CEQ) was created by Title II of NEPA and is modeled after the Council of Economic Advisors created by the Employment Act of 1946. President Nixon expanded the CEQ's mandate by Executive Order 11514, directing it to issue guidelines to federal agencies for the preparation of environmental impact statements (EISs) and to coordinate federal programs related to environmental quality.[2]

The CEQ established NEPA requirements for all federal agencies, including procedures for preparing EISs. The CEQ's NEPA regulations may be found in 40 CFR 1500 (i.e., Chapter 40, Section 1500 of the CFR). CFR stands for Code of Federal Regulations, which is where all federal regulations are codified (published).[3]

Individual agencies, including the Department of Energy, have established their own implementing regulations and Orders to meet or exceed the CEQ requirements. The DOE's regulations for NEPA compliance are codified in 10 CFR 1021 and DOE Order 451.1A, National Environmental Policy Act Compliance Program.[4]

There are several types of NEPA documents that a federal agency may prepare to document the potential environmental impacts of a proposed action and its alternatives. The two most common NEPA documents are an Environmental Assessment (EA) and an

Environmental Impact Statement (EIS). If an agency is unclear whether a proposed action may cause significant environmental impacts, an EA is normally first prepared.

An EA is used as a screening document to determine whether an action will have significant impacts to the environment. If there are potential significant impacts, the agency must prepare an EIS. If, as a result of the analysis in an EA, there is no potential for significant impacts, the agency will make a finding of no significant impact (FONSI). CEQ regulations describe an EA as a concise public document that also serves to aid an agency's compliance with NEPA when no EIS is necessary and to facilitate preparation of an EIS when one is necessary. An EA should include a brief discussion of the need for the proposal, of alternatives, of the environmental impacts of the proposed action and alternatives, and a listing of agencies and persons consulted. A FONSI is supposed to briefly present the reasons why an action will not have a significant impact on the human environment. It must include the EA or a summary of the EA in supporting the FONSI determination.[5]

An agency may skip the EA and commence preparation of an EIS if it is clear that the proposed action is a major federal action that may significantly affect the quality of the human environment (40 CFR 1502.3). In general, an EIS is a much more thorough environmental analysis than an EA, and the process for preparing an EIS is more deliberate and includes a significant amount of public involvement.[6]

The major steps in the NEPA process for preparing an EIS are as follows: issuing a Notice of Intent (NOI) to begin the EIS process; gathering input from federal agencies, state and local governments, Native American tribes, and other stakeholders (the public) during a process known as "scoping"; preparing the draft EIS; holding public meetings to discuss the draft EIS; receiving a responding to public comments on the draft EIS; preparing the final EIS; and issuing a Record of Decision (ROD). Decisions are not made in an EIS; rather, an EIS is one tool federal decision-makers must consider when deciding among various alternatives for a program or project. The major steps in the EIS process are further explained below.[7]

- A federal agency first issues an NOI to prepare an EIS. The NOI is published in the Federal Register to inform the public that an EIS will be prepared and to formally announce the beginning of the scoping process. The NOI describes the proposed action and alternatives the agency is considering; provides information on issues and potential impacts; and invites comments, questions, and suggestions (both written and oral) on the scope of the EIS. An agency will generally hold a scoping meeting at any site potentially affected by a proposed action or the alternatives to receive these scoping comments. The comments provided during scoping aid the federal agency in determining the alternatives, issues, and environmental impacts to be analyzed in the EIS. DOE regulations require that at least one scoping meeting be held to facilitate the collection of public comments.

- The draft EIS is the next step in the EIS process. It describes, analyzes, and compares the potential environmental impacts of the proposed action and the alternatives that could be chosen to accomplish the purpose and need to which the agency is responding. The draft EIS also provides information on the methodologies and assumptions used for the analyses. If one or more preferred alternative(s) exist at this stage of the EIS process, they will be identified in the draft EIS.

- Once the draft EIS is published and distributed, a minimum of 45 days is provided for federal agencies, state and local governments, Native American tribes, and the public to comment on the draft EIS. The public comment period begins upon publication of a Notice of Availability (NOA) for the draft EIS in the Federal Register. At least one public meeting is held to solicit public comments on the draft EIS. Other methods for submission of comments generally include U.S. mail, fax, and e-mail. Comments received are considered in the preparation of the final EIS.

- Following the public comment period, a final EIS is prepared, published, and distributed to the public. The final EIS reflects consideration of all comments received on the draft EIS, contains the agency's responses to those comments, and provides revised EIS text. In addition, the final EIS will identify the agency's preferred alternative(s), if they were not identified in the draft EIS. The release of the final EIS is announced by publishing an NOA in the Federal Register.

- Once the final EIS is published, a minimum 30-day waiting period is required by CEQ Regulations before a Record of Decision (ROD) can be made. The ROD notifies the public of the agency's decision on the proposed action and discusses the reasons for that decision. The ROD will include consideration of other decision factors such as costs, technical feasibility, agency statutory mission, and/or national objectives.

The NEPA process does not dictate that an agency select the most environmentally beneficial alternative. Rather, the NEPA process ensures that accurate environmental studies are performed; that they are done with public involvement and full public disclosure; and that public officials make decisions based on an understanding of the potential environmental consequences.[8]

A Programmatic Environmental Impact Statement (PEIS) is a specific type of EIS that is prepared for large programs. A PEIS is prepared to aid an agency in making broad programmatic decisions before the program has reached a stage of investment or commitment to implementation likely to determine subsequent development or restrict later alternatives (40 CFR 1502.4(c)(3)). Following the preparation of a PEIS and ROD, an agency may prepare project-specific EISs or EAs to implement the PEIS decisions. An agency may also prepare a Programmatic EA to aid in making broad programmatic decisions for programs that are not likely to cause significant environmental impacts.[9]

In the early years, the threat of litigation over the EIS requirement caused many federal agencies to overreact by including in their statements every possible environmental reference that could be found. This resulted in lengthy statements that neither decision-makers nor the public would read. Today, CEQ regulations emphasize the need to reduce excessive paperwork and focus on the essential information that is needed by decision makers and the public.[10]

References for Appendix B

1. Thomas F.P. Sullivan, ed., *Environmental Law Handbook,* (Rockville, MD: Government Institutes, Inc., 1997), 404.

2. Ibid., 406.

3. James Rose, DOE headquarters, e-mail to author, 3 February and 7 February 2000.

4. Ibid.

5. Sullivan, *Environmental Law Handbook*, 416.

6. James Rose, DOE headquarters, e-mail to author, 3 February and 7 February 2000.

7. Ibid.

8. Ibid.

9. Ibid.

10. Sullivan, *Environmental Law Handbook*, 404.

APPENDIX C

Nonnuclear Reconfiguration Program

Introduction

In the *National Defense Authorization Act for Fiscal Years 1988/89* (Public Law 100-180), Congress directed the DOE to conduct a study and prepare a plan for the modernization of the NWC. This mandate led to a series of studies that gave birth to the Nonnuclear Reconfiguration Program.

This program was very difficult to manage from two standpoints. First, it involved plant closures in Ohio, Florida, and Colorado. The attendant loss of jobs created strong political opposition in those states. Second, the organizations at DOE headquarters in Washington, D.C., lacked a common sense of direction (see the discussion in Chapter 11 on the National Nuclear Security Administration). These organizations all marched to their own drummers. None had complete authority over the program but each had the power to stop or delay the portion of the program that involved their area of responsibility.

Chronology of Events

January 12, 1989: *The Nuclear Weapons Complex Modernization Report (Modernization Report)* was submitted to Congress. It called for extensive modernization of NWC facilities through the year 2010. This report was based on the assumption that the Cold War would continue indefinitely, which drove the U.S. to have a large nuclear weapons stockpile and to expect to continue developing and producing new weapon systems.

March 9, 1989: James D. Watkins was sworn in as Secretary of Energy.

September 29, 1989: Secretary Watkins established the Modernization Review Committee to review the assumptions and recommendations in the *Modernization Report*. By this time, it appeared that the Cold War was winding down, which had a major impact on the assumptions used in the *Modernization Report.*

June 1990: The Modernization Review Committee (subsequently renamed the Complex Reconfiguration Committee) established five panels to develop recommendations on various aspects of a modernized NWC.

- Privatization Planning Panel
- Site Evaluation Panel
- Weapons Design Standardization Panel
- Technology Assessment and Selection Panel
- Weapons Research, Development, and Testing Consolidation Panel

Chairmanship of the Privatization Planning Panel (PPP) was assigned to the DOE's Albuquerque Operations Office (DOE/AL). The PPP was chartered to examine all nonnuclear manufacturing activities and determine which of them could be transferred to the private sector and which should be retained within the NWC. This charter divided the PPP's efforts into two phases. Phase 1 was to identify manufacturing activities that were potentially suitable candidates for transfer to the private sector. Phase 2 would then develop a plan for implementing increased privatization.

November 21, 1990: President George H. W. Bush declared the end of the Cold War as relations eased with the Soviet Union. On December 25, 1991, the Soviet Union formally disintegrated.

January 1991: The *Phase 1 Report of the PPP* was published. It showed that the NWC had already attained a high degree of privatization and that increased large-scale privatization did not make economic sense without decisions to terminate operations at selected plants and consolidate the NWC. As a result, Phase 2 of the PPP was cancelled.

The PPP showed that 80 to 90 percent of the cost of a product in the NWC was due to overhead (e.g., accounting, budgeting, construction, environment, facilities, health, human resources, maintenance, payroll, safety, security, utilities, waste management, etc.). The direct cost was a very small part of the total. Also, the overhead was largely fixed and would not change if additional products were transferred to the private sector. Large cost savings could be achieved only through reductions in overhead, which required plant closures.[1]

January 1991: The DOE published the *Nuclear Weapons Complex Reconfiguration Study* as developed by the Complex Reconfiguration Committee. This study recommended that the DOE consider consolidating nonnuclear manufacturing and procurement activities into one "dedicated" nonnuclear site. In this context, "dedicated" meant a site that did not have other ongoing missions (such as the laboratories).[2]

February 11, 1991: The Secretary issued a Notice of Intent (NOI) in the *Federal Register* to prepare a Programmatic Environmental Impact Statement (PEIS) for the Reconfiguration of the NWC. It would address a broad range of DOE activities, both nuclear and nonnuclear. This PEIS was initiated pursuant to the National Environmental Policy Act of 1969 and its implementing regulations (40 CFR, Parts 1500 – 1508).

April 2, 1991: The DOE's Assistant Secretary for Defense Programs tasked DOE/AL to begin developing a Nonnuclear Consolidation Plan (NCP). The term "consolidation" was later discarded in favor of "reconfiguration." The purpose of this plan was to analyze alternatives and make recommendations on how best to consolidate nonnuclear activities at a single dedicated site.

September 1991: The NCP was completed. Four guiding criteria were used in the NCP analyses. Consolidation should be accomplished in a manner that (1) minimizes risks to the environment, safety, and health; (2) minimizes technical risks to the weapons program; (3) minimizes consolidation costs; and (4) minimizes the amount of time to consolidate. The major recommendations in the NCP were as follows:[3]

- Select the Kansas City Plant as the one dedicated nonnuclear site.
- Transfer most of the nonnuclear activities out of the Mound, Pinellas, and Rocky Flats plants to the Kansas City Plant.
- Transfer some activities from Mound, Pinellas, and Rocky Flats to other existing DOE sites (e.g., tritium activities to the Savannah River Site and neutron generators to Sandia National Laboratories) or to the private sector.

November 1991: DOE/AL presented the results of the NCP to Secretary Watkins. DOE/AL also recommended deleting nonnuclear reconfiguration from the overall PEIS and preparing an Environmental Assessment (EA) instead. There were two reasons. One, the types of activities to be transferred already existed at the proposed receiver sites, so the probability of a significant environmental impact was very low. Two, it would save substantial time. This EA could be completed much faster than the overall PEIS.

December 16, 1991: In a press conference, Secretary Watkins announced that the DOE would pursue the recommendations in the NCP and that an EA would be developed for these actions. If the EA did not result in a Finding of No significant Impact (FONSI), then nonnuclear reconfiguration would become an element of the overall PEIS, with subsequent delays in its implementation.

December 23, 1991: The Assistant Secretary for Defense Programs directed DOE/AL to begin detailed planning for the proposed reconfiguration of nonnuclear activities. The responsibility for preparing the EA was retained at DOE headquarters.

DOE headquarters decided that the EA should be expanded into a "Programmatic" EA and analyze alternatives for consolidation at the Mound, Pinellas, and Rocky Flats plants in addition to the Kansas City Plant. DOE/AL disagreed with this decision and argued that, as shown in the NCP, it did not make sense to consolidate at any of these three plants from the standpoint of cost, time or technical risk. This decision made the EA much more complicated and time consuming. Further, it undermined the recommendations in the NCP, which encouraged the political opposition.

DOE headquarters also decided to retain the responsibility for managing the design of the neutron generator facility at Sandia National Laboratories (SNL). DOE/AL argued that this job should be delegated to Sandia. However, DOE headquarters gave the design job to Fluor Daniel, an architect/engineering firm with whom they had an existing contract. In developing the NCP, DOE/AL had assumed that an existing building at Sandia (Building 870) could be modified to produce neutron generators at a cost of approximately $75 million. DOE headquarters and Fluor Daniel disregarded this idea and designed a completely new building. The resulting cost estimate was in excess of $300 million, which jeopardized the entire Nonnuclear Reconfiguration Program. After this estimate was presented to DOE headquarters, they gave the design job back to SNL.

January 21, 1992: DOE/AL established a Nonnuclear Reconfiguration Program Office. This office then established a Reconfiguration Planning Team with representatives from each involved site. This team developed a plan that had an operations component and a facilities component. The operations component addressed weapon program activities, and the facilities component addressed construction and capital equipment activities.

January 28, 1992: In his State of the Union Address, President Bush announced substantial reductions in the size and character of the nuclear weapons stockpile and in the number and types of new weapons to be produced. These reductions resulted in a production rate that was approximately 50 percent of the rate used in the NCP.

March 1992: DOE released the NCP along with an addendum that analyzed the effects of the stockpile reductions on the recommendations in the NCP. The addendum showed that direct weapons production and support activities were reduced by only a small percentage. The reason for this disproportionate reduction is that the NWC had already been reduced to the point where its size was capability-driven, not capacity-driven. Although the numbers used in the NCP were altered by the stockpile reductions, the relative rankings of the consolidation alternatives remained unchanged.

By this time, the DOE's announced plans were being attacked by a large number of individuals and groups at the sites targeted for closure. The NCP was a focal point for these attacks. As a result, the NCP was reviewed by the DOE's Inspector General, who is the "watchdog" for DOE, and the General Accounting Office, which is the "watchdog" for Congress. These reviews concluded that the NCP was accurate. In addition, over the next two years, various Congressional committees tasked the DOE to answer a host of questions and to conduct several additional studies.

April 1992: As directed by Congress, DOE/AL prepared the *Supplemental Cost Study for Nonnuclear Consolidation.* This study showed that the nature of the fixed portions of overhead costs prevented any meaningful cost reductions without actually terminating the operation of a plant. It also showed that consolidation of the remaining manufacturing work to support the nuclear weapons stockpile was essential to maintaining key technologies needed to meet any future national security requirements.[4]

April 9, 1992: The DOE/AL Program Manager for Nonnuclear Reconfiguration established 26 Activity Transfer Groups. These groups were tasked to develop the detailed plans needed for the timely and effective transfer of activities.

May 1992: DOE/AL delivered five budget quality conceptual design reports (CDRs) to DOE Headquarters. Decisions and approvals on facilities activities, such as these CDRs, had to go through a different bureaucratic channel and process than was used for the weapons activities at DOE Headquarters. This split made management of the overall program considerably more difficult.

June 17, 1992: President Bush and Russian President Yeltsin announced an agreement on further reductions in strategic nuclear weapons. This agreement would reduce the number of warheads on strategic weapons in the U.S. stockpile by nearly two-thirds. As a result, DOE/AL decided to revise portions of its reconfiguration plans to collocate some additional production activities with design activities at the laboratories.

August 1992: As directed by Congress, DOE/AL prepared the *Two-Site Nonnuclear Consolidation Study*. This study analyzed alternatives for consolidating nonnuclear manufacturing activities at any two of the current three dedicated nonnuclear plants: Mound, Pinellas, and Kansas City. It also estimated and compared the annual operating costs for the three two-site alternatives with the one-site alternative at Kansas City. None of the two-site options were as good as the single-site option at Kansas City in terms of retaining technical competence while achieving maximum savings in operating costs.[5]

October 1992: DOE/AL provided DOE Headquarters with new CDRs for SNL and LANL along with revised CDRs for Kansas City and Savannah River. These CDRs reflected the revised plans in response to the Bush-Yeltsin agreement.

October 1992: The Energy and Water Development Appropriations Act of 1993 and the National Defense Authorization Act for fiscal Year 1993 required the Secretary of Energy to submit a report to the Congressional Committees on Appropriations and to the Congressional Defense Committees. This report was to contain an analysis of the projected relevant costs and benefits of the proposed reconfiguration (i.e., Kansas City as the one dedicated nonnuclear plant) and of each alternative (i.e., Mound, Pinellas, and Rocky Flats as the one dedicated nonnuclear plant). DOE then had to wait ninety days before any funds could be obligated to implement nonnuclear reconfiguration.

These Acts required the report to include life cycle cost analyses using discounted cash flow techniques (per guidelines published by the Office of Management and Budget) projected out through the year 2050. In addition, these Acts required the Secretary to certify that each of the proposed activity transfers and associated plant closures would be cost effective. They also required the Secretary to certify that these transfers would not increase technical, environmental, safety, or health risks in the operation of facilities in the Department. DOE Headquarters tasked DOE/AL to develop this report.

December 1992: DOE/AL completed the *Nonnuclear Reconfiguration Cost Effectiveness Report* and submitted it to DOE headquarters. This report showed that the proposed reconfiguration met all of the above criteria.[6]

January 3, 1993: The START II Treaty was signed by President Bush and Russian President Yeltsin, which formalized their agreement of June 17, 1992.

January 15, 1993: Secretary Watkins submitted the *Nonnuclear Reconfiguration Cost Effectiveness Report* to Congress along with the required certifications.

January 22, 1993: Hazel R. O'Leary was sworn in as Secretary of Energy.

March 8, 1993: Senator John Glenn and Congressman Tony Hall from Ohio asked Secretary O'Leary to decertify the *Nonnuclear Reconfiguration Cost Effectiveness Report*. She declined this request but agreed to subject it to an independent review.

April 6, 1993: Secretary O'Leary appointed three independent consultants to analyze the cost effectiveness of DOE's plans. These consultants were appointed with the agreement of the governors, senators, and involved members of the House of Representatives from each of the eight affected states (Colorado, New Mexico, Kansas, Missouri, Ohio, South Carolina, Georgia, and Florida). These consultants reviewed the *Nonnuclear Reconfiguration Cost Effectiveness Report* and visited each involved site.

May 24, 1993: Each of the three independent consultants submitted a report to Secretary O'Leary that said, in effect, the DOE's plans were cost effective and should be implemented.

May 27, 1993: After reviewing these reports, the Secretary announced her intent to proceed with the nonnuclear reconfiguration process. At this point, the major political opposition to the Nonnuclear Reconfiguration Program was over.

June 1993: The *Nonnuclear Consolidation Environmental Assessment* was completed.[7]

July 8, 1993: DOE issued a proposed Finding of No Significant Impact (FONSI) based on the Nonnuclear Consolidation Environmental Assessment. The public was given 30 days to review and comment on the proposed FONSI and EA.[8]

July 20, 1993: Secretary O'Leary approved the start of Title I work (preliminary design) for construction at the Kansas City Plant, Sandia National Laboratories, and Los Alamos National Laboratory.

September 8, 1993: Secretary O'Leary issued a FONSI based on the EA for nonnuclear reconfiguration. Issuance of the FONSI enabled DOE to proceed with the implementation of nonnuclear reconfiguration.[9]

The DOE/AL Program Manager directed all sites to proceed with the operations component of nonnuclear reconfiguration. This direction authorized the sites to begin activity transfers from donor to receiver sites and to begin qualification activities at the receiver sites.

October 1, 1993: DOE/AL issued a revised Production Site Mission Assignments document to formally transfer production responsibilities from the three donor sites to the four receiver sites in accordance with the plans for nonnuclear reconfiguration.

October 26, 1993: Secretary O'Leary issued an Action Memorandum to authorize continued work on the facilities component of the program. This authorization addressed definitive design activities at the Kansas City Plant, Sandia National Laboratories, and Los Alamos National Laboratory and authorized construction on several subprojects at the Kansas City plant. It also authorized the start of Title 1 work (preliminary design) for those projects that were not covered in the July 20 authorization.

February 7, 1994: President Clinton's FY 1995 budget was sent to Congress. This budget reflected significant reductions from the projected Stockpile Support budget levels used in the nonnuclear reconfiguration plans. No one in Washington, D.C., contacted the DOE/AL Program Manager to assess the impact of these reductions prior to this decision.

February 8, 1994: The DOE/AL Program Manager issued a call to all involved sites to revise their nonnuclear reconfiguration plans to reflect the reduced Stockpile Support budget. The baseline for the Nonnuclear Reconfiguration Program was revised with direction to cease production activities at the Mound, Pinellas, and Rocky Flats plants by the end of FY 1994, which was one year earlier than previously planned. In addition, a few activities such as the CAP Assembly (which was an existing component that used old technology and was retained in the program as a backup to its successor, the Acorn, that used new technology) were deleted from the program. These deletions added some technical risk to the program.

DOE/AL directed the three donor sites to build an inventory of products by September 30, 1994, that would support the nuclear weapon stockpile until the receiver sites were ready to take their place. Inventory quantities were a function of the time it would take the receiver sites to begin production on their new missions. Neutron generators were the most complicated product to transfer and had the longest transfer time, five years. The first delivery of neutron generators from Sandia was thus due in October 1999.

September 30, 1994: Production activities were terminated at the Mound, Pinellas, and Rocky Flats plants. Product inventory, equipment, and people were then transferred to the four receiver sites, Kansas City Plant, Sandia National Laboratories, Los Alamos National Laboratory, and the Savannah River Site.

The receiver sites subsequently completed their facilities and construction work and established production capabilities as defined in the Nonnuclear Reconfiguration Program plans. All deliveries of nuclear weapons components to the DoD during the transition period were made on schedule.

Summary

In spite of many difficulties, the Nonnuclear Reconfiguration Program was accomplished on schedule and within budget. It cost approximately $440 million to implement and resulted in cost savings of about $250 million per year. By consolidating activities it has also helped the NWC maintain technical competence in the low work load environment after the Cold War. The Nonnuclear Reconfiguration Program was a notable success for the DOE, for the DoD, and for the Nation.

References for Appendix C

1. U.S. Department of Energy, Albuquerque Operations Office, *Phase 1 Report of the Privatization Planning Panel* (Albuquerque: Albuquerque Operations Office, January 1991), v-vi and 46-50.

2. U.S. Department of Energy, *Nuclear Weapons Complex Reconfiguration Study*, DOE/DP-0083 (Washington, D.C.: U.S. Department of Energy, January 1991), 4-5 and 30-33.

3. U.S. Department of Energy, Albuquerque Operations Office, *Nonnuclear Consolidation Plan* (Albuquerque: Albuquerque Operations Office, September 1991), ii-iii and 40-41.

4. U.S. Department of Energy, Albuquerque Operations Office, *Supplemental Cost Study for Nonnuclear Reconfiguration* (Albuquerque: Albuquerque Operations Office, April 1992), 12.

5. U.S. Department of Energy, Albuquerque Operations Office, *Two-Site Nonnuclear Consolidation Study* (Albuquerque: Albuquerque Operations Office, August 1992), ii-iii and 29.

6. U.S. Department of Energy, *Nonnuclear Reconfiguration Cost Effectiveness Report*, DOE/DP-0112P (Washington, D.C.: U.S. Department of Energy, January 1993), i-iii and 43.

7. U.S. Department of Energy, *Nonnuclear Consolidation Environmental Assessment*, DOE/EA-0792 (Washington, D.C.: U.S. Department of Energy, June 1993).

8. U.S. Department of Energy, *Proposed Finding of No Significant Impact: Consolidation of the Nonnuclear Component Within the Nuclear Weapons Complex* (Washington, D.C.: U.S. Department of Energy, July 8, 1993).

9. U.S. Department of Energy, *Finding of No Significant Impact: Consolidation of the Nonnuclear Component Within the Nuclear Weapons Complex* (Washington, D.C.: U.S. Department of Energy, September 8, 1993).

APPENDIX D

Nuclear Weapons Treaties

Nuclear weapon treaties have had a major impact on the workload and size of the NWC. A brief summary of the most important treaties and proposed treaties is as follows.[1]

Limited Test Ban Treaty (LTBT)

The purpose of this treaty is to ban tests in the atmosphere, outer space, and under water. This treaty does not ban tests underground, but it does prohibit nuclear explosions in this environment if they cause radioactive debris to be present outside the territorial limits of the State under whose jurisdiction or control the test is conducted. The LTBT was signed in Moscow in August 1963, ratified by the U.S. Senate in September 1963, and became effective in October 1963. This treaty involved the governments of the United States, United Kingdom of Great Britain and Northern Ireland, and the Union of Soviet Socialists Republics. The LTBT is of unlimited duration.[2]

Anti-Ballistic Missile Treaty (ABM)

This treaty limits anti-ballistic missile systems of the United States and the Soviet Union through an agreement that each may have two ABM deployment areas. Both parties agreed to limit the improvement of their ABM technology. The ABM Treaty was signed in Moscow in May 1972, ratified by the U.S. Senate in August 1972, and became effective in October 1972. This treaty is between the United States and the Union of Soviet Socialist Republics.[3] The U.S. has expressed a desire to modify or abandon this treaty in anticipation of its National Missile Defense Program, but as of this writing, no such action has been taken.

Strategic Arms Limitation Talks (SALT I)

This agreement freezes the number of strategic ballistic missile launchers and permits an increase (agreed upon level) in submarine–launched ballistic missile (SLBM) launchers. SALT I was signed in Moscow in May 1972 and became effective in October 1972. These talks involved the United States and the Union of Soviet Socialistic Republics.[4]

Threshold Test Ban Treaty (TTBT)

This treaty establishes a nuclear test "threshold" by prohibiting underground tests having a yield exceeding 150 kilotons (equivalent to 150,000 tons of TNT). The TTBT was signed in July 1974, ratified and became effective in December 1990. This treaty involved the United States and the Union of Soviet Socialist Republics.[5]

Peaceful Nuclear Explosions Treaty (PNET)

This treaty governs all nuclear explosions outside the locations specified under the Threshold Test Ban Treaty. As with the TTBT, the "peaceful" explosions (such as big earth moving projects) must be conducted in compliance with the LTBT (e.g., underground with no radioactive release outside a country's borders) and cannot exceed 150 kt in yield for any single explosion. Aggregate explosions up to 1.5 megatons are permitted if each explosion can be verified to be less than 150 kt. The PNET was signed in Washington and Moscow in May 1976 and became effective in December 1990. This treaty involved the United States and the Union of Soviet Socialist Republics.[6]

Strategic Arms Limitation Talks (SALT II)

The purpose of the SALT II negotiations was to agree on a long-term comprehensive treaty providing limits on strategic offensive weapons systems. SALT II negotiations began in November 1972. The agreement was signed in Vienna in June 1979. These talks involved the United States and the Union of Soviet Socialistic Republics. President Reagan declared that the Soviet Union had violated its political commitment to observe the SALT II Treaty in 1984 and 1985. Therefore, in May 1986, President Reagan stated that "the United States must base decisions regarding its strategic force structure on the nature and magnitude of the threat posed by Soviet strategic forces and not on standards contained in the SALT structure."[7]

Intermediate-Range Nuclear Forces Treaty (INF)

The INF treaty eliminated all nuclear-armed, ground-launched ballistic and cruise missiles with ranges between 500 and 5,500 kilometers. This treaty resulted in the elimination of 846 long- and short-range U.S. INF missile systems and 1846 Soviet INF missile systems. The INF was signed in Washington in 1987, ratified in May 1988, and became effective in December 1988. This treaty involved the United States and the Union of Soviet Socialist Republics.[8]

Strategic Arms Reduction Treaty (START I)

The purpose of this treaty was to equal the level of strategic offensive arms. Both sides agreed to reduce the number of strategic delivery vehicles (ICBMs, SLBMs, and heavy bombers) from about 2500 to 1600 and to reduce the number of accountable warheads on these vehicles from about 10,200 to 6000. These reductions were to be carried out in three phases over seven years (after the treaty became effective).

START I was signed in July 1991 between the United States and the Soviet Union. Five months later, the Soviet Union dissolved and became four independent states — Belarus, Kazakhstan, Russia, and Ukraine. In May of 1992, Belarus, Kazakhstan, Russia, and Ukraine became parties to the START I treaty as legal successors to the Soviet Union. The U.S. Senate ratified the treaty in October 1992 and Russia ratified it in November 1992. Russia decided not to exchange the instruments of ratification until Belarus, Kazakhstan, and Ukraine reached an agreement on the dismantlement of their nuclear forces and join the NPT. In December 1994, the five parties to the START I Treaty exchanged instruments of ratification at the Budapest summit.[9]

Strategic Arms Reduction Treaty (START II)

START II is a bilateral treaty between the U.S. and Russia that will reduce deployed accountable strategic warheads to no more than 3500 for each side (down from 6000 in START I) and will eliminate all MIRVed ICBMs. START II was signed in January 1993 by U.S. President George H. W. Bush and Soviet President Boris Yelstin. This treaty was ratified by the U.S. Senate in January 1996. It was not ratified by the Russian Duma until April 2000 and then only with some modifications. The U.S. Senate has not approved these modifications. Consequently, this treaty is still not in effect.

The proposed reductions were originally targeted to be complete by 2003. However, in 1997, both sides agreed to extend the completion date to 2007.[10]

Non-Proliferation Treaty (NPT)

The NPT obligates the five acknowledged nuclear-weapon states (United States, Russian Federation, United Kingdom, France, and China) to not transfer nuclear weapons, other nuclear explosive devices, or their technology to any nonnuclear weapons state. Nonnuclear weapon states agree not to acquire or produce nuclear weapons and are obligated to accept nuclear safeguards agreements with the International Atomic Energy Agency (IAEA) to preclude diversion of nuclear materials from peaceful activities to other uses. The treaty was opened for signature (U.S., UK, and USSR signed) in July 1968 and became effective in March 1970. China signed the NPT in March 1992, and France signed in August 1992. Over 180 nonnuclear-weapon states are parties to the NPT. Israel, India, and Pakistan are not parties to the NPT.[11]

Comprehensive Test Ban Treaty (CTBT)

The CTBT prohibits "any nuclear weapon test or any other nuclear explosion" either for weapons or peaceful purposes. The treaty includes provisions for an International Monitoring System, On–Site Inspections (OSI), and Confidence Building Measures. The CTBT was signed in September 1996; however the U.S. Senate voted it down for ratification in October 1999. As of

October 2001, all but three (India, Pakistan, and North Korea) of the 44 nations required for Entry into Force have signed the CTBT, but only 31 of those 44 countries have ratified. Overall, 160 countries have signed and 76 have ratified.[12]

Strategic Arms Reduction Treaty (START III)

In March 1997, at the Helsinki Summit, the U.S. and Russian Presidents agreed to begin negotiations on a START III agreement immediately after START II is ratified, but no formal negotiations have yet begun. Proposals for START III include further reductions in the number of strategic nuclear warheads to 2000 to 2500 for each side.[13]

Cooperative U.S. – Former Soviet Union (FSU) Programs

Following the breakup of the Soviet Union, the Nunn-Lugar Act of 1991 put in motion a set of programs aimed at reducing the likelihood of accidents or thefts of nuclear weapons or materials. Through these efforts, the U.S. has worked with Russia and other FSU states to support safe, secure implementation of START I agreements (e.g., the destruction of delivery systems and the transportation and storage of nuclear weapons downloaded from such systems); to consolidate and secure fissile materials; and to verifiably remove weapons grade fissile materials from the stockpiles.[14]

Moscow Treaty

On May 24, 2002, U.S. President George W. Bush and Russian President Vladimir Putin signed the Strategic Offensive Reductions Treaty (SORT). Because the signing took place in Moscow it is commonly called the Moscow Treaty. The U.S. Senate ratified it on March 6, 2003. This treaty requires both sides to reduce their number of operationally deployed strategic nuclear warheads to between 1,700 and 2,200 by December 31, 2012.

This treaty does not require the destruction of any nuclear weapons or delivery systems. It merely changes their operational status. Each side can keep an unlimited number of nuclear weapons in storage. Also, it does not contain any verification measures to create confidence that either country is carrying out the required changes in operational status.

References for Appendix D

1. Larry S. Walker and Richard L. Lucero, Sandia National Laboratories, memorandum to author, 16 February 2000.

2. David B. Thompson, *A Guide to Nuclear Arms Control Treaties* (Los Alamos: Los Alamos Historical Society Publications, 2001), 18-20, 37-38.

3. Ibid., 22.

4. Ibid., 21-22.

5. Ibid., 38-41.

6. Ibid., 39.

7. Ibid., 22-23.

8. Ibid., 23-24, 117-128.

9. Ibid., 24-25, 163-199; and U.S. Department of Energy, *Final Programmatic Impact Statement for Stockpile Stewardship and Management: Summary*, DOE/EIS-0236 (Washington, D.C.: U.S. Department of Energy, September 1996), S-13.

10. Thompson, *A Guide to Nuclear Arms Control Treaties*, 25-26, 209-224; and U.S. Department of Energy, *Final Programmatic Impact Statement for Stockpile Stewardship and Management: Summary*, S-13.

11. Thompson, *A Guide to Nuclear Arms Control Treaties*, 20-21, 79-105.

12. Ibid., 41-49.

13. Ibid., 225-226.

14. Ibid., 241-254

GLOSSARY

Atom: The basic component of all matter. The atom is the smallest unit of an element that has all the characteristics of that element. Atoms consist of a nucleus of protons and neutrons surrounded by electrons.

Atomic mass unit (amu): A quantity of mass equal to one-twelfth of the mass of the carbon12 isotope ($_6C^{12}$).

Atomic number: The number of protons in the nucleus of an atom.

Ballistic: The trajectory of a vehicle after the propulsive force is terminated and the vehicle is acted upon only by gravity and aerodynamic drag.

Beryllium: The fourth-lightest element. Some nuclear weapon parts are made of beryllium.

Binding Energy: The amount of energy that must be put into a nucleus to break it into its constituent particles.

Chain reaction: A reaction in which a neutron from a fissioned atom hits another atom and causes it to fission.

Cold War: A conflict over ideological differences between the United States and the Soviet Union that lasted from the late 1940s until the early 1990s and carried on by methods short of sustained military action.

Critical mass: The quantity of fissionable material needed to support a sustaining chain reaction.

Cross section: The probability that any particular nuclear reaction will take place with a given incident particle.

Cruise missile: A guided missile that uses aerodynamic lift to offset gravity and propulsion to counteract drag. A cruise missile's flight remains within the Earth's atmosphere.

Depleted uranium: Uranium that, through the process of enrichment, has been stripped of most of the uranium-235 it once contained so that it has more uranium-238 than natural uranium.

Deuterium: A naturally occurring isotope of hydrogen. It has one proton and one neutron.

Electron: A negatively charged lightweight particle that orbits the nucleus.

Element: A substance that cannot be separated into simpler substances by ordinary chemical means. There are 92 naturally occurring elements (e.g., hydrogen, helium, lithium).

Enrichment: The process of separating different isotopes of the same element. The three elements that have been isotopically enriched in large quantities for use in nuclear weapons production are uranium, lithium, and hydrogen.

Environmental assessment (EA): A written environmental analysis that is prepared pursuant to the National Environmental Policy Act to determine whether a Federal action would significantly affect the environment and thus require preparation of a more detailed environmental impact statement. If the action would not significantly affect the environment, then a finding of no significant impact is prepared.

Environmental impact statement (EIS): A document required of Federal agencies by the National Environmental Policy Act for major proposals significantly affecting the environment. A tool for decision making, it describes the positive and negative effects of the undertaking and alternate actions.

Finding of no significant impact (FONSI): A document by a Federal agency briefly presenting the reasons why an action will not have a significant effect on the human environment and will not require an environmental impact statement.

Fissile: Capable of being split by slow (low-energy) neutrons as well as by fast (high-energy) neutrons. Uranium-235 and plutonium-239 are fissile materials.

Fission: The splitting of a heavy atomic nucleus into two lighter nuclei, accompanied by the release of energy and generally one or more neutrons. Heavy nuclei contain a large number of protons and neutrons (e.g., uranium-235 contains 92 protons and 143 neutrons.) Fission can occur spontaneously or be induced by neutron bombardment.

Fusion: The process whereby the nuclei of lighter elements, especially the isotopes of hydrogen (deuterium and tritium), combine to form the nucleus of a heavier element, such as helium, with the release of substantial amounts of energy and neutrons.

Half-life: The time it takes for one-half of any number of unstable atoms to decay. Each isotope has its own characteristic half-life. They range from small fractions of a second to billions of years.

Heavy water: Water (H_2O) that contains deuterium atoms in place of hydrogen atoms (i.e., D_2O).

Highly-enriched uranium (HEU): Uranium with more than 20 percent of the uranium-235 isotope, used for making nuclear weapons and also as fuel for some nuclear reactors. Weapons-grade uranium is a subset of this group.

Implosion: The sudden inward compression and reduction in volume of fissile material with ordinary explosives in a nuclear weapon.

Initiator: A device that produces a timed burst of neutrons to initiate a fission chain reaction in a nuclear weapon. Initiators made of polonium-210 and beryllium were located at the center of the fissile cores of early atomic weapons.

Intercontinental ballistic missile (ICBM): A rocket-propelled vehicle capable of delivering a warhead to intercontinental ranges. An ICBM consists of a booster, one or more reentry vehicles, possibly penetration aids, and in the case of a MIRVed missile, a post-boost vehicle.

Intermediate-range ballistic missile (IRBM): A rocket-propelled vehicle with a range capability from about 1500 to 3000 nautical miles.

Ion: An atom that has gained or lost an electron and thus carries an electrical charge.

Isotopes: Forms of the same chemical element that differ only by the number of neutrons in their nucleus. Most elements have more than one naturally occurring isotope. Many more isotopes have been produced in nuclear reactors or accelerators.

Kiloton (kt): A quantity of energy equal to the explosion of 1000 tons of TNT.

Limited life component (LLC): A weapon component that decays with age and must be replaced periodically. Neutron generators and reservoirs are limited life components because they contain tritium.

Low-enriched uranium (LEU): Uranium that has been enriched until it consists of about three percent uranium-235 and 97 percent uranium-238. Used as reactor fuel.

Mass Defect: The difference between the mass of a nucleus and the sum of the masses of its constituent nucleons.

Mass number (aka atomic mass number): The number of protons and neutrons in the nucleus of an atom.

Medium-range ballistic missile (MRBM): A rocket-propelled vehicle with a range capability from about 600 to 1500 nautical miles.

Megaton (Mt): A quantity of energy equal to the explosion of one million tons of TNT.

Moderator: A material used to slow down fast neutrons. A good moderator reduces the speed of neutrons in a small number of atomic collisions but does not absorb them to any great extent. Heavy water and very pure graphite are good moderators.

Molecule: Consists of atoms that have been chemically combined (e.g., H_2O).

Multiplying chain reaction: A condition in which the rate of nuclear fission events increases. A nuclear weapon is the result of a very rapidly multiplying chain reaction.

Nuclear weapons complex (NWC): A nationwide group of government-owned and contractor-operated laboratories and production plants that are currently administered by the U.S. Department of Energy. The NWC is responsible for the research, development, design, manufacture, testing, assessment, certification, and maintenance of the Nation's nuclear weapons and the subsequent dismantlement of retired weapons.

Natural uranium: Uranium that has not been through the enrichment process. It consists of 99.3 percent uranium-238 and 0.7 percent uranium-235.

Neutron: A massive, uncharged particle that comprises part of an atomic nucleus.

Neutron generator: A device that produces a timed burst of neutrons to initiate a fission chain reaction in a nuclear weapon.

Nucleon: A term that refers to the two constituent parts of a nucleus (protons and neutrons).

Nucleus: The cluster of protons and neutrons at the center of an atom that determines its identity and chemical and nuclear properties.

Permissive Action Link (PAL): A system that prevents a nuclear weapon from being armed until a prescribed code or combination is inserted.

Pit: The central core of the primary stage of a nuclear weapon consisting of fissile materials surrounded by a tamper and sometimes by a sealed metal shell.

Primary: Provides the initial source of energy to initiate a nuclear chain reaction for a nuclear weapon. Consists of a central core, called the pit, surrounded by a layer of high explosive. The pit is typically composed of plutonium-239 and/or highly enriched uranium surrounded by a tamper.

Programmatic environmental impact statement (PEIS): A legal document prepared in accordance with the requirements of 102(2)(C) of the National Environmental Policy Act which evaluates the environmental impacts of proposed Federal actions that involve multiple decisions potentially affecting the environment at one or more sites.

Proton: A massive, positively charged particle that comprises part of an atomic nucleus.

Record of decision (ROD): A document prepared in accordance with the requirements of 40 CFR 1505.2 that provides a concise public record of DOE's decision on a proposed action for which an EIS was prepared. A ROD identifies the alternatives considered in reaching the decision, the environmentally preferable alternative(s), factors balanced by DOE in making the decision, and whether all practicable means to avoid or minimize environmental harm have been adopted and, if not, why they were not.

Sealed pit: A pit that is hermetically closed to protect the nuclear materials from the environment.

Secondary: Provides additional explosive energy release for the detonation of a nuclear weapon. Activated by the explosion from the primary. Can be composed of lithium deuteride, uranium, and other materials. Within the secondary, lithium is converted to tritium, which undergoes fusion with deuterium to create a thermonuclear explosion.

Short-range ballistic missile (SRBM): A rocket-propelled vehicle capable of delivering a warhead at ranges up to about 600 nautical miles. Pershing and Lance are SRBMs.

Sustaining chain reaction: A condition in which the rate of nuclear fissions remains constant. This occurs in a nuclear reactor after it reaches its desired power level.

Supercritical mass: The quantity of fissionable material needed to support a multiplying chain reaction.

Tamper: The portion of a fission device that surrounds the fissile components and provides neutronic and/or inertial enhancement of the fission reaction. It is not a nuclear component.

Thermonuclear weapon: A nuclear weapon that uses fission to start a fusion reaction. Commonly called a hydrogen bomb or "H-bomb."

Tritium: The heaviest isotope of the element hydrogen. It has one proton and two neutrons. Tritium is produced in nuclear reactors and has a half-life of 12.3 years. Tritium is used to boost the explosive power of most modern nuclear weapons.

Warhead: Collective term for the package of nuclear assembly and nonnuclear components that can be mated with a delivery vehicle or carrier to produce a deliverable nuclear weapon.

Weapons-grade uranium: Uranium that contains over 90 percent of the uranium-235 isotope.

Yield: A measure of the energy produced by a nuclear explosion. It is generally expressed as the quantity of TNT required to produce an equivalent amount of energy.

BIBLIOGRAPHY

Albright, Joseph, and Marcia Kunstel. *Bombshell.* New York: Times Books, 1997.

The story of espionage during the Manhattan Project with a focus on Ted Hall, who was one of the spies at Los Alamos.

Arms, Thomas S. *Encyclopedia of the Cold War.* New York: Facts on File, Inc., 1994.

An extensive set of articles covering all of the major events and players in the Cold War.

Benson, Louis Benson, and Michael Warner, eds., *Venona: Soviet Espionage and the American Response, 1939-1957.* Washington, D.C. : National Security Agency and Central Intelligence Agency, 1996.

A summary of the U.S. project that deciphered encrypted Soviet diplomatic messages along with copies of selected messages that revealed the network of spies in the U.S.

Bernstein, Jeremy. *Hitler's Uranium Club: The Secret Recordings at Farm Hall.* Woodbury, NY: AIP Press, 1996.

An edited and annotated version of the secretly recorded conversations among the top ten scientists involved in the German nuclear program during WWII.

Bidwai, Praful, and Achin Vaniak. *New Nukes: India, Pakistan and Global Disarmament.* New York: Interlink Publishing Group, Inc., 2000.

A history of the nuclear programs and nuclear tests in India and Pakistan.

Brian, Denis. *Einstein, A Life.* New York: John Wiley & Sons, Inc., 1996.

A biography of the genius who developed the theoretical foundation for the release of nuclear energy.

Brinton, Crane, John B. Christopher, and Robert Lee Wolff. *Modern Civilization.* Englewood Cliffs, NJ: Prentice-Hall, Inc., 1961.

An excellent history of the last five centuries.

Burgess, William F., Jo Anne McCormick, and Eileen Pingitore. *History of the Production Complex: The Methods of Site Selection.* Prepared by History Associates Incorporated for the U.S. Department of Energy, Office of Nuclear Materials, Washington, D.C., under Nevada Operations Office Contract No. AC08-87NV1594. Washington, D.C.: U.S. Department of Energy, 1987.

Provides the rationale and criteria used for selecting the major sites in the Nuclear Weapons Complex.

Calaprice, Alice. *The Quotable Einstein*. Princeton: Princeton University Press, 1996.

An informative, entertaining, and well-organized set of quotes from the most famous scientist of the twentieth century.

Carr, B. H. *Pantex History: 1942 to 1992*. Amarillo: Pantex Plant Report, 1992.

A brief account of the significant events in the first forty years of operation of the Pantex Plant.

Commission on Maintaining United States Nuclear Weapons Expertise (the Chiles Commission). *Report to the Congress and Secretary of Energy*. Washington, D.C.: General Services Administration, March 1999.

A review of the DOE's efforts to attract scientific, engineering, and technical personnel within the NWC along with recommendations for improvement.

Compton, Arthur Holly. *Atomic Quest*. New York: Oxford University Press, 1956.

A very readable account of the Manhattan Project by a Nobel prize winning scientist who was one of its most important participants.

Dahl, Per F. *Heavy Water and the Wartime Race for Nuclear Energy*. Bristol and Philadelphia: Institute of Physics Publishing, 1999.

An exciting account of the German efforts to obtain heavy water, which they needed in order to make a nuclear reactor, and the Allied actions that stopped them.

Durant, Will, and Ariel Durant. *The Lessons of History*. New York: Simon and Schuster, 1968.

Reflections on the messages revealed in the ten volumes that comprise the Story of Civilization, which was their life's work.

Dyson, Freeman. *Weapons and Hope*. New York: Harper and Row, 1984.

A prominent physicist's view of the nuclear controversy in America.

Fehner, Terrence R., and Jack M. Holl. *Department of Energy 1977-1994: A Summary History*. Washington D.C.: History Division, Executive Secretariat, Human Resources and Administration, U.S. Department of Energy, November 1994.

Explains the origins, goals, and achievements of the Department of Energy.

Feld, Bernard T., and Gertrude Weiss Szilard, eds., *The Collected Works of Leo Szilard: Scientific Papers*. Cambridge: The MIT Press, 1972.

Contains copies of many interesting documents including a patent application in 1934 for the concept of using neutron-induced chain reactions to liberate energy.

Fermi, Laura. *Atoms in the Family*. Chicago: University of Chicago Press, 1954.

The story of Enrico Fermi as written by his wife.

Furman, Necah Stewart. *Sandia National Laboratories: The Postwar Decade*. Albuquerque: University of New Mexico Press, 1990.

Describes the evolution of Sandia National Laboratories from its origin in 1945 as a division of Los Alamos Scientific Laboratory to its role in 1955 as nuclear ordnance engineer for the nation.

Gaddis, John Lewis. *We Now Know: Rethinking Cold War History*. Oxford: Clarendon Press, 1997.

A comprehensive history of the Cold War that draws on information from sources that were unavailable until the conflict was over.

Glasstone, Samuel. *Sourcebook on Atomic Energy*. Princeton: D. Van Nostrand Company, Inc., 1958.

Sponsored by the Atomic Energy Commission, this classic text covers everything from atomic structure to nuclear reactors.

Goodchild, Peter. *Edward Teller: The Real Dr. Strangelove*. Cambridge: Harvard University Press, 2004.

A very thorough and interesting biography of one of the most controversial scientists of the twentieth century.

Gosling, F. G. *The Manhattan Project: Making The Atomic Bomb*. DOE/MA-0001. Washington, D.C.: U.S. Department of Energy, History Division, Executive Secretariat, Management and Administration, January, 1999.

A history of the origins and development of the American atomic bomb program during World War II.

Groves, Leslie R. *Now It Can Be Told*. New York: Harper, 1962.

The story of the Manhattan Project as told by the general who managed it.

Gusterson, Hugh. *Nuclear Rites: A Weapons Laboratory at the End of the Cold War*. Berkeley and Los Angeles: University of California Press, 1996.

An anthropologist's study of the Lawrence Livermore National Laboratory that helps to explain why people have such diverse views about nuclear weapons.

Halberstam, David. *The Fifties*. New York: Villard Books, 1993.

A sweeping social, political, economic, and cultural history of the ten-year period that the author regards as seminal in determining what our nation is today.

Hewett, Richard G., and Oscar E. Anderson, Jr. *The New World, 1939/1946.* University Park: The Pennsylvania State University Press, 1962.

The first volume in the official history of the Atomic Energy Commission. It includes an extensive amount of information on the Manhattan Project and the transition to civilian control of atomic energy after World War II.

Hewlett, Richard G., and Francis Duncan. *Atomic Shield, 1947/1952.* University Park and London: The Pennsylvania University State Press, 1969.

The second volume in the official history of the Atomic Energy Commission. It covers events related to the NWC from the first days of the Atomic Energy Commission in 1947, and their hope for peaceful uses of atomic energy, through the transition to a much enlarged NWC in 1952 with a focus on weapons.

Hewlett, Richard G., and Jack M. Holl. *Atoms for Peace and War: 1953-1961.* Berkeley and Los Angeles: University of California Press, 1989.

The third volume in the official history of the Atomic Energy Commission. It is largely focused on President Eisenhower's efforts to slow the nuclear arms race.

Haynes, John Earl, and Harvey Klehr. *Venona: Decoding Soviet Espionage in America.* New Haven and London: Yale University Press, 1999.

A thorough description of the top-secret U.S. program to decrypt the Soviet Union's messages. This program uncovered the three spies who stole secrets for the atomic bomb for the Soviet Union.

Hill, Kenneth L. *Cold War Chronology: Soviet-American Relations, 1945-1991.* Washington: Congressional Quarterly, Inc., 1993.

An extensive listing of the events related to the Cold War along with a short description or analysis of each event.

Johnson, Leland. *Sandia National Laboratories: A History of Exceptional Service in the National Interest.* SAND97-1029. Albuquerque: Sandia National Laboratories, 1997.

A comprehensive history of Sandia from its origins in 1945 to its role as a multiprogram national laboratory in 1996.

Johnson, Leland, and Daniel Schaffer. *"Oak Ridge National Laboratory: The First 50 Years (1942-1992)."* Oak Ridge National Laboratory Review, vol. 25, nos. 3 and 4, 1992.

A history of the Oak Ridge National Laboratory that includes its involvement in the Manhattan Project.

Johnson, Leland. *Tonopah Test Range: Outpost of Sandia National Laboratories.* SAND96-0375. Albuquerque: Sandia National Laboratories, 1996.

A brief history of the Tonopah Test Range and the other nonnuclear test sites in the NWC.

Jones, Vincent C. *Manhattan: The Army and the Atomic Bomb.* Washington, D.C.: Center of Military History, United States Army, 1985.

A comprehensive study of the role of the U.S. Army Corps of Engineers in the Manhattan Project.

Kahn, Herman. *On Thermonuclear War.* Princeton: Princeton University Press, 1961.

A rational and dispassionate analysis of deterrence that describes many shocking nuclear war scenarios.

Kurzman, Dan. *Blood and Water: Sabotaging Hitler's Bomb.* New York: Henry Holt and Company, 1997.

The dramatic story of Allied actions during World War II that prevented German scientists from obtaining heavy water needed to build a nuclear reactor.

Lemert, Ann Arnold. *First You Take a Pick and Shovel: The Story of the Mason Companies.* Lexington, KY: The John Bradford Press, 1979.

A history of the company that built and operated the Burlington and Pantex Plants and the Clarksville and Medina Modification Centers.

Los Alamos Public Relations Office. *Los Alamos:1943-1945; Beginning of an Era.* 1979 reprint, Los Alamos: Los Alamos Historical Society, 1986.

A brief history of Los Alamos and its mission to create the first atomic bomb.

Maydew, Randall C. *America's Lost H-Bomb.* Manhattan, KS: Sunflower University Press, 1997.

Describes the most serious accident involving a U.S. nuclear weapon. It also highlights other accidents involving U.S. nuclear weapons.

McCullough, David. *Truman.* New York: Simon & Schuster, 1992.

A meticulously detailed, elegantly written biography of President Truman.

Melzer, Richard. *Breakdown: How the Secret of the Atomic Bomb Was Stolen During World War II.* Sante Fe: Sunstone Press, 2000.

An explanation of the weaknesses in security at Los Alamos during the Manhattan Project.

Menon, Raja. *A Nuclear Strategy for India.* New Delhi: Sage Publications, Inc., 2000.

A history of the nuclear program in India along with the key events that led to nuclear tests in Pakistan.

Norris, Robert S., *Racing for the Bomb: General Leslie R. Groves, The Manhattan Project's Indispensable Man.* South Royalton: Steerforth Press, 2002.

An outstanding biography of General Groves that provides valuable insight on his role in the Manhattan Project.

Pais, Abraham. *Subtle Is The Lord – The Science and Life of Albert Einstein.* Oxford: Oxford University Press, 1982.

A scientific biography of Albert Einstein.

Porro, Jeffry, ed. *The Nuclear Age Reader.* WGBH Educational Foundation and the Corporation for Public Broadcasting. New York: McGraw-Hill, Inc., 1989.

Examines the origins of the nuclear competition between the U.S. and the Soviet Union and the impact of that competition on the world.

Powers, Thomas. *Heisenberg's War.* New York: Alfred A. Knopf, 1993.

A fascinating story of the German efforts to develop an atomic bomb.

Prange, Gordon W. *At Dawn We Slept: The Untold Story of Pearl Harbor.* New York: McGraw-Hill Book Company, 1981.

A detailed account of the Japanese attack on the United States at Pearl Harbor.

Rhodes, Richard. *Dark Sun.* New York: Simon & Schuster, 1995.

A history of the development of the hydrogen bomb and the espionage activities of the Soviet Union.

Rhodes, Richard. *The Making of the Atomic Bomb.* New York: Simon & Schuster, 1986.

A history of the development of the first atomic bomb, including the evolution of physics in the first half of the twentieth century.

Richanbach, Paul H., David R. Graham, James P. Bell, and James D. Silk. *The Organization and Management of the Nuclear Weapons Program,* (the 120-Day Study). Institute for Defense Analyses Report, ADA-323402. Alexandria, VA: U.S. Department of Commerce, National Technical Information Service, March, 1997.

A review of the DOE's management practices and organization with an analysis of the functions performed at Headquarters Defense Programs, operations offices, and applicable area and site offices.

Rowe, James Les. *Project W-47.* Livermore: JA A RO Publishing, 1978.

Describes the activities at Wendover, Utah, in 1945 to assemble atomic bombs and dummy bombs used for training by the 509th Composite Group.

Schwartz, Stephen, I., ed. *Atomic Audit: The Costs and Consequences of U.S. Nuclear Weapons Since 1940.* Washington, D.C.: Brookings Institution Press, 1998.

The first comprehensive effort to tally the total costs of the U.S. nuclear weapons program. It explains the process by which the stockpile was expanded and how policymakers viewed the costs and consequences at the time.

Secretary of Energy Advisory Board, Task Force on Alternative Futures for the Department of Energy National Laboratories (the Galvin Commission). *Alternative Futures for the Department of Energy National Laboratories*. Vol. 1. Washington, D.C.: U.S. Department of Energy, February 1995.

An examination of the options for change within the DOE laboratories with some proposed alternatives for meeting the economic, environmental, defense, scientific, and energy needs of the nation.

Sime, Ruth Lewin. *Lise Meitner: A Life in Physics*. Berkeley and Los Angeles: University of California Press, 1996.

An excellent biography of Lise Meitner that describes her contributions to physics and her struggles as a woman in a man's world.

Skates, John Ray. *The Invasion of Japan: Alternative to the Bomb*. Columbia: University of South Carolina Press, 1994.

A thorough explanation of the policies and problems in the Pacific faced by U.S. leaders during World War II.

Spanier, John, *American Foreign Policy Since World War II*. 12th ed., rev. Washington: CQ Press, A Division of Congressional Quarterly, Inc., 1992.

Describes the international roles played by the U.S. since WWII with a focus on the superpower rivalry and the Cold War.

Stanton, Doug. *In Harm's Way: The Sinking of the USS Indianapolis and the Extraordinary Story of Its Survivors*. New York: Henry Holt and Company, 2001.

A fascinating description of the errors that led to the sinking of the Indianapolis and the horrors endured by its survivors.

Sullivan, Thomas F. P., ed. *Environmental Law Handbook*. 14th ed. Rockville, MD: Government Institutes, Inc., 1997.

A textbook that covers all of the major environmental laws in the U.S.

Szasz, Ferenc Morton. *The Day the Sun Rose Twice*. Albuquerque: University of New Mexico Press, 1984.

A thoroughly researched account of the world's first nuclear test at the Trinty site in New Mexico.

Szilard, Leo. *The Collected Works of Leo Szilard: Scientific Papers*. Edited by Bernard T. Feld and Gertrude Weiss Szilard. Cambridge, MA: The MIT Press, 1972.

A collection of scientific papers and patents by the scientist who first developed the concepts of neutron-induced chain reactions and critical mass. Szilard also drafted the letter signed by Albert Einstein to President Roosevelt that ultimately led to the U.S. government's program to develop an atomic bomb.

Thompson, David B. *A Guide to the Nuclear Arms Control Treaties*. Los Alamos: Los Alamos Historical Society Publications, 2001.

An excellent source of information on nuclear arms control treaties.

Tibbets, Paul W. *Flight of the Enola Gay*. Columbus, Ohio: Mid Coast Marketing, 1989.

An autobiography by the pilot who dropped the atomic bomb on Hiroshima.

U.S. Atomic Energy Commission, Albuquerque Operations Office. *The Story of Albuquerque Operations*. AL Pamphlet 3100-2. Albuquerque: Atomic Energy Commission, 1973.

A brief history of the government office that manages the weapons programs in the NWC.

U.S. Department of Energy. *Classification Bulletin WNP-90*. Washington, D.C.: U.S. Department of Energy, July 29, 1994.

Provides the latest declassified information on a variety of subjects, including the total number of weapons in the U.S. stockpile from 1945 to 1961.

U.S. Department of Energy. *Nuclear Weapons Complex Reconfiguration Study*. DOE/DP-0083. Washington, D.C.: U.S. Department of Energy, January 1991.

Presents an overview of the problems in the NWC, provides a vision for the future, and charts a course by which to achieve that vision.

U.S. Department of Energy. *Nonnuclear Reconfiguration Cost-Effectiveness Report*. DOE/DP-0112P. Washington, D.C.: U.S. Department of Energy, January 15, 1993.

Analyzes the projected costs and benefits of each alternative considered in the Nonnuclear Consolidation Environmental Assessment.

U.S. Department of Energy. *Nonnuclear Consolidation Environmental Assessment*. DOE/EA-0792. Washington, D.C.: U.S. Department of Energy, June 1993.

Analyzes the environmental impacts of various alternatives for consolidating the nonnuclear component of the NWC.

U.S. Department of Energy. *Finding of No Significant Impact: Consolidation of the Nonnuclear Component Within the Nuclear Weapons Complex*. Washington, D.C.: U.S. Department of Energy, September 8, 1994.

Documents the decision to close the Mound, Pinellas, and Rocky Flats plants.

U.S. Department of Energy. *Final Programmatic Environmental Impact Statement for Stockpile Stewardship and Management.* DOE/EIS-0236. Washington, D.C.: U.S. Department of Energy, September 1996.

Assesses the environmental impacts of the ongoing program and proposed actions for maintaining the safety and reliability of the nuclear weapons stockpile without underground testing and with no new-design weapons production.

U.S. Department of Energy. *Record of Decision: Programmatic Environmental Impact Statement for Stockpile Stewardship and Management.* Washington, D.C.: U.S. Department of Energy, December 19, 1996.

Documents the decisions made for the Stockpile Stewardship and Management Program based on the information and analysis in the Programmatic Environmental Impact Statement.

U.S. Department of Energy, Albuquerque Operations Office. *Phase 1 Report of the Privatization Planning Panel.* Nuclear Weapons Complex Reconfiguration Study. Albuquerque: Albuquerque Operations Office, January 1991.

Analyzes 120 manufacturing activities in the NWC to determine which ones could be privatized and thereby facilitate nonnuclear consolidation.

U.S. Department of Energy, Albuquerque Operations Office. *Nonnuclear Consolidation Plan.* Albuquerque: Albuquerque Operations Office, September 1991.

Provides a plan for consolidating the nonnuclear component of the NWC by closing operations at the Mound, Pinellas, and Rocky Flats plants.

U.S. Department of Energy, Albuquerque Operations Office. *Supplemental Cost Study for Nonnuclear Reconfiguration.* Albuquerque: Albuquerque Operations Office, April 1992.

Shows how the fixed portions of overhead costs prevent any meaningful cost reductions without terminating the operation of a plant.

U.S. Department of Energy, Albuquerque Operations Office. *Two-Site Nonnuclear Consolidation Study.* Albuquerque: Albuquerque Operations Office, August 1992.

Shows how a single-site alternative is more cost effective than any of the two-site alternatives for nonnuclear consolidation.

U.S. Department of Energy, Nevada Operations Office. *United States Nuclear Tests: July1945 through September 1992.* DOE/NV-209, Revision 15. Washington, D.C.: U.S. Department of Energy, December 2000.

Lists chronologically and alphabetically by name all nuclear tests conducted by the United States from July 1945 to September 1992.

U.S. Department of Energy, Office of Environmental Management. *Closing the Circle on the Splitting of the Atom*. DOE/EM-0266. Washington, D.C.: U.S. Department of Energy, January 1995.

Describes nuclear weapon production processes from uranium mining to final assembly, the environmental contamination generated by these processes, and the problems associated with cleanup.

U.S. Department of Energy, Office of Environmental Management, Office of Strategic Planning and Analysis. *Linking Legacies*. DOE/EM-0319. Washington, D.C.: U.S. Department of Energy, January 1997.

A comprehensive analysis of nuclear weapons production processes and their links to specific quantified environmental impacts.

U.S. Energy Research and Development Administration, Albuquerque Operations Office. *The Story of Albuquerque Operations*. AL Pamphlet 3100-2. Albuquerque: Albuquerque Operations Office, 1975.

A brief history of the government office that manages the weapon programs in NWC. This is an update from the 1973 pamphlet.

Warner, Sir Frederick, ed. *Nuclear Test Explosions*. Chichester, England: John Wiley & Sons, Ltd., 2000.

An extensive compilation of information about world-wide nuclear testing.

Welsome, Eileen. The Plutonium Files. New York: The Dial Press, Random House, Inc. 1999.

A disturbing account of radiation accidents and medical experiments conducted on American citizens.

Wheeler, Keith. *The Fall of Japan*. Chicago: Time-Life Books, Inc., 1983.

An easy-to-read presentation of the war against Japan with many interesting pictures and anecdotes.

Weisberger, Bernard A. *Cold War, Cold Peace: The United States and Russia Since 1945*. New York: American Heritage, 1984.

An analysis of the historical roots of the Cold War and the factors that made it continue for so long.

PHOTO CREDITS

For permission to reprint photographs not in Sandia's photographic collection, I am grateful to:

Figure 1.1, Albert Einstein, 1922: Courtesy of The Burndy Library, Dibner Institute for the History of Science and Technology.

Figure 1.2, Niels Bohr, 1922: Courtesy American Institute of Physics, Emilio Segre Visual Archives, W. F. Meggers Collection, photo number A1.

Figure 1.4, Enrico Fermi: Courtesy of the Argonne National Laboratory.

Figure 1.6, Albert Einstein and Leo Szilard: Courtesy of Time Life Pictures Syndication.

Figure 1.7, Franklin D. Roosevelt: Courtesy of the Franklin Delano Roosevelt Library.

Figure 1.8, Glenn Seaborg: Courtesy of the Lawrence Berkeley National Laboratory.

Figure 1.9, U.S.S. Shaw Explodes During the Japanese Air Raid: Courtesy of the National Archives and Records Administration, photo number NWDNS-90-G-16871.

Figure 1.10, J. Robert Oppenheimer: Courtesy of the Los Alamos National Laboratory.

Figure 2.1, General Leslie R. Groves: Courtesy of the Los Alamos National Laboratory.

Figure 2.6, Harry S Truman: U. S. Army, Courtesy of the Harry S Truman Library.

Figure 2.8, Groves and Oppenheimer at Trinity: Courtesy of the Los Alamos National Laboratory.

Figure 2.9, Colonel Paul W. Tibbets: Courtesy of the National Archives and Records Administration, photo number 208-LU-13H-5.

Figure 3.1, Werner Heisenberg in 1927: Courtesy of the American Institute of Physics, Emilio Segre Visual Archives, Segre Collection, photo number A15.

Figure 3.2, Heisenberg and Bohr in 1934: Photograph by Paul Ehrenfest, Jr., Courtesy of the American Institute of Physics, Emilio Segre Visual Archives, Weisskopf Collection, photo number C13.

Figure 3.3, Walther Bothe: Photograph from Ullstein Bilderdienst, Courtesy of the American Institute of Physics.

Figure 3.4, Harold Urey, Argonne National Laboratory: Courtesy of the American Institute of Physics, Emilio Segre Visual Archives, photo number F1.

Figure 3.5, Heavy Water Plant at Vemork: Courtesy of the Norwegian Industrial Museum.

Figure 3.6, The Ferry "Hydro" at the Railhead on Lake Tinn: Courtesy of the Norwegian Industrial Museum.

Figure 4.1, Roosevelt at Quebec Conference: Courtesy of the Franklin Delano Roosevelt Library.

Figure 4.2, Klaus Emil Julius Fuchs: Courtesy of the Los Alamos National Laboratory.

Figure 4.3, Theodore A. Hall: Courtesy of the Los Alamos National Laboratory.

Figure 4.4, David and Ruth Greenglass: Courtesy of the National Archives and Records Administration.

Figure 4.5: Harry Gold: Courtesy of the National Archives and Records Administration.

Figure 4.6, National Security Agency Seal: Courtesy of the National Security Agency.

Figure 4.7, Julius and Ethel Rosenberg: Courtesy of AP Wide World Photos.

Figure 6.1, Edward Teller: Courtesy of the Lawrence Livermore National Laboratory.

Figure 6.4, Dwight D. Eisenhower: U.S. Navy, Courtesy of the Dwight D. Eisenhower Library.

Figure 7.2, Bravo shot: Courtesy of the Los Alamos National Laboratory, photo number CN59-59.

Figure 9.1, John F. Kennedy: Courtesy of The History Place.

Figure 9.2, Castro and Khruschev: Courtesy of Kurt Wiersma, Webmaster, from the website, "Thinkquest Library."

Figure 9.3, Berlin Wall: Courtesy of Frederik Ramm, from the website, "Berlin Wall."

Figure 9.5, Soviet Missile Installations in Cuba: Courtesy of Kurt Wiersma, Webmaster, from the website, "Fourteen Days in October, The Cuban Missile Crisis."

Figure 10.2, Bomb Hoisted Aboard the U.S.S. Petrel: U. S. Air Force, Courtesy of the National Atomic Museum.

Figure 11.1, Ronald Reagan: Courtesy of the Ronald Reagan Library.

Figure 11.3, Berlin Wall Being Destroyed: Courtesy of Associated Press Television.

Figure 11.4, Presidents Bush and Gorbachev: Courtesy of the George Bush Presidential Library.

INDEX

Accelerator Production of Tritium (APT), 179-180

AEC-DoD Agreement of 1953, 101

adaption kit, 92, 134, 203

Advisory Committee on Human Radiation Experiments, 194

Advisory Committee on Uranium, see Uranium Committee

Afghanistan, 1979 invasion, 166

air-launched cruise missile (ALCM), 166

Alamogordo, New Mexico, 34, 116, 118

alarm clock, 96, 114

Albright, Joseph, 74

Albuquerque Microelectronics Operation (AMO), 136

Albuquerque Operations Office (AL), xi, 157, 159-160, 170, 184, 216-224

Alsos, 46-47

Amchitka, Alaska (test site), 118-119

American Car and Foundry (ACF), 98

Anti-Ballistic Missile Treaty of 1972, 165, 226

anti-Semitism, 8-9

arming, fusing and firing (AF&F), 135

Army Corps. of Engineers, 21

artillery-fired shells, 123

Aryan physics, 48

Aston, Francis W., 6-7, 10

Atlas Facility, 178

atomic demolition munitions (ADM), 90-91

Atomic Energy Act

- of 1946, 79, 85, 203
- of 1954, 108, 197

Atomic Energy Commission (AEC), 79-80, 98, 158

AEC-DoD Agreement of 1953, 204-206

atomic mass unit, 7-8

atomic number, 3

atomic structure, 2-4

Atoms for Peace Program, 106-109, 117

Barking Sands, see Kauai Test Facility

Barovsky, Vladimir, 69

Baruch, Bernard, 80-81

Baruch Plan, 80, 189

Batista, Fulgencio, 140

Bay of Pigs, 141-142

Bell, Daniel, 28

Berlin

- blockade and airlift of 1948-49, 81, 107, 141
- uprising of 1953, 139
- crisis of 1960-61, 140
- wall, 116, 142-144, 167

beryllium, 29-30, 89, 129, 132, 134, 171

Bethe, Hans, 9, 11,18, 66, 104

Bikini Atoll (test site), 114, 118

binding energy, 6-8

Bhagavad-Gita, 18, 35

bismuth, 30

Bloch, Felix, 9, 18

Bock's Car, 38

boosting, 96, 161

Bothe, Walther, 51-52
Bohr, Neils, 3, 9, 11, 13, 49-51
bombs (nuclear)
  Little Boy, 32-34, 36, 89, 113
  Fat Man, 33, 35-36, 38-39,83, 89
  Mark III and Mark IV, 121
  B14 and B15, 100
  B28, 133
  B61, 155
  B83, 166
  B90, 169
bomb shelters, 143
Born, Max, 64
Bradbury, Norris, 113
Braun, Werner von, 152
Briggs, Lyman J., 11
Burlington Plant, 84, 148, 156
Bush, George, H. W., 160, 168-169, 216, 220-222, 230
Bush, George W., 231
Bush, Vannevar, 12-13, 15, 21, 48, 67, 104
calutron, 27, 40
capacitors, 133
carbon-14, 193
Carlsbad, New Mexico (test site), 119
Carter, James "Jimmy", 91
Castro, Fidel, 141
Cavendish Laboratory, 74
Central Intelligence Agency (CIA), 142
Central Nevada (test site), 118
cesium-137, 193
Chadwick, James, 5
chain reaction, 5, 11-12, 14, 29, 33, 46, 59
Chambers, Whittaker, 101
Checkpoint Charlie, 143
Chernobyl, 160, 195
Chevalier, Haakon, 104
Chiles Commission, 183
Christmas Island (test site), 118
Christy, Robert, 106
Churchill, Winston, 31, 34, 36, 65, 80, 196
Clarksville Modification Center, 134, 148
Clinton, William J., 177, 183, 194, 224
Cockcroft, John, 5
Cohen, Lona and Morris, 63, 69, 73
Cold War
  overview of, xii-xiii
  and Yalta agreements, 31
  beginning of, 80-83
  intensification of, 96, 139
  and McCarthyism, 101
  and Berlin Wall, 116
  and Cuban Missile Crisis, 147
  ending of, 161, 165, 167-168
  causes of, 189-190
  greatest danger during, 147, 197-198
  and Nonnuclear Reconfiguration Program, 170, 173, 217, 225
COLEX, 100
Combined Policy Committee, 65
commercial light water reactor (CLWR), 179-180
communism, collapse of, 167-168
Complementarity Principle, 50
Comprehensive Test Ban Treaty (CTBT), 177, 230-231
Compton, Arthur, 16, 24
Conant, James, 13, 24, 102

conceptual design report (CDR), 220-221

Concurrent Design and Manufacturing (CDM), 172

Contained Firing Facility, 178

Corporal, 90

Council on Environmental Quality (CEQ), 209, 212-213

Council on Foreign Relations, 103

critical mass, 5, 67

Cuban missile crisis, 146-147, 197

Curie, Marie and Pierre, 29

Dana Plant, 99, 133

Davis gun, 123

Dayton facility, 30, 84

Dean, Gordon, 98, 104, 203

Deibner, Kurt, 46

Department of Energy (DOE), creation of, 158

détente, 165

deuterium, 3-4, 6, 53, 88, 96-99, 113-114, 129-130, 133, 161

Development and Production Manual, 180-181, 205

detonators, 33, 86, 134, 155, 171, 204

Doepel, Robert, 52

Donne, John, 34

Dr. Strangelove, 152

Dulles, John Foster, 139

Duma, Russian, 169-170, 230

Durant, Will and Ariel, 199

Dyson, Freeman, 195-196

Edgewood Test Range, 123-124

Eidal Manufacturing Company, 98

Einstein, Albert, xii, 1, 9, 11, 48

Eisenhower, Dwight D., 102, 106-109, 116-117, 139-140, 143

electromagnetic separation, 15, 17, 22, 27-28

ELEX, 100

Energy Research and Development Administration (ERDA), 158

Enewetak Atoll (test site), 113-114, 118

enhanced nuclear detonation safety (ENDS), xiv, 155

Enola Gay, 36

Enrico Fermi Award, 106

environmental assessment (EA), 171, 209-210, 212, 218

environmental impact statement (EIS), 178-180, 209-212

Erb, Otto, 127

Espionage, General Act of 1917, 73

exclusion barrier, 155-156

Falkenhorst, Nikolaus von, 55, 57

Fallon, Nevada (test site), 119

Farm Hall, 47

Farmington, New Mexico (test site), 119

Fat Man, see bombs (nuclear)

Federal Civil Defense Administration (FCDA), 143

Federal Register, 211, 217

Fernald Feed Materials Production Center, 89, 132, 148, 162, 197

Fermi, Enrico, 6-7, 11-12, 15, 24-25, 102

finding of no significant impact (FONSI), 171, 210, 218, 222

Fluor Daniel, 219

Fogel, 75

fissile material, 14, 17, 27, 51, 192, 196, 231

fission, discovery of, 10

fission-fusion-fission concept, 113-114

flexible response, 144

Franck, James, 18

Frisch, Otto, 9-11

Fuchs, Klaus Emil Julius,64-67, 69, 71-72, 75, 101

fusion, 95-97, 130, 157

Gaddis, John Lewis, 189

Galvin Commission, 178, 182

Galvin, Robert, 178

Gamow, George, 9, 81

gas centrifuge, 15, 17, 22

gaseous diffusion, 15, 17, 22, 28, 40, 65-66, 75, 99, 133, 147, 162, 192

General Advisory Committee (GAC), 102-104

General Electric X-Ray Department, 129, 132

Glenn, John, 222

Gold, Harry, 63, 66-67, 70-72

Gorbachev, Mikhail, 167, 169

Gordon, John, 184

Goudsmit, Samuel, 48-49

Grand Valley, Colorado (test site), 119

Gravel Gerties, 87

Greenglass, David and Ruth, 64, 70, 72-73, 75

Greenhouse (nuclear test series), 96, 113

ground-launched cruise missile (GLCM), 167

Groves, Leslie R., 5, 21-24, 28, 35, 39, 46, 54, 64, 104, 200

gun assembly, 32-34

Gusterson, Hugh, 193

Hahn, Otto, 10, 49

Haigerloch, 47

Hall, Theodore (Ted), 64, 67, 73-75

Hall, Tony, 222

Hanford, 24-26, 29, 86, 88-89, 148, 161-162, 179, 192, 197

Harris Semiconductor, 136

Hattisburg, Mississippi (test site), 119

Hechingen, 47

Heereswaffenamt, 45

Heisenberg, Werner, 45-51, 54

highly-enriched uranium (HEU), see uranium, enriched

Hiroshima, 36, 39, 113, 196

Hitler, Adolph, 9, 48-49, 55, 64

heavy water, 4, 25-26, 53-59, 87-88, 161

Heroya, 58

high energy rate forgings (HERF), 161

Hirohito, Emperor, 40

Hiss, Alger, 101

Holloway, Marshall, 113

Honest John, 90, 203

Hope, Bob, 120

House Un-American Activities Committee (HUAC), 101

Hungary

- 1956 anti-Communist revolt, 139
- rejects communism at polls, 167

Hydro, ferry, 58-59

hydrogen bomb, 95, 103-104

Idaho National Engineering Laboratory (INEL), 179

implosion, 34-35, 66-67, 70, 84

initiator, 29-30, 33, 67, 69, 84-85, 99, 129, 132

Institute for Advanced Study, 105

Institute for Defense Analyses, 183

Interim Committee, 32

Intermediate-Range Nuclear Forces (INF) Treaty, 168, 229

International Atomic Energy Authority (IAEA), 80, 107, 230

Inyokern, California, 84, 132

iron curtain, 80

isotopes, 3, 14-15, 27, 29, 88, 97, 99-100, 192

Jefferson, Thomas, 199

Johnston Atoll (test site), 118

Johnson, Lyndon, 106

Joint Committee on Atomic Energy, 79

K-25 Plant, 22-23, 40, 66, 147, 162, 192, 197

Kahn, Herman, 152

Kansas City Plant (KC)

- origin of, 86,
- and AMO, 136
- and South Albuquerque Works, 148
- and PAL devices, 152
- and strong links and weak links, 156
- in DOE organization, 159-160
- and Nonnuclear Reconfiguration Program, 170-173, 218, 221, 223-224
- current mission, 174
- downsizing of, 178

Kansas City Site Office (KCSO), 184

Kaiser Wilhelm Institute, 46

Kauai Test Facility, 123, 173

Kellex Corporation, 66

Kennedy, John F., 140-144, 146, 152

Khrushshev, Nikita, 139-144, 146, 196

Kirtland Air Force Base, 157-158

Kissinger, Henry, 152

Kistiakowski, George, 9

Konopinski, Emil, 18

Korean War, 83, 107

Kroger, Peter and Helen, 73

Kuczynski, Jurgen and Marcia, 64-65

Kunstel, Marcia, 74

Lackland Air Force Base, 135

Lake Tinn, 58

Lance, 91-92

large-scale integrated (LSI) circuits, 135-136

Las Vegas Bombing and Gunnery Range, 88, 122

Lawrence, Ernest O., 14-15, 98

Lawrence Livermore National Laboratory (LLNL)

- origin of, 98-99
- and Kauai, 123
- Sandia facility at, 132
- became national laboratory, 156
- in DOE organization, 159-160
- current mission, 175
- and National Ignition Facility, 178
- and Galvin Commission, 178

Lebaron, Robert, 203

Lee, Wen Ho, 198

Lenard, Philip, 48

lightning arrestor connectors (LAC), 133

Lilienthal, David, 82, 104

limited life components (LLC), 131

Limited Test Ban Treaty (LTBT), 119, 192, 227-228

Lippman, Walter, 81

lithium, isotopes of, 4-5, 87, 97, 99-100, 115-116, 180

lithium deuteride, 97, 99, 115

Little Boy, see bombs (nuclear)

Little John, 90

Livermore Site Office (LSO), 184

Los Alamos National Laboratory (LANL)

- origin of, 23-25,
- enriched uranium to, 28
- and Z Division, 30, 85-87
- and Little Boy, 37
- espionage at, 64, 66-68, 75-76
- and Edward Teller, 96, 98, 105-106
- and thermonuclear tests, 113
- and Kauai, 123,
- neutron generator concept, 129
- beryllium component production, 134
- became national laboratory, 156-157
- in DOE organization, 159-160
- and Nonnuclear Reconfiguration Program, 171-172, 223-224
- current mission, 175
- pit production capability, 178-179
- Galvin Commission, 178
- and Wen Ho Lee, 198

Los Alamos Site Office (LASO), 184

Los Lunas Test Range, 121

low-enriched uranium (LEU), see uranium, enriched

Luce, Clare Booth, 79

Mael, Norway, 58

Manhattan Engineer District (MED)/Manhattan Project

- and Szilard's patent, 5
- origin of, 21
- selection of Los Alamos site, 23
- and uranium enrichment, 27-28
- creation of Z Division, 30-31
- and first nuclear weapons, 32, 34
- compared to German program, 49
- transfer to AEC, 79-80, 156
- and Salton Sea, 121
- espionage during, 64, 68, 71, 75, 105
- and Edward Teller, 95
- comparison to NWC in 1994, 173
- characterized by, 182
- cost of, 190
- experiments on health effects of radioactive materials, 193-194

Manufacturing Development Engineering (MDE), 100-101, 171-172

Mark 3, see reentry vehicles

Mark 5, see reentry vehicles

Marshall, George C., 81

Marshall, James C., 21

Marshall Islands, 113

Marshall Plan, 81

mass defect, 6-8

mass number, 3

massive retaliation, 139

McCarthyism, 101-102, 106, 198-199

McCarthy, Senator Joseph R., 101-102

Medina Modification Center, 135, 148

Meitner, Lise, 10-11

Microelectronics Development Laboratory (MDL), 136

Military Application of Uranium Disintegration (MAUD) Committee, 15

Military Industrial Complex, 109

Military Liaison Committee (MLC), 79, 203-204

miniaturization, 135

Minuteman intercontinental ballistic missile (ICBM) 146

Missiles and Rockets Agreement of 1953, 92, 203-206

mixed oxide (MOX), 179

moderator, 6, 12, 29, 51, 53

Modernization Review Committee, 215-216

Modern strategic bomb, see bombs, B83

Moerschner, Ingeborg, 52

Moromoto, Shigeyoshi, 38

Moscow Treaty, 231

Mound Laboratory/Plant, 84, 134, 171, 218, 221, 224

Multiple independently-targeted reentry vehicles (MIRV), 145, 230

Murphee, Eger, 15

Nagasaki, 38-40, 197

National Aeronautic and Space Administration (NASA), 123, 136

National Atomic Museum, 154

National Defense Research Committee, 13

National Environmental Policy Act (NEPA), 160, 170, 196, 209, 217

National Ignition Facility (NIF), 177

National Nuclear Security Administration (NNSA), xi, 182-184

National Security Agency (NSA), 71, 74

NNSA Service Center, 184

Naval Ordnance Test Station (NOTS), 84

Nellis Air Force Range (test site), 118

Neumann, John von, 9

neutron, discovery of, 3

neutron bomb, 91

neutron detectors, 133

neutron generators, 128-133, 171, 218-219, 224

neutron tube target loading, 171

Nevada Operations Office (NV), 158-160, 184

Nevada Site Office (NSO), 184

Nevada Test Site (NTS)

- origin of, 88, 157
- weapons tests, 118-119
- storage of contaminated materials, 154
- in DOE organization, 159-160
- and Nonnuclear Reconfiguration Program, 173
- current mission, 175
- Atlas Facility, 178
- testing and human health, 193

Newport, Indiana, 99

Nichols, Kenneth D., 28

Nixon, Richard M., 102, 165, 209

Nonnuclear Consolidation Environmental Assessment, 223

Nonnuclear Consolidation Plan (NCP), 170-171, 217-220

Nonnuclear Reconfiguration Cost Effectiveness Report, 222

Nonnuclear Reconfiguration Program, 170-173, 177, 215, 219, 224-225

Non-Proliferation Treaty (NPT), 230

Norsk Hydro Plant, 52-57

North Atlantic Treaty Organization (NATO), 82, 142, 168

notice of availability (NOA), 211-212

notice of intent (NOI), 210-211, 217

nuclear fission, see fission

nuclear reactors (prototype, test, and research)

- CP1, CP2, and CP3, 25-26
- Test Pile 305, 26
- X-10, 26, 30

nuclear tests

- United States
- Bravo, 114-115
- George, 113
- Mike, 113-114
- Ruth and Ray, 99
- Shot Grable, 90-91
- Trinity, 34-35
- Soviet Union
  - Joe 1, 82
  - Joe 4, 114

Nuclear Regulatory Commission (NRC), 158

Nuclear Security Enterprise, 186

Nuclear Weapons Complex (NWC)

- defined, xi, 16
- electrical consumption of, 133
- in 1942, 22-25
- from 1943 to July 1945, 31
- in September 1945, 40
- in 1947, 84-85
- in 1948, 85-86
- in 1949, 86-87
- from 1950 to 1951, 87-89
- from 1952 to 1953, 100
- from 1954 to 1957, 133
- in 1958, 134
- from 1962 to 1967, 148
- from 1975 to 1979, 156
- from 1982 to 1989, 161-162
- in 1994, 173

Nuclear Weapons Complex Modernization Report, 215-216

Nuclear Weapons Complex Reconfiguration Study, 170, 172, 217

nuclear weapons, cost of, 190-191

Nuclear Weapons Stockpile Memorandum, 158, 160

Oak Ridge, 22, 25-27, 75

Oak Ridge National Laboratory (ORNL), 27

Oak Ridge Operations Office (OR), 157, 159-160

Oakland Operations Office (OAK), 159-160, 184

Office of Amarillo Site Operations (OASO), 159-160

Office of Civil Defense Mobilization (OCDM), 143

Office of Environmental Management, 161, 191

Office of Kansas City Site Operations (OKCSO), 159-160

Office of Kirtland Site Operations (OKSO), 159-160

Office of Los Alamos Site Operations (OLASO), 159-160

Office of Santa Fe Directed Operations, 157

Office of Scientific Research and Development (OSRD), 13

O'Leary, Hazel, 178, 194, 222-223

one-point safe, 157

Operation Barbarossa, 64

Operation Freshman, 54

Operation Gunnerside, 55

Oppenheimer, J. Robert, 17-18, 23-24, 34, 67, 98, 102-106

OREX, 100

Oxnard Facility, 161, 172

Oxnard Field, 30-31, 121

Paducah Gaseous Diffusion Plant, 99, 147-148, 191

Palomares, Spain (nuclear weapon accident), 153

Pantex Plant (PX)

- origin of, 89
- closure of Medina and Clarksville, 148
- storage of contaminated materials, 154
- closure of Burlington, 156
- in DOE organization, 159-160
- current mission, 174
- downsizing of, 178

Pantex Site Office (PSO), 184

Paris Summit Conference, 140

Parker, James, 198

Peacekeeper, land-based intercontinental ballistic missile (ICBM), 167

peaceful nuclear explosions, 116

Peaceful Nuclear Explosions Treaty (PNET), 228

Pearl Harbor, 16

Peierls, Rudolf, 9, 64-66

Permissive Action Link (PAL), xiv, 151-152

Pers, 75

Pershing, 90

Pershing II, intermediate-range missile, 167-168

Personnel Security Questionnaire (PSQ), 85

Persons, Addison, 132

Phases, weapon program, 169, 205-206

Picatinny Arsenal, 86, 92, 134, 204

Pinellas Plant, 132, 156, 171, 218, 221, 224

pits, plutonium, 33, 86, 97, 148, 154, 171, 175, 178-179

Plowshare Program, 119

plutonium, 14-17, 21, 23, 29, 33-36, 51, 67, 82, 86, 88, 113, 117, 132, 162, 178-179, 192, 194

Polaris, submarine-launched ballistic missile (SLBM), 146

polonium, 29-30, 129, 132

Portsmouth Gaseous Diffusion Plant, 99, 147-148, 192

Portland Naval Research Base, 73

Poseidon C3, submarine launched ballistic missile (SLBM), 135, 204

Potsdam Declaration, 36, 39

Powers, Francis Gary, 140

Precision Forge, 161

primary, 96

Privatization Planning Panel, 216-217

Production and Planning Directive (P&PD), 158-160

programmatic environmental impact statement (PEIS), 170, 177-179, 212, 217-218

protium, 3-4, 6

pumpkins, 120

"Q" clearance (origin), 85

Quantum, 75

quantum mechanics, 45, 50, 64, 67

Quebec Conference/Agreement, 65

Rabi, Isidor I., 9, 11, 102, 104, 106

radiation-hardened microelectronics, 135-136

radioisotopic thermoelectric generators (RTG), 133

RAND Corporation, 152

Reagan, Ronald, 165-166

Reard, Louis, 118

record of decision (ROD), 177-180, 210, 212

reentry vehicles, 145

- Mark 3, 135, 203
- Mark 4, 135
- Mark 5, 135

Reis, Vic, 182

Relativity, Special Theory of, 1, 10

reservoirs, 97, 131, 162, 174

Rhodes, Richard, 105

Rickover, Hyman G., 85

Rifle, Colorado (test site), 119

Rjukan, Norway, 53

Robinson, C. Paul, 199

Rock Island Arsenal, 84, 98

Rocky Flats Plant

- origin of, 89
- and beryllium components, 134
- and uranium components, 147
- and plutonium pits, 148, 178
- and Oxnard Facility, 161-162
- and Nonnuclear Reconfiguration Program, 171-172, 218, 221, 224
- storage and disposition of waste fissile materials, 178-179
- ceased nuclear operations, 197

Roosevelt, Franklin D., , 11, 13, 21, 31, 34, 65, 67

Rosenberg, Julius and Ethel, 63-65, 70, 72-73, 102

Rossi, Bruno, 9, 68

Rutherford, Ernest, 2, 4

S-50 Plant, 22, 40

Salton Sea (test site), 121-122

Salt Wells Plant, 84, 132

Sandia Base, 30-31, 87, 158

Sandia National Laboratories (SNL)

- origin of, 87
- and MDE, 100
- and nonnuclear test sites, 121-124
- and wooden bomb concept, 127
- and neutron generators, 129
- origin of SNL/CA facility, 132
- radiation-hardening and miniaturization, 135
- ENDS concept, 155-156
- and Nonnuclear Reconfiguration Program, 171-173, 218-219, 221, 223-224
- current mission, 175

Sandia Site Office (SSO), 184

Santa Fe Operations Office, 157

Sergeant, 90

Savannah, nuclear-powered cargo ship, 108

Savannah River Operations Office (SR), 159-160

Savannah River Plant/Site (SRS)

- origin of, 87-89
- and tritium components, 132
- storing contaminated materials, 154
- in DOE organization, 159-160
- and Nonnuclear Reconfiguration Program, 172, 224
- current mission, 174
- tritium supply and recyling, 179
- contamination at, 192
- reactor operations ceased at, 197

Savannah River Site Office (SRSO), 184

Sax, Saville, 68-69, 73
Scioto Ordnance Works, 85, 99
Seaborg, Glenn, 14-15, 102
sealed pits, 128-129
secondaries, 97, 99
Segre, Emilio, 9, 34
Sequoyah #1 and #2, 180
Serber, Robert, 18
Shippingport, Pennsylvania, nuclear reactor, 108
site mission assignments, 174-175, 223
Sloan Kettering Institute, 74
Smith, Cyril, 102
Sommerfeld, Arnold, 48
South Albuquerque Works, 98, 148
Soviet Union, disintegration of, 168
Speer, Albert, 49, 51
Spoon River Plant, 89
Sputnik, 139
SS-20, intermediate-range ballistic missiles (IRBM), 166
standard notation, 3
Stagg Field, 24
Stalin, Joseph, 31, 36, 82, 107, 189
Stealth, fighter and bomber, 122-123
Stark, Johannes, 48
Stimson, Henry L., 23, 32
stockpile (nuclear weapon), 83, 169-170
Stockpile Life Extension Program (SLEP), 180-182
Stockpile Stewardship and Management, 177-178
Storage and Disposition of Weapon-Usable Fissile Material, 178-179
Strassman, Fritz, 10
Strategic Arms Limitation Talks (SALT)
SALT I, 165-166, 229
SALT II, 228-229
Strategic Arms Reduction Talks, 166
Strategic Arms Reduction Treaty (START)
START I, 169-170, 180, 229
START II, 169-170, 180, 221, 229
START III, 231
strategic nuclear weapons, 144
Strategic Offensive Reductions Treaty (SORT), xiii, 231-232
Strauss, Lewis, 102, 229
strong links, 155-156
strontium-90, 191
Super, 103
Supplemental Cost Study for Nonnuclear Consolidation, 219
Sweeney, Charles W., 38
Szilard, Leo, 5, 9, 11-12, 15
tactical nuclear weapons, 90-92, 123
tamper, 67
Task Force on Alternative Futures, 182
Teller, Edward, 9, 11, 18, 95-96, 103-106, 113-114, 152
Teller-Ulam concept, 96, 113
Tennessee Valley Authority (TVA), 133, 180
terradynamics, 123
thermal batteries, 127, 133
thermal diffusion, 22, 28
thermonuclear weapons, 95-96, 99-100, 113-116
Third World, 165-166
Thomas, Charles A., 30
Three Mile Island, 160, 195

Threshold Test Ban Treaty (TTBT), 119, 228

Thule, Greenland (nuclear weapon accident), 154

Tibbets, Paul, 35-37, 120

Tinian Island, 35-37, 120

Tonapah Test Range, 122-123

tracer studies, 193

triad, 144

Trident II D5, submarine launched ballistic missile (SLBM), 135, 166-167

Trinity, 34

Trinitite, 35

tritium, 4, 87, 97-98, 129-133, 162, 171, 174, 179-180, 218

Tritium Extraction Facility (TEF), 179-180

Tritium Supply and Recycling, 179-180

Truman Doctrine, 81

Truman, Harry S, 32, 36, 71, 79, 81-82, 87, 96, 102-103, 139, 143, 197

Two-Site Nonnuclear Consolidation Study, 221

U-2 reconnaissance aircraft, 140, 146

Ulam, Stanislaw, 9, 96

Uncertainty Principle, 45, 50

United Nations, 80

United States Enrichment Corporation, 148

University of California Radiation Laboratory (UCRL), 98

Uranium Committee, 11-13, 15

uranium, enriched, 17, 21-23, 25, 28, 32, 51, 75, 99, 117, 133, 147-148, 162, 178-179, 192

uranium pile, 12, 15, 17, 24

Uranverein, 46

Urchin, 29-30

Urey, Harold, 15, 53, 65

U.S.S. Indianapolis, 35-36

U.S.S. Missouri, 39

U.S.S. Petrel, 153

U.S.S. Shaw, 16

Van Vleck, John, 18, 67

Vela Project, (Hotel, Sierra, and Uniform), 119

Venona Project, 70-75

Vemork, 53, 56, 58

warheads (nuclear)

- W19, 90
- W25, 129
- W31, 204
- W33, 123
- W34, 133
- W48, 123
- W49, 152, 204
- W68, 204
- W70, 91
- W79, 123
- W76, 135
- W80, 166
- W82, 123, 169
- W84, 167W85, 167-168
- W87, 167
- W88, 167
- W89, 169
- W91, 169

Walton, Ernest, 5

Warsaw Pact, 89

Watkins, James T., 160-161, 215, 218, 222

Watts Bar #1, 180

weak links, 155-156

Weapons Evaluation Test

Laboratory (WETL), 148

Weisskopf, Victor, 9

Weizacher, Carl Friedrich von, 47, 49

Weldon Spring Plant, 132, 148

Wendover Army Air Force Base, 120-121

Wheeler, John, 14

Wigner, Eugene, 9

Wilson, Carol, 192

wooden bomb concept, 127

Y-12 Plant

- origin of, 22-23
- and enriched uranium, 28, 40
- and uranium components, 86, 147
- and lithium, 99
- and metal case work, 148
- in DOE organization, 157, 159-160
- and heavy water, 161
- current mission, 174
- downsizing of, 178
- storage of highly-enriched uranium, 179

Y-12 Site Office (YSO), 184

Yalta, 31

Yatskov, Anatoly, 67, 69-70

Yeltsin, Boris, 73, 220-222, 230

York, Herbert, 96

Yucca Flats (test site), 122

Z Division, 30-31, 84-85

About the Author

Charles Loeber worked as an engineer on the design and production of nuclear weapons for more than 40 years. He served in a variety of organizations, including the Department of the Army, the Department of Energy, and Sandia National Laboratories. Over time, his interest in the history of the Nuclear Weapons Complex grew into a hobby, and he became an authority on the subject.

He has been giving presentations on the History of the Nuclear Weapons Complex to audiences around the country for more than 20 years. This book is based on those presentations.

Mr. Loeber retired from Sandia in 1995. He is now serving as a consultant to Sandia, the Department of Energy, and others. His favorite recreational activities are playing with grandchildren and running, especially in the Sandia Mountains near Albuquerque, New Mexico.